Conflict and Consensus

RELIGIOUS FREEDOM AND
THE SECOND VATICAN COUNCIL

By the same author:

American Pluralism and the Catholic Conscience

Conflict and Consensus

RELIGIOUS FREEDOM AND
THE SECOND VATICAN COUNCIL

Richard J. Regan, S.J.

THE MACMILLAN COMPANY, NEW YORK
COLLIER-MACMILLAN LTD., LONDON

The translation of *The Declaration on Religious Freedom* is taken from *The
Documents of Vatican II*, published by Guild Press, America Press, Association
Press, and Herder and Herder, and copyrighted © 1966 by The America Press.
Used by permission.

IMPRIMI POTEST: Robert A. Mitchell, S.J.
Provincial of the New York Province
April 3, 1967

NIHIL OBSTAT: John B. Amberg, S.J.
Censor Deputatus

IMPRIMATUR: ✠ Cletus F. O'Donnell
Vicar General, Archdiocese of Chicago
April 12, 1967

*The nihil obstat and imprimatur are official declarations that a book or
pamphlet is free of doctrinal or moral error. No implication is contained
therein that those who have granted the nihil obstat and imprimatur agree
with the contents, opinions, or statements expressed.*

To my friend and mentor
JOHN COURTNEY MURRAY
whose work made this book necessary,
and whose help made it possible.

Acknowledgments

AS THE DEDICATION OF THIS BOOK INDICATES, my primary debt is to John Murray. It is a testimony to his care for history that he preserved so carefully and completely the record of the Secretariat's work; it is a testimony to his selflessness that he was willing to open his files to an interested student; it is a testimony to his patience that he would endure reliving a long history to help reconstruct events for one not privy to them. Fr. Murray not only provided me with the material necessary for a study of the Declaration's genesis, he also discussed the principal issues with me fully and openly. I appreciate his help deeply, and I cherish his friendship always.

This book is substantially identical with the dissertation submitted to the Political Science Department of the University of Chicago in partial fulfillment of the requirements for the Ph.D. degree. I owe a broad debt to all in the department, faculty and students, who helped to develop my patterns of thought, but I wish to express special appreciation to those professors most closely associated with this study: Mr. Leonard Binder, chairman of the department, who encouraged me to undertake this project when the opportunity arose in the spring of 1966; Mr. Joseph Cropsey, chairman of the faculty committee, who advised me on the dissertation; Messrs. Nathan Leites and Aristide Zolberg, who also assisted me as faculty advisers.

Other expressions of appreciation are also very much in order. The Jesuit community of Woodstock College received me graciously and facilitated my work in every way. The Jesuit community of Saint Peter's College offered generous help, material and fraternal, in the final days of completing the manuscript. My sister, Mrs. Joan Sheridan, devotedly typed the final copy with care and dispatch, at considerable personal sacrifice. Fr. Leo Martin, S.J., provided spiritual solace during the many trials of composition. To all I offer my sincere thanks.

Richard J. Regan, S.J.

Contents

I

Introduction

WHEN POPE JOHN determined to convoke an ecumenical council of Catholic bishops, he certainly could not have seen far beyond the threshold of the door that he was opening. Like many an Old Testament prophet, he was a "mouthpiece" moved by the Spirit to announce God's grace to men without full consciousness of the message's import or dimensions. The Declaration on Religious Freedom is one among many products of John's decision, and the history of its framing forms the subject of this book.

Religious freedom was not the most pressing problem facing church or state on December 7, 1965, when the Declaration was promulgated.[1] In most respects, the Church's relation to religious freedom was a relic of a nineteenth-century polemic. The context out of which that polemic arose had long since passed, and Catholics generally recognized the right to religious freedom both as a political reality and a theological truth. What disturbed this otherwise happy development was the apparently adverse authority of the nineteenth-century papacy to which the thinning, geographically isolated ranks of Catholic fundamentalists appealed. Professional anti-Catholics and many Catholic professionals found themselves agreed on the negative value which they thought the Church placed on religious freedom. As a result, liberal Catholics and inquiring non-Catholics alike looked to the Council for a new, authoritative statement to dispel the shadow over the Church's commitment to religious freedom where it existed and to its insti-

1

tution where it did not. For this reason, the Declaration on Religious Freedom is addressed without distinction to all men and indeed is the only document of the Council so addressed.[2]

The French and American revolutions constitute the watershed which separates older questions of church and state from the modern problem of religious freedom. The Church as a unit had fought countless battles with emperors and kings to protect her own freedom. Indeed, despite serious exceptions in practice, the Church long affirmed the right of the individual to freedom from coercion in the profession of the Catholic faith.[3] But, as with other political freedoms, the freedom of religious exercise was intimately related to the character of the *anciens régimes* and necessarily circumscribed when government was the prerogative of an elite. Paternal government could hardly welcome religious diversity any more than the diversity implicit in the freedoms of speech, press, and assembly. With the two major political revolutions at the end of the eighteenth century, human society for the first time sought to maximize and institutionalize the values of individual freedom and equality. For the Church, which laid unique claims to divine authority and hierarchical organization, the application of these values of the new political order to the religious sphere of action posed many serious theoretical and practical problems.

Unfortunately for the Church, the nineteenth-century papacy expressed its reaction to only one of these revolutions. Nineteenth-century heirs of the Jacobins had appropriated the term "democracy" to describe a political model of popular sovereignty in which the will of the people dominated all other human values and all divine commands as the ultimate source of morality; such a "democracy" established a secular religion whose central mystery incarnated right and duty in the decisions of an omnipotent majority. There was, of course, no possibility of a satisfactory, much less an ideal, relationship between the Church and such a political organization.

With the European historical context in mind, it is no surprise that the nineteenth-century papacy did not conceive of the possibility, much less the implications, of a responsible, democratic society which was neither paternal nor Jacobin. The nineteenth century in Europe was a century of liberalism, not a century of democracy. During the last century, despite gradual extension

of the franchise, universal suffrage—the trademark of democracy—
existed in only two European countries, France and Switzerland,
both of which were hostile to the Church's freedom. Even in
England, the Lords were not shorn of their residual power until
resolution of the constitutional crisis of 1910–11, and universal
suffrage did not become a complete reality until 1918.[4]

Parenthetically, we should note that there is nothing inconsistent or even strange about the fact that the liberal governments
of the nineteenth century were paternal rather than democratic
in character. The central doctrine of classical liberalism was not
universal suffrage or majority decision but the autonomy of the
self-sufficient individual. This doctrine is ultimately more compatible with anarchic than with democratic principles, since
democracy is a genuine pattern of social organization, however
decentralized its ultimate process of decision making. Unlike
classical liberalism, democracy does not challenge the objective
and perfective, the creative and dynamic, nature of social organization itself.

What the classical liberal of the nineteenth century essentially
wanted was a freedom from society itself and a *gendarme* government to preside over a world in which only the economically fit
would survive. This was the vision which the liberal elite would
prescribe for the masses. The classical liberal crusaded for a
suffrage broad enough to include himself, but he feared that
further extension of the franchise to the masses would swell the
ranks of his adversaries both on the tradition-bound right and
on the radical left. The peasant might support a return to the
old order, and the industrial worker might support radical intervention by governments in economic affairs. His fears were fully
justified; the nineteenth-century partics of classical liberalism were
doomed everywhere in Europe when modern democracy and universal suffrage became twentieth-century realities.

The nineteenth-century papacy intuited correctly that Latin
liberalism was a new form of paternalism, and that this liberal
paternalism sought to prescribe by omission a substantive set of
values as normative for society. Since paternal society by definition
assumes the immaturity of "the many," the Latin liberals under-
took to prescribe every good considered socially important. In this
context, then, the Latin liberal profession of religious freedom

and separation of church and state implied indifference to, or even denial of, the Church's unique claims.

Latin liberals of the nineteenth century made no effort to conceal their paternal aspirations to free unenlightened subjects from the bondage of what they characterized a medieval and anachronistic superstition. While preaching a self-styled "freedom of conscience" and a "free church in a free state," in actual practice they displayed hostility and even violence toward the Church. In the name of liberty, the Latin liberals suppressed and despoiled the religious orders, secularized education without respect to the wishes of Catholic parents, and required civil ceremonies for the validity of marriages.[5] Fact as well as theory supported the papal argument that liberalism was yoked to paternalism and implied hostility to the Church.

The truth is that nineteenth-century popes were exclusively absorbed with paternal society and the nature of its relation to the freedom of religious exercise. They gave no attention to the possibility of a democratic society untainted by Jacobinism and its implication for religious freedom. The explanation of their restricted conception of political problems in general and the freedom of religious exercise in particular lies more in history and psychology than in theology and philosophy.

The overwhelmingly dominant pattern of political organization and consciousness in the Europe of the nineteenth century was paternal. Democracy and the associated political freedoms, including that of religious exercise, were novel and emerging concepts not yet freed from association with the excesses of the French Revolution in the minds of Europeans trained in the old tradition. Leo XIII, for example, had been schooled at the Academy of Noble Ecclesiastics, served as papal governor of Benevento and Perugia during the early period of the Italian revolutionary turmoil, and spent the thirty years before his election to the papal throne as bishop of the latter city. He was thus in Perugia throughout the events of the *risorgimento*.[6] Understandably, the nineteenth-century papacy failed to penetrate the novel, and even suspect, pattern of democratic political organization not yet maturely established in Europe.

There was, indeed, one democratic society, both nonpaternal and non-Jacobin, both genuinely democratic and friendly to the

Church's mission—the United States. But of the uniqueness and ingenuity of the American pattern of political organization and its constitutional affirmation of religious freedom the nineteenth-century papacy nowhere indicated any recognition. Leo XIII did note, in a letter significantly entitled *Longinqua oceani,* that the Catholic Church in America was "free to live and act without hindrance," but he added that "it would be very erroneous to draw the conclusion that in America is to be sought the type of the most desirable status of the Church, or that it would be universally lawful or expedient for State and Church to be, as in America, dissevered and divorced."[7] Indeed, the Church in America herself "would bring forth more abundant fruits if, in addition to liberty, she enjoyed the favor of the laws and the patronage of the public authority."[8] Thus, Leo failed to discern the significance of the American experiment and the political implications of democratic government for the Church. His failure to do so, however historically conditioned, delayed official recognition of religious freedom by the Church beyond the middle of the twentieth century.

The nineteenth-century papal analysis of the relation of the paternal state to religious freedom was not designed for, nor applicable to, a responsible democracy. Unlike the paternal polity, the democratically organized society does not aim to prescribe through public law every phase of the common good. The democratic polity does not separate a special class of rulers to specify the good for their subjects, nor do citizens in a democratic polity look to their leaders for a specification of all goods worthwhile for the community. As a result of this difference of function, therefore, religious freedom in a democratic state does not imply indifference to religion or rejection of the Church's claims. Religious freedom in the constitutional law of a democratic state implies no public profession of an ontological equality of all religions or none in the law of God. Because the democratic state has no aim to make every major prescription of the social good for its citizens— whom democratic theory presumes to be mature enough to act responsibly on their own—the religious freedom enshrined in public law conveys no anti-Catholic ontological or theological presuppositions.

The nineteenth-century papacy, then, did not recognize the

political and ethical implications of modern democracy. That patrician popes missed the significance and underestimated the vitality of democracy is historically conditioned: democracy itself was only then in the process of emergence in Europe. But the most important reason why they failed was that the nineteenth-century apostles of religious freedom never argued their case on democratic principles. Liberals like Cavour and Crispi in Italy and Gambetta and Ferry in France proposed religious freedom—accompanied by a program openly pledged to limit the Church's liberty—in the interest of a dogmatic secular humanism or an indifferent religious subjectivism. Nineteenth-century popes never understood the character of modern democracy, but their Latin liberal counterparts never offered them the example of truly democratic principles.

In spite of the limitations of his political consciousness, Leo XIII did thoroughly dismantle the medieval theoretical framework of church-state relations. Bellarmine had begun the process by discarding the "direct power" thesis of the more sanguine canonists; Leo continued the process by discarding Bellarmine's own "indirect power" theory. Leo clearly distinguished the spiritual and temporal societies and defended the "excellence and nobleness" of each.[9] Indeed, Leo was the first pope in history to affirm the legitimacy of the principle of toleration for non-Catholic religions.

But Leo did not transcend his patrician background and the political context of nineteenth-century Latin Europe. He identified the state with organized human society, and he required of the former what the Christian dispensation had always required of the latter, namely, a one-hundred-per-cent commitment to Christian principles and practice.[10] Hence, the public profession and propagation of non-Catholic religions could be, at best, only tolerated by "Catholic" states. The source of the confusion between state and society, of course, was Leo's culturally conditioned identification of human society with its paternal instance. If the ruler was regarded as a "father" of the community, then it was easy to think that his concern for the welfare of the community was all inclusive.

A half century after the death of Leo XIII, another patrician occupied the chair of Saint Peter and guided the Church in her earthly pilgrimage. The times had vastly changed. Classical liberalism, a doctrine essentially geared to government by the select, "enlightened" few, had been caught in a pincer movement by the rise of mass parties and had passed off the main stage of world history with World War I. The new threat to the Church came not from those who exaggerated the autonomy of the individual, but from those who exalted the cult of collectivity: the new threat to the Church came from the totalitarian mass parties of the left and the right which had come to power in Russia, Italy, and Germany and which threatened the most cherished values of Western civilization.

Where Leo XIII emphasized the genuine authority of the state against the efforts of the liberals to abdicate it, Pius XII stressed the limitations on the state's authority against the attempts of the dictators to deify it. Where Leo emphasized what the state must do to protect citizens from the abuse of freedom, Pius stressed what the state must refrain from doing because of the right of citizens to freedom. Where Leo proposed profession of the Catholic religion through legal establishment, Pius asked for the freedom of the Church to carry on her mission. Where Leo emphasized the specification of religious and moral goods through legal formulae as a matter of logical necessity, Pius stressed the concrete conditions which help the individual to achieve his own perfection and "so promote his attainment of his supernatural end."[11]

In his sixth and final Christmas message of World War II, Pius had occasion to speak hopefully of the future. The Axis dictatorships were doomed, and Pius took the opportunity to recognize the advent of a post-war world order in which democracy would play the key role. The Pope went far beyond Leo XIII's condescending admission that the Church does not condemn any form of government in itself, noting that the "democratic form of goverment is considered by many today to be a natural postulate of reason itself."[12] He further acknowledged that civil liberty and equality on the basis of human freedom and dignity are essential ideals of democracy, and that self-rule and free communication are "two rights of the citizens which find their expression in a democracy."[13] By these statements, Pius did more than acknowledge and tolerate democracy as the only alternative to the totalitarian heresies; he clearly indicated that he understood democratic processes and approved what he understood.[14]

That Pius in 1944 should understand the democratic process is no more surprising than Leo's failure to do so before the turn of the century. Democracy had emerged as the dominant form of government in Europe at the end of World War I and proved its sustaining power in World War II. In contrast to the totalitarian powers, the democracies honored human freedom and the Church's. Indeed, as papal secretary of state, Pius had traveled widely and witnessed personally the responsible workings of modern democracy.

Thus Pius added to the political consciousness of the papacy a dimension beyond that of his nineteenth-century predecessors. He explicitly recognized the existence and desirability of, even the natural and rational exigency for, the democratic organization of modern society. Moreover, he recognized the necessary political implications of such a democratic organization of society for human freedom. It is interesting to note that both Leo XIII and Pius XII related freedom to equality, although with different emphases. For Leo paternal society's denial of political equality implied limits on the freedom of the ruler's subjects; for Pius the political equality of citizens implied their freedom.

But despite the fact that Pius perceived in the transition of modern society from paternal to democratic principles even a natural postulate of reason, and despite the fact that he defended vigorously the rights of the person against the claims of totalitarian governments, he did not explicitly affirm religious freedom as a human right. Human consciousness, including that of the Church, is conditioned by history more than logic, and Pius advanced the argument only far enough to acknowledge religious freedom as a civil right, even a moral imperative, within the constitutional context of democratic society.

His successor, John XXIII, expanded further the papacy's consciousness of man's dignity in his encyclical letter *Pacem in terris*. As a person endowed with intelligence and freedom, man has rights and duties of his own, which are inviolable and inalienable.[15] Specifically, in the matter of religious exercise: "Every human being has the right to honor God according to the dictates of an upright conscience, and the right to profess his religion privately and publicly."[16] Not only did John recognize that the rights of man limit the competence of government, but he saw as a sign of the times that the "paramount task" of government is to protect and promote these rights and duties of citizens, especially by constitutional guarantees.[17]

Thus, John XXIII seemed to draw from Pius XII's premises the unqualified conclusion that religious freedom is a right proper to the human person. In one sentence of one encyclical, John appeared to work a veritable Copernican revolution in the theology of religious freedom. Where his predecessors, including Pius XII, approached the value of freedom, religious or otherwise, from the context of social organization, John seemed simply to affirm freedom, religious or otherwise, as a human right and from the context of freedom to approach the problems of social organization. Where Leo XIII and even Pius XII were preoccupied primarily with the establishment question and only secondarily touched the question of religious freedom, John XXIII affirmed religious freedom directly and left the establishment question completely aside. As a result of John's revolution, limitations on religious freedom seemed to be henceforth required to assume the burden of proof hitherto demanded by the papacy of religious freedom.

Yet John's single sentence on religious freedom invited many questions: (1) What precisely is religious freedom? (2) When is conscience upright? (3) Does the unbeliever have a right to the free exercise of disbelief? (4) Does a man in bad faith have a right to religious freedom? (5) What is the ground of religious freedom? (6) How far does the public profession of one's religion extend? (7) Does religious freedom include more than the right to profess publicly one's religion? and (8) Under what conditions is religious freedom defeasible? Here the Declaration on Religious Freedom took up the task begun by Pius and framed by John.

The primacy which American bishops accorded a conciliar statement on religious freedom amused many Europeans, who, understanding the nineteenth-century papal polemic against Jacobin democracy and sectarian liberalism, attached less importance to such a statement. As already indicated, however, the reasons for concern were real enough. American Catholics, who identified themselves with their country's authorship of the constitutional right to the free exercise of religion, had experienced a more bitter questioning of the Church's relation to religious freedom by non-Catholics than had Catholics elsewhere. It is also noteworthy that the main opposition to the Declaration on Religious Freedom came from the bishops of a nation committed to the paternal organization of society, showing that the basic issue posed by the Declaration on Religious Freedom was not simply religious freedom but freedom simply.

Religious freedom, in the sense of immunity from coercion by individuals, groups, or governments in religious matters, is a modern, technical term. As such, it must be distinguished from other uses of the term: (1) physical freedom, or free will itself, *i.e.*, the ability of individual men to determine for themselves whether or how to act; (2) psychological freedom, or the human consciousness of the capacity to act with responsibility; (3) moral freedom, or the human ability to determine whether or how to act in relation to God and the moral order; (4) evangelical freedom, or the freedom by which man is delivered from the power of sin through the truth of the gospel and the grace of the Holy Spirit; and (5) ecclesiastical freedom, or the freedom which belongs to the Church by the mandate of Christ in the fulfillment of her mission.[18] Unfortunately for the history of the Declaration on Religious Freedom, these distinctions were not always recognized in debate either by the conservative opposition to or by all liberal proponents of the Declaration.

This does not mean that the modern, technical use of the term "religious freedom" is without relation to the other uses.[19] For religious freedom has its foundation in the other freedoms, although in different ways: if man did not have free will or was unconscious of his freedom, all discussion of religious freedom would lack meaning; man's moral duty to worship God according to the dictates of his conscience is one reason why he has the right to immunity from coercion in religious matters; under the leaven of the gospel, Christians have increasingly recognized the right of all men to the free exercise of religion; lastly, in the course of fulfilling her mission, the Church has made men more conscious of their dignity and of the limits of government. Moreover, religious freedom enables the other freedoms to be exercised more easily and more completely.

Freedom, like peace, is indivisible. This is true not only in the sense that religious freedom intimately relates to other political freedoms, e.g., of speech, press, and assembly, but also in the sense that religious freedom has radical import for the internal life of the Church. Although the right of citizens to religious freedom in the *polis* differs in kind from the right of Christian men and women to freedom within the Church, the ideal of freedom ineluctably unites the two rights, both theoretically and practically. This is one of the great undeveloped areas in which the Church has yet to elaborate a comprehensive theology transcending sporadic insights. Such a task, however, is beyond the scope of this historical study.

One important theological question posed by the Declaration is that of the development of dogma: How did the Church's unequivocal affirmation of religious freedom develop? How did the Church's understanding of the relation of the Christian message to the right of citizens to religious freedom grow, especially through the nineteenth and twentieth centuries? Since the Declaration on Religious Freedom represents the fruition of a process of evolution, the doctrine of religious freedom presents an invaluable microcosm of the more general process by which doctrine develops and thus offers theologians a unique opportunity to study the structure of the process itself. An elaborate treatment of this question is also beyond the scope of the present work.

The aim of the present study is principally historical, to record and evaluate the principal events surrounding the framing of the Declaration on Religious Freedom for the service of future theological and political analysts. If the Declaration is important, its legislative history is important, especially for understanding the document itself. The study does not pretend to be comprehensive or without assumptions. Every selection involved in the writing of history presupposes interpretation; the conscientious historian can only hope to articulate clearly his view of events and cite all the evidence relevant to it. Following the advice of an American Catholic who experienced first hand the consequences of ambiguity in the Church's relation to religious freedom, we now turn to that record.

Notes

1. *The Documents of Vatican II*, eds. Walter M. Abbott, S.J., and Joseph Gallagher (New York: America, 1966), p. 696.
2. *Ibid.*, p. 688, n. 24.
3. See, for example, *Codex iuris canonici*, c. 1351.
4. See Carlton J. H. Hayes, *A Political and Cultural History of Modern Europe* (New York: Macmillan, 1937), Vol. II, pp. 482–84, 891.
5. *Ibid.*, pp. 553–56, 564–67, 572–73, 586–87, 589.
6. See *Leo XIII and the Modern World*, ed. Edward T. Gargan (New York: Sheed and Ward, 1961), pp. 15–20.
7. Cf. Leo XIII, *Longinqua oceani*, Acta Sanctae Sedis, Vol. XXVII (1895), p. 390; the translation is from *The Great Encyclical Letters of Pope Leo XIII*, ed. John J. Wynne, S.J. (New York: Benzinger, 1903), p. 255.
8. *Ibid.*
9. Leo XIII, *Immortale Dei*, ASS, XVIII (1885), p. 166; the translation is from *The Church Speaks to the Modern World: The Social Teachings of Leo XIII*, ed. Etienne Gilson (Garden City: Image, 1954), p. 168.
10. *Ibid.*, p. 163.
11. Pius XII, *Summi pontificatus*, Acta Apostolicae Sedis, Vol. XXXI (1939), p. 433.
12. Pius XII, *Già per la sesta volta*, AAS, XXXVII (1944–45), p. 13; the translation is from *Selected Letters and Addresses of Pius XII*, ed. G. D. Smith (London: Catholic Truth Society, 1949), p. 305. For the Leonine acceptance of different forms of government, see *Immortale Dei, loc. cit.*, p. 162.
13. *Ibid.*, pp. 13–14; trans. in Gilson, *op. cit.*, pp. 305–306.
14. On the Leonine doctrine of toleration, see *Immortale Dei, loc. cit.*, p. 174, and *Libertas praestantissimum*, ASS, XX (1887–88), p. 610.
15. John XXIII, *Pacem in terris*, AAS, LV (1963), p. 259.
16. *Ibid.*, p. 260; the translation is that of America Press, p. 14.
17. *Ibid.*, pp. 273–79; trans., pp. 21–26.
18. These distinctions were made in the introductory report to the *textus re-emendatus*; "Relatio, pars altera," *Schema declarationis de libertate religiosa* (Rome: Vatican Polyglot Press, 1965), p. 40.
19. The relation of "religious freedom" in the technical sense to the other uses of the term is discussed in *op. cit.*, pp. 40–41.

II

The Preparations

THE DECLARATION ON RELIGIOUS FREEDOM, promulgated on December 7, 1965, began its conciliar gestation almost five years before. On December 27, 1960, the submission of the Secretariat for Christian Unity charged with the task of drafting a text on religious freedom met at Fribourg, Switzerland, in the offices of Bishop François Charrière.[1] The group adopted as the basis for future discussion a paper submitted by Bishop Emile De Smedt of Bruges (Belgium).[2]

The first chapter at the outset distinguished forms of tolerance which ask the Church to renounce her faith in truths about God and the supernatural communion which He has established with men from the virtue of tolerance which ought to govern relations among men who do not agree in the area of convictions; De Smedt's draft condemned the former and defended the latter.[3] The first ground of tolerance as thus defined was based on the nature of man.[4] From the viewpoint of the most fundamental exigencies of the natural law, the objective sense of interpersonal relations includes the obligation of valuing and treating another as a subject, not as an object or means or thing. As a subject, the human person is called to a conscious and free life by which he is constituted master of his actions. He must decide moral value himself, for he is affected morally by his acts only insofar as he apprehends that his acts are good or bad in judgments of conscience and acts freely in conformity or deformity with these judgments. In this sense, the autonomy of the human person admits of no substitute in moral decisions. It also admits of no violation: if one violates the spiritual interiority of the human person, if one prevents him from developing himself consciously and freely, if one prevents him from forming his own judgment of conscience and from assuming personally the responsibility of his destiny, one reduces him to the rank of an object and a thing.

This intangible dignity of the human person determines the positive content of tolerance. The doctrine of tolerance does not proclaim a "freedom of conscience" which authorizes man to form his conscience according to whim. No one can say that he is sincerely interested in the formation of his conscience if he is not animated by love of truth and if he is not concerned with realizing in his actions the demands of truth according to the rules of prudence. Positive tolerance has nothing in common with moral or religious indifference.

But the doctrine of tolerance does recognize a "freedom of conscience" which respects and values persons who, in spite of a search for truth, have formed and are following an erroneous conscience. One respects and values in this case the person who errs in good faith, not the error itself. The fact that a person works to form his conscience sincerely reveals the fundamental value of his moral attitude. Moreover, it is only by means of the judgment of conscience that truth can penetrate a person's actions; a man can comform his acts to norms only insofar as they are known and pass into the judgments of conscience.

Positive tolerance is based, then, on the respect of the dignity of the human person who consciously and freely pursues his destiny. But it is also a fruit of love, which is the highest expression of interpersonal relations. As love is richer than tolerance, it not only implies the respect and value of the other as subject and person, it is driven to work for the true good of the other. Since this effort is directed toward a person, however, it should choose means in conformity with the value of the other as person. To prevent and overcome error, it should use means worthy of the human order, such as education, exposition, counsel, and especially the example of a life oriented toward the demands of truth and inspired by love of truth.

The second ground advanced by De Smedt was based on the nature of the act of faith.[5] The act of faith is above all the fruit of the grace of God, and an attempt to impose faith on another by force would be as temerarious as trying to put oneself in the place of God. Moreover, on the part of man, the act of faith is a free response to divine initiative. An imposed faith is thus a contradiction in terms, not only in relation to the free will of God but also in relation to the free adhesion which it presupposes in man.

The third ground presented by the Fribourg draft was based on the practical demands of the situation facing the Church in the modern world.[6] In the question of tolerance, Pius XII underlined the importance of "superior norms," such as the common good of the universal church and of the kingdom of God in the whole world. In no country can Catholics who form a majority take an attitude toward religious freedom which would have a deleterious effect on the condition of Catholics who in other countries constitute only a minority. The world is a unity, and one must take account of the consequences that a particular attitude would have in other parts of the world. Tolerance partakes of the practice of Christian charity, but it does not exhaust it. The mission of charity is vaster; it demands not only that the Church practice tolerance toward those who do not share her faith but also that she protect her own faithful. That is why she insists on the education of Catholic children in Catholic schools. It is why she insists on a solid religious and moral formation of the faithful.

Appended to the chapter on tolerance were three notes.[7] The first urged the necessity of avoiding the formula "the rights of truth." In the proper sense of the term, truth has no rights; only human persons (or societies composed of human persons) are the possessors of rights. Of course, the person has obligations with regard to truth, but these obligations can be expressed without appeal to the inaccurate term "rights of truth."

The second note deplored use of the term "dogmatic intolerance." Its use is in part responsible for the pejorative meaning the term "dogma" has for non-Catholics. Of course, Catholics do not admit that the truths of faith are entirely relative. But that commitment can be expressed without use of the unfortunate term "dogmatic intolerance," which appears to yoke intolerance to dogma.

The third note emphasized the distinction of Pius XI between "freedom of conscience" and "freedom of consciences." The latter term avoids the contamination of religious indifferentism and expresses only the ideal of true freedom, which consists in forming and following one's conscience with a sincere effort to conform it to objective reality.

Chapter II took up the theme of Catholics working together with those not of their faith in the cultural development of human society.[8] The work of promoting science, technology, the arts, the economic order, social and political institutions, and the organization of international relations is profane in the sense that the scientific knowledge and technique necessary to achieve human goods are not given by revelation but have their source in the natural gifts which the Creator has confided to men. Moreover, such tasks are essentially social in nature. No individual has the time or the capacities to realize by himself all the cultural values of which he has need to live a truly human life. The collaboration of men to realize human culture can develop to the maximum all its potential only if all the richness of different human groups and different lands are bound up in it. Thus Catholics have an obligation to take an active part in collaboration toward secular goals. But, since the world is pluralist, they must collaborate in the human cultural endeavor with those who do not share their religious convictions.

Two reasons determine for a Christian the dignity and the grandeur of his participation in the cultural endeavor incumbent on mankind. First, the Christian knows that he has been created in the image of God and participates in God's power of lordship over the rest of creation. In this scheme, the work by which man exercises mastery over earth and develops himself takes on a religious meaning. Second, he sees in his work an exercise of the great commandment which Jesus gave to his disciples, that of fraternal charity. These two principles define the place of the Christian in the world of secular values: he must develop his natural gifts, and he must be faithful to the law of charity.

If the secular world has its own autonomy, it is no less true that it is subject to the order of moral values. These principles of the moral life, proclaiming the dignity of the person, are intrinsically and substantially open to the natural light of reason; they can be known by those who are not Christians and do not believe in God. In the area of secular values, the Christian can live in communion of word and action with all men who, without sharing his faith, pursue the realization of a truly human order. The Church accepts and counsels cooperation on the common ground of the Decalogue, of the whole Decalogue in collaboration with those who admit the existence of God, and of the second table in encounter with those who do not adhere to a religious faith but recognize practically the objective demands of the dignity of the human person.

As to the forms of collaboration, the Fribourg draft distinguished two cases. When the freedom of the Catholic to be faithful to his conscience is respected, Catholics may take their place in groups where they collaborate with non-Catholics. This form of collaboration presupposes as indispensable conditions that Catholics intensify their own religious life and reinforce their ties to their religious community in works and associations of a religious nature. When, however, prospective partners do not have respect for the freedom of Catholics or pursue goals and adopt means with which Catholics cannot agree, participation by Catholics in the same organizations would create an ambiguous situation. In these cases, Catholics must regretfully form their own groups to work for secular goals. But, even if permanent collaboration is impossible, Catholics will still cooperate with others each time that limited objectives permit.

Chapter III took up the broad theme of relations between church and state.[9] In contrast to the theocracy of the Old Testament, the New Testament prescribes other principles to govern relations between the Church and civil society. Christ founded a Church with a religious mission for all times and addressed to all men. Moreover, Christ established a decisive distinction between Caesar and God, between the temporal power of the state and the spiritual power of the Church. As a consequence, the state cannot require religious faith of a citizen for participation without restriction in civic life, and the state must recognize the limits of its power in relation to the fact that the Christian dispensation is essentially supernatural, coming from above and irreducible to human efforts.

What has the Church of right to expect from temporal societies? The state, taking account of its temporal finality, ought to proclaim its respect for religious values by means proper to itself, *i.e.*, by civil acts in favor of citizens and their associations. The state must protect the inalienable and inviolable rights of the human persons who form its body of citizens. To be able to act conformably to truth, the human person has the duty, and the correlative right, to search for truth in the different areas which benefit his existence; this right is today called freedom of thought. To orient his moral life, the human person has the duty, and the corresponding right, to form and follow his conscience; this right is today called freedom of conscience. To live the requirements of his relation to God sincerely grasped in conscience, the human person has the duty, and the corresponding right, to be faithful to his conscience in the area of religion; this right is today called freedom of religion.

The promulgation of these rights, especially religious freedom, is fully in accord with the teaching of the Church on the dignity of the human person and on the act of faith. The confirmation of religious liberty by public law corresponds perfectly to the confinement of the state's role to the temporal sphere and shows its respect for the supernatural transcendence and psychological structure of the act of faith. Moreover, if the legal expression of the rights of the human person is to be efficacious, it must assure the genuine exercise of these rights in external activities. The state must guarantee to its citizens the freedoms of speech, association, propagation, worship, etc.

But there are limits to these freedoms. Although personal rights are essentially intangible, their exercise is necessarily limited. When a man acts in a social context, his actions can have effects harmful for others, for the common good, and for public morality. It belongs to the competence of civil authority to make and enforce the laws required to prevent citizens and associations from breaking the norms which protect human dignity. The interventions of the state imposed on the exercise of personal rights ought to be based exclusively on the demands of the common good and to be applied equally to all citizens, without distinction of religious belief.

To Chapter II were appended two notes.[10] The first disavowed the classic nineteenth-century distinction between "thesis" and "hypothesis." The distinction is vague, open to the reproach of opportunism, and suggests that the theocracy of the Old Testament is ideal even for the Church of the New Testament. The second note condemned the expression that "the state has an obligation to worship God." Although the state must serve God, public worship is the responsibility of the Church. The service of the state to God must correspond to its temporal structure. It is realized by recognizing the transcendence of religious values, which the state must respect, by proclaiming the rights of the human person, including religious freedom, and by legally limiting the exercise of rights to eliminate abuses which are contrary to the demands of the common good.

The Fribourg draft foreshadowed the main lines of argument which were to appear in the first two texts on religious freedom submitted to the Council by the Secretariat. As did the first two conciliar texts, the Fribourg draft grounded the right of religious freedom on the moral duty to follow a sincerely formed conscience and the free supernatural character of the act of faith. The Fribourg draft, of course, was open in this respect to the questions later raised against the derivative conciliar texts: Does the moral duty to follow one's sincerely formed conscience establish a right to act according to the dictates of a sincerely formed but erroneous conscience? Does the right of the human person not to be coerced *against* his conscience establish the right of the human person not to be restrained from acting in society *according to* the dictates of a sincerely formed but erroneous conscience? If the right to the free exercise of religion is dependent on sincerity of conscience, may not the state deny freedom of religious exercise to persons acting in bad faith, judge which consciences are sincere, and in effect, make religious freedom a concession from the state rather than a right?

As did the first two conciliar texts on religious freedom, the Fribourg draft limited the free exercise of religion by the demands of the common good. Here, too, the document was open to an objection made against the derivative conciliar texts: Is not the common good the precise ground on which the conservative opposition always argued against the right to religious freedom? While the Fribourg draft did touch the constitutional question of the state's competence in religious matters, it obscured the distinction between state and society in its treatment of the limits on the free exercise of religion.

Three other objections, unrelated to successive drafts, can be raised specifically against the Fribourg document. First, the initial chapter curiously spoke of tolerance, while modern man claims religious freedom not as a concession but as a right, and the arguments advanced in this section clearly transcended the ordinary understanding of the term "tolerance." Second, the argument of the first chapter was artificially separated from the argument of the third chapter, with which it formed a logical whole. Third, the second chapter was a lengthy, unnecessary, and clumsy digression from the main theme of the document.

Yet all these criticisms should not obscure the contribution of the Fribourg draft to the final conciliar Declaration on Religious Freedom. As a first draft, it served as a basis of future discussion and unambiguously affirmed the right to religious freedom in both the internal and external fora. Perhaps most important of all, it highlighted the dignity of the human person, his unique value as subject, on which the ultimate declaration would rest so strongly.

The Secretariat revised and reworked the Fribourg draft in the succeeding months. In the *motu proprio* of February 2, 1962, John XXIII announced that the Council would convene on October 11, 1962, and Cardinal Augustin Bea, president of the Secretariat, submitted its product on religious freedom to the Central Commission on June 18 for presentation to the Council Fathers.[11]

The draft submitted at this time began with an introduction urging all men to defend the honor of God and the dignity of the human person.[12] Not only should men seek in charity truths and values common among them, but at the same time they should also attend to the rights and duties of human persons. Chapter I, on promoting the good of the faith in charity, then took up the question of religious freedom.[13] Catholics must work to teach all nations and spread the light of life to all men by the natural and supernatural means employed by the Lord Himself, namely, preaching, example, witness, and even the shedding of their own blood. But they must avoid all overt or covert works of a base proselytism, all improper and unworthy means, such as bribes, enticements, blandishments, lies, threats, and force.

The Church urges that her sons and daughters, living truth in charity and striving to bring all men to the true faith, take care always that those created in the image of God give assent to the faith only with full liberty and in good conscience. They must abstain, therefore, from all force. The person in error concerning the faith must be respected, and the Church has always supported his right to religious freedom. Indeed, this religious freedom, or immunity from external coercion, is demanded by the nature of the act of faith itself. On the one hand, faith is a free gift of God, and on the other, faith demands a free homage to God. The Church accordingly commands that "no one should be compelled against his will to embrace the Catholic faith."

The right to follow conscience in religious matters must be observed not only by the faithful, who can acknowledge the constitution of the act of faith, but absolutely by all men and the community of men. For the human person can fulfill the will of God only insofar as he perceives the divine law through the medium of a dictate of conscience. Hence the man who obeys his sincerely formed conscience intends to obey God; he must be judged worthy of respect and can be hindered by no force from following his conscience.

The exclusion of external coercion in religious matters preached by the Church extends beyond freedom of thought or freedom of public worship; it embraces the right to observe and proclaim private and public duties toward God and toward men as conscience dictates. It includes the right to apply and diffuse moral principles in matters familial, social, hygienic, and economic. This right to religious freedom belongs both to individual men and to associations of men who are brought by the demands of conscience to follow or promote a particular religious conception of life.

These personal rights would not be really and effectively recognized if the right of men to act in the external forum according to the dictates of conscience were denied. The only limitation on the public exercise of the freedom of conscience is that imposed by the common good. For this reason, the Church condemns discrimination, harm, and persecution of men because of their nationality, race, or color. Specifically, in religious matters, she asserts that the right to exercise freedom of conscience in the external forum, provided that the common good is protected, must always and everywhere be recognized.

Chapter I closed with a brief comment that religious freedom everywhere is especially urgent in modern times because of the many relationships by which men of different religious beliefs are joined together. An annotation at this point added that the growing interaction among peoples of the world makes it more necessary than ever for Catholics in individual nations to observe the right to religious freedom for the common good of the universal Church.

Chapter II exposed in three paragraphs and two annotations the role of Catholic cooperation with non-Catholics in the task of developing human society.[14] Moral norms flowing from the very dignity of the human person offer a common foundation for constructing a truly human order, but they are not the only or the highest norms. The Christian, in ordering his life and perfecting his work, can and ought to be governed by the precept of charity, whereby the task of human creativity and social service are ordered to building up the Body of Christ and to the glory of God. The Church must be vigilant that Catholics collaborate duly and generously with non-Catholics, and that Catholics are at the same time mindful of their duties as Catholics. To assure the latter, it is helpful that Catholics join Catholic associations for a spiritual foundation of their work with non-Catholics.

Chapter III, on relations between the Church and civil society, was divided into three sections.[15] In the first section, as in the Fribourg document, the universal spiritual mission of the Church was sharply distinguished from the theocracy of the Old Testament. As a consequence, civil society must limit itself to the secular order and give to the Church the freedom to fulfill her mission. Nor, since the Church's mission is universal, can she be narrowed to the limits of a so-called national church.

The second section of Chapter III structured the exercise of religious liberty in the framework of civil society. The state may not espouse "in a positive way" the view that all religions are of the same value, but "modern civil societies," in their practical ordering of civil life, may establish religious freedom and the political equality of all religions before the law. Moreover, since the dignity of the human person requires that every citizen be able to follow the dictates of his conscience in the exercise of his religious life, no one can be hindered by civil society from exercising his right, provided that the public order is not affected and the needs of the common good are satisfied. The state cannot impose on citizens the profession of a particular religion as a condition of full participation in national and civil life. But it does belong to civil authority to protect against abuses by laws which respond to the needs of the common good and apply equally to all citizens without distinction as to religious profession.

The third section of Chapter III expressed the ardent desire that the Church receive subsidies from civil society for its activities serving the common good, subsidies which should also be given proportionately and within the limits of the public good to non-Catholic religious communities. Civil society, like every human community, is bound to serve God. But it must offer this service according to its own proper nature, *i.e.*, by attending in its legislation to the norms of divine law and by fulfilling faithfully its own proper mission received from God. Protecting and promoting personal dignity and the virtue of citizens by an appropriate order of law performs that service to God.

The draft submitted to the Central Commission on June 18, 1962, differed from the Fribourg draft in many respects of varying importance: it eliminated all reference to tolerance; it defined religious freedom; it reversed the order of arguments from conscience and faith in favor of religious freedom; it simplified Chapter II, leaving the burden of theological analysis to the annotations; Chapters I and III were better developed and integrated, both logically and stylistically; the new draft was more aware of the transition from the order of conscience to the order of action according to conscience; it closely related religious freedom to the political equality of citizens; and it cited three times as many scriptural passages as the Fribourg document, presumably in an effort to strengthen its theological base.

But the main questions raised by the Fribourg draft remained unanswered, and several new ones posed. The draft of June 18, 1962, used the terms "civil society" and "state" interchangeably in Chapter III and thus accepted a key plank in the conceptual frame of the conservative opposition. (The conservatives' logic was hard to fault if they succeeded in defining the terms of discourse.) Moreover, the draft introduced, and failed to develop adequately, the idea of proportionately equal subsidies to religious communities for undefined services to the common good, an intricate issue of church-state relations only indirectly related to the core of religious freedom.

The Secretariat, however, was not the only agency of the Council concerned with relations between Church and state. The Theological Commission, under the presidency of Cardinal Alfredo Ottaviani (Curia), had evolved in its own schema on the Church a chapter "On the Relations between Church and State and on Religious Tolerance." Indeed, at the same session (June 12–20, 1962) in which Cardinal Bea presented the Secretariat's draft on religious freedom to the Central Commission, the Theological Commission submitted its own schema to that body.[16]

Chapter IX of the Theological Commission's proposed schema on the Church was phrased in the scholastic and juridical terms classic to the manuals of theology, especially after the writings of Leo XIII.[17] It distinguished at the outset the ends of the Church and civil society; each is supreme in its own order, not subject to the other, and equipped with its own executive, legislative, and judicial power. Since, however, the two societies exercise their powers over the same persons and frequently the same objects, they cannot neglect one another if they both are to prosper together.

The power of the Church extends to everything by which men attain their eternal salvation, but everything which pertains only to man's temporal happiness is subject to civil authority. In those things which pertain to the goals of both societies, such as marriage and education, the rights of the civil power must be so exercised that, in the judgment of the Church, the higher goods of the supernatural order suffer no harm. In all other temporal matters, provided that the law of God is observed, the Church respects the autonomy of civil society. Moreover, the Church, in fufilling her own mission, secures for civil society great advantages. By preaching Christian doctrine, she works to develop good citizens; she warns rulers to exercise their office for the benefit of the citizens; and she inculcates the observance of both the natural and supernatural laws by which the whole order among citizens and nations should be established in peace and justice.

On its part, civil power cannot be indifferent to religion. Since it was instituted by God to help men to acquire truly human perfection, it ought not only to offer its citizens the capacity to procure temporal goods but also to aid them to acquire more readily spiritual goods helpful to leading their human life in a religious context. Among these goods none is more capital than the recognition and fulfillment of duties owed to God. Civil power in its public acts embodies the "person" of society. Since God is the author of civil society and the source of all goods which flow to its members through it, civil society must honor and worship God specifically as He shows Himself in the present economy of salvation in the true Church of Christ.

The state, therefore, must associate itself with the public worship offered by the Church not only through its citizens but also through those who are charged with the authority to represent civil society. Civil power, and not only the individual citizen, has the duty to receive the revelation of God proposed by the Church, and civil power must conform its laws to natural, divine, and ecclesiastical law. The civil power must protect in a special way the full liberty of the Church to fulfill her mission. Lastly, civil authority has a grave obligation to exclude from its regime, legislation, and public action everything which the Church may judge to hinder the attainment of eternal life.

The doctrine explained above, however, can be applied integrally only in a state in which the citizens profess the Catholic faith. Although a government can never compel anyone to embrace the Catholic faith unwillingly, it must promote intellectual, social, and moral conditions "in which even the less educated may persevere more easily in their received faith." Therefore, as a government protects public morality, so it can regulate the public manifestations of non-Catholic religious worship and defend its citizens against the diffusion of false doctrines which, in the judgment of the Church, imperil eternal salvation, in order to safeguard citizens from the seduction of error and preserve the unity of faith.

But the demands of Christian charity and prudence require

that the state act in such ways that neither the state nor the Church suffers harm. Therefore the state can rightfully institute according to circumstances a system of legal tolerance to avoid evils, such as civil discord or impeding conversion to the Catholic faith, and to promote a greater good, such as civic cooperation and a more efficacious achievement of the Church's supernatural mission. In this matter, not only goods of the national scene but also goods of the universal Church must be considered. By tolerance, a "Catholic" government follows the example of divine Providence which permits evil out of which it draws good.

In those states in which a great part of the citizens do not profess the Catholic faith, a "non-Catholic" government must conform itself in religious matters at least to the precepts of the natural law. In these circumstances, the government must grant civil liberty to all forms of religious worship not contrary to "natural religion." Such liberty is not opposed to Catholic principles, since it is appropriate for the good of the Church and the commonwealth. Moreover, lest the Church or commonwealth suffer harm, Catholic citizens seeking to vindicate the rights of the Church should seek the judgment of ecclesiastical authority, whose function it is to judge what is the good of the Church in particular circumstances and to "direct" citizens in civil actions in defense of the Church.

Chapter IX closed with a ringing affirmation that the principles governing relations between Church and state were immutable, despite the moderation in their application which circumstances might require. (When the first schema on the Church was placed before the Council, on December 1, 1962, the title to Chapter IX was simplified to "The Relations between the Church and the State," and the whole application of the chapter's blueprint to "Catholic" and "non-Catholic" states was suppressed, though still implicit.[18])

The obvious opposition between the schema of the Secretariat and that of the Theological Commission on the subject of religious freedom evoked formidable discussion at the June 12–20 session of the Preparatory Central Commission.[19] In the face of this discussion, which was proceeding without issue, Cardinal Pietro Ciriaci (Curia) proposed to refer the matter to the Pope.[20] In July the Pope responded characteristically by creating an *ad hoc* commission, headed by Ciriaci and composed of Bea, Ottaviani, Msgr. Jan Willebrands, and Fr. Sebastian Tromp, S.J.[21] (The latter two men were the secretaries of the Secretariat and Theological Commission, respectively.) The role of the *ad hoc* commission, of course, was to seek an accord between the two drafts on religious freedom.

The secretariat asked Bishop De Smedt and Fr. Jérôme Hamer, O.P., rector of the Dominican faculty of Saulchoir, to come to Rome to prepare a new text taking account of the Theological Commission's position.[22] The new draft, edited by De Smedt, Willebrands, and Hamer, was submitted to Ciriaci and Tromp on July 16.[23]

The new draft, called a pastoral decree, left intact the introduction and first two chapters of the previous schema submitted by the Secretariat.[24] But the new Chapter III, "On the Relations between the Church and Civil Society," was composed of paragraphs taken bodily from both Chapter IX of the Theological Commission's schema on the Church and Chapter III of the Secretariat's previous schema on religious freedom.[25] The result can only be described as a crazyquilt.

The new Chapter III incorporated the draft of the Theological Commission on the distinction between the Church and civil society, on the subordination of the end of the state to the end of the Church, on the power and limits of the Church, and on the duties of the Church toward civil society.[26] Even on the religious duties of governments, the new text repeated most of Chapter IX of the schema on the Church: governments cannot be indifferent to religion; governments must assist citizens to gain spiritual advantage; governments in their public acts representing the whole society must honor God according to the present plan of salvation centered in the true Church; governments must conform their laws to natural, divine, and ecclesiastical laws; governments must particularly protect the freedom of the Church to fulfill integrally her mission; and governments have a grave obligation to exclude from regime, legislation, and public action everything which the Church may judge to hinder citizens from achieving the goal of salvation.[27] Two religious duties, however, were removed from the list: the duty of the state to associate itself with the public worship offered by the Church and the duty of governments to receive the revelation proposed by the Church. In addition, two paragraphs were inserted from the Secretariat's old Chapter III: civil society must restrict itself to the secular sphere, and the Church cannot be reduced to the limits of a "national" church.[28]

At this point, the new draft of Chapter III departed radically from the text and argument of the Theological Commission. It dropped all reference to "Catholic" and "non-Catholic" states and avoided altogether the concept of religious tolerance. Instead, the new draft took up the themes of religious freedom in civil society and peaceful relations between religious communities and civil society.[29]

Apparently forgetting that the point had already been made in Chapter I, Article 2, the new draft of Chapter III incorporated the Theological Commission's disclaimer on the use of force in cases of conversion to the Catholic faith.[30] After disavowing the doctrine of religious indifference and affirming the advantage to civil society if all citizens were Catholic, the new draft of Chapter III even expanded the affirmation of religious freedom advanced in the previous draft of the Secretariat: civil society may not prevent anyone from following in the internal and external fora the dictates of his conscience, even when objectively and invincibly in error, and from adhering publicly to any form of religious worship not contrary to "natural religion."

Moreover, civil society can rightfully deny the exercise of this religious freedom only when it disturbs public order or harms the common good. Indeed, it is precisely the common good of civil society, of the world-wide human community, and even of the Catholic Church in the modern world which most acutely demands recognition of the personal right to follow conscience. This is why nations and international organizations are invited to bend their efforts to safeguard and promote religious freedom and the equality of all citizens. In this way, they imitate the example of divine Providence which permits evils out of which greater goods can be drawn. The last three paragraphs on religious freedom were taken verbatim from the Secretariat's previous schema: the state cannot impose on citizens the profession of a particular religion as a condition of full participation in national and civil life, and it belongs to civil authority to prevent abuses by means of laws which respond to the needs of the common good and are applied to all citizens without religious discrimination.[31]

On the peaceful relations between religious communities and civil society, the new draft of Chapter III repeated the first two paragraphs of the previous Secretariat schema: civil society must grant and enshrine in public law freedom of religious bodies and other religiously inspired associations which citizens form consistent with the common good, and the Catholic Church and other religious communities should receive proportionate subsidies from civil society for services to the common good.[32] Two succeeding paragraphs were adapted from Chapter IX of the Theological Commission's schema: Catholic citizens have the obligation of securing the freedom of the Church to fulfill her mission and must strive that the Church and the state offer one another mutual aid, and in doing this, Catholic citizens must follow the judgment of the Church, to whom it belongs to evaluate the good of the Church in varying circumstances and direct citizens in their civic actions in defense of the Church.[33]

The conclusion of Chapter III was an amalgam typical of the entire new draft: one paragraph adopted from Chapter IX of the Theological Commission's schema and one paragraph adopted from the Secretariat's previous schema.[34] The first paragraph disavowed laicism and affirmed the immutability of the principles governing relations between Church and state, no matter what the regime or circumstances. The second paragraph acknowledged the obligation of civil society to worship God by recognizing publicly the divine majesty and by fulfilling faithfully its mission, especially in protecting and promoting by public law the personal dignity and virtue of its citizens.

The new draft of Chapter III radically limited the effectiveness and even the internal consistency of the schema's affirmation of religious freedom. Not only was the hybrid text an affront to good style, it skirted the laws of logic without even a becoming intellectual blush. On the level of style, the new draft might as well have asked Picasso to retouch Raphael. On the level of logic, the new text attempted to incorporate the concepts and premises of the conservative opposition to religious freedom into its defense. The logical temerity and ideological timidity of the July draft was matched only by its short life.

But the reasons why, against all logic, the attempt was made are not hard to find. The Secretariat was not yet an equal of the Theological Commission, and religious liberty involved theological issues other than the strictly ecumenical question of cooperation with non-Catholics in fostering Christian unity. Moreover, at this moment before the opening of the Council, the Secretariat had no way of knowing how strong liberal sentiment would be among the Council Fathers.

On July 20, 1962, Willebrands visited Ciriaci in order to explain the new draft of the schema on religious freedom.[35] In the meantime, on the preceding day, Tromp had written to Willebrands to inform the Secretariat that the Theological Commission would rewrite on its own, without the advice or consent of the Secretariat, a new chapter on Church-and-state relations (Chapter IX) for the proposed Constitution on the Church.[36] He assured Willebrands that he would speak with him later on the problem of tolerance and religious freedom. Willebrands replied to Tromp, by letter on July 25, that he could not accept the *modus operandi* proposed by Tromp because the problems of religious freedom and of relations between Church and state were interrelated and, therefore, fell within the competence of both the Secretariat and the Theological Commission.[37]

In the same letter of July 25 Willebrands asked to meet with Tromp to discuss the question more fully. On July 28 Tromp wrote to assure Willebrands that there was no reason to be disturbed about the Theological Commission's proposed course of action; he said that he hoped to be able to see Willebrands soon.[38] On July 31 Willebrands wrote to inform Tromp that he was obliged to leave Rome on August 4 and that he therefore desired to see Tromp before that date.[39] On August 2 Tromp and Willebrands did meet, but Tromp insisted that the meeting was altogether unofficial and that he was not authorized as Secretary of the Theological Commission to speak with Willebrands.[40] On this basis, they discussed relations between Church and state but not the question of religious freedom.

With this unsatisfactory issue of the Tromp-Willebrands exchange, no rapport between the Theological Commission and the Secretariat was possible. It was perfectly clear that the Theological Commission did not wish any compromise with the Secretariat on the subject of religious freedom, and that wish was well founded on the radical incompatibility of the two groups' positions. Predictably, then, the device of an *ad hoc* commission to reconcile differences between Chapter IX of the Theological Commission's proposed Constitution on the Church and the Secretariat's schema on religious freedom was doomed to failure because the two schemata were unequivocally separated by the principle of contradiction. The preconciliar history of the schema on religious freedom closed on this pessimistic note, and this was only the first skirmish in a series of battles before the final victory.

Notes

1. Memo of Fr. Jérôme Hamer, O.P., a *peritus* (expert) assisting the Secretariat, on successive drafts of the Declaration on Religious Freedom, p. 1. (Mimeographed, in the files of Fr. John C. Murray, S.J., Woodstock College, Woodstock, Maryland). See also Hamer, "Histoire du texte de la Déclaration," *Vatican II: La liberté religieuse*, eds. Hamer and Yvs. M.-J. Congar, O.P. (Les Éditions du Cerf: Paris, 1967), p. 53. Hamer indicates *ibid.*, n. 2, that the subcommission was composed of himself and Canon Bavaud, professor of the Fribourg seminary and consultant of Charrière, in addition to the two bishops.
2. *Ibid.* The De Smedt paper is hereafter referred to as the Fribourg draft.
3. Fribourg draft (mimeographed, the Murray files), pp. 1–2.
4. *Ibid.*, pp. 2–3.
5. *Ibid.*, pp. 3–4.
6. *Ibid.*, p. 4.
7. *Ibid.*, p. 5.
8. *Ibid.*, pp. 6–9.
9. *Ibid.*, pp. 10–12.
10. *Ibid.*, p. 13.
11. For the *motu proprio* of February 2, 1962, see Xavier Rynne, *Letters from Vatican City* (New York: Ferrar, Straus and Co., 1963), p. 93. For the date of Bea's submission of the Secretariat's draft on religious freedom, see Hamer, Memo, p. 1, and "Histoire . . . ," *op. cit.*, p. 57. See also Pietro Pavan, "The Declaration on Religious Freedom." *Information. Documentation on the Conciliar Church*, Doss. LXVI–XXIV (November 23, 1966), pp. 1–2. But

the date of June 20 is given in "Note sur le schéma 'De libertate religiosa' présenté par le Secrétariat pour l'unité des Chrétiens," October 30, 1963, p. 1. (Mimeographed, the Murray files.) The date given in the "Note" possibly refers in shorthand form to the whole session of the Central Commission from June 12 to 20.

12. *Schema constitutionis de libertate religiosa* (Rome: Vatican Polyglot Press, 1962, p. 5.

13. *Ibid.*, pp. 6–9.

14. *Ibid.*, pp. 10–11.

15. *Ibid.*, pp. 12–15.

16. Hamer, "Histoire . . . ," *op. cit.*, p. 60. In his Memo, p. 1, he states that the Theological Commission submitted its draft on the same day as Bea presented the Secretariat's, June 18. The Secretariat's "Note" also claims a common date, but lists June 20 as the date.

17. Typewritten copy of the chapter, the Murray files.

18. *Schema constitutionis dogmaticae de Ecclesia* (Rome: Vatican Polyglot Press, 1962), pp. 64–79. For the date of conciliar introduction, see Rynne, *op. cit.*, p. 214.

19. "Note," p. 1.

20. *Ibid.*

21. *Ibid.*

22. *Ibid.*

23. *Ibid.*

24. "Decretum de libertate religiosa," 1962, pp. 1–5. (Mimeographed by the Secretariat, the Murray files.)

25. *Ibid.*, pp. 6–12.

26. *Ibid.*, pp. 6–8.

27. *Ibid.*, pp. 8–9.

28. *Ibid.*, p. 9.

29. *Ibid.*, pp. 9–12.

30. *Ibid.*, p. 3.

31. *Ibid.*, pp. 11–12.

32. *Ibid.*

33. *Ibid.*

34. *Ibid.*

35. "Note," p. 1.

36. *Ibid.*

37. *Ibid.*

38. *Ibid.*, p. 2.

39. *Ibid.*

40. *Ibid.*

III

The First Text

SEVERAL EVENTS DURING AND AFTER the First Session of the Council strengthened immeasurably the authority of the Secretariat and its position on religious freedom. First, on October 19, 1962, eight days after the Council opened, Pope John elevated the Secretariat to a rank of equality with the conciliar commissions and authorized it to present its own schemas to the Council.[1] Indeed, in November, the schema on religious freedom was formally listed among those scheduled to be discussed at the Council, although with the note: "This schema is in a special commission to be put in accord with the schema 'On Religious Tolerance.' "[2] Second, in the closing week of the First Session, the conciliar debate on the Theological Commission's Constitution on the Church, including Chapter IX, revealed a broadly based and general opposition to that juridically oriented and conservative draft, and this opposition further strengthened the Secretariat's pastorally oriented and liberal position on religious freedom.[3] Finally, on April 11, 1963, four months after the First Session of the Council closed, Pope John XXIII published his moving encyclical *Pacem in terris*, and its unflinching focus on human freedom, including religious freedom explicitly, now became the doctrine in possession, a new "thesis" supporting the argument of the Secretariat, not that of the Theological Commission.[4]

At a plenary meeting of the Secretariat on February 16 to 18, 1963, two months after the close of the first session, a new draft on religious freedom was accepted.[5] Conscious of both its own increased authority and the diminished prestige of the Theological Commission, the Secretariat withdrew its ill-conceived and ill-executed attempt to compromise with the conservative opposition on the proposition of religious freedom. The new draft was considerably shorter: it left completely aside the subject of relations between Church and state which had hitherto composed the third chapter of the schema; chapter divisions were dropped altogether; and explicit references to cooperation with non-Catholics eliminated, although two of the three paragraphs of what formerly formed Chapter II of the schema were retained in the new draft.[6] The schema now focused exclusively on the theme of religious freedom proper and even added two paragraphs spelling out violations of religious freedom: death, despoliation, deprivation, and denial of social or civic equality.[7]

This succinct draft on religious freedom was discussed anew at another meeting of the Secretariat on May 18 and underwent some minor modifications.[8] Growing awareness of the problem of limiting public action in the name of conscience led to two changes. The modified new draft affirmed only that a man following conscience is worthy of respect; it did not claim, as did previous drafts, that there was no right to prevent him from following conscience. On the other hand, another modification apparently equated the only admitted limit to action according to conscience, the common good, to the objective order of the rights of God and the inalienable rights and freedoms of the human person. The difficulty of formulating limits to the exercise of religious freedom would preoccupy future conciliar deliberations on religious freedom. The text thus modified was definitively approved by the Secretariat on May 30, 1963.[9]

Following a meeting on July 3 and 4 of the Commission coordinating the preparation of schemata between sessions of the Council, the Secretariat incorporated the schema on religious freedom into the schema on ecumenism as a fifth chapter.[10] On July 9 Cardinal Bea explained the structural change to Cardinal Amleto Cicognani, president of the Coordinating Commission, and the latter accepted the incorporation.[11] Two days later Cardinal Bea sent the text to Cardinal Cicognani for printing.[12]

Again the draft on religious freedom met opposition from the

Theological Commission, less directly this time but with no less effectiveness.[13] Although the new Constitution on the Church submitted to the Council for discussion at the beginning of the Second Session no longer dealt at all with the question of relations between Church and state, and thus no longer conflicted even by implication with the Secretariat's draft on religious freedom, the Theological Commission did not grant permission for the printing of the latter's text.[14] This was accomplished by inaction rather than by a positive refusal; the curial forces at the Council employed here as elsewhere the familiar tactic of delay. By the end of October, with the schema on ecumenism scheduled as the next topic for discussion in the Council after consideration of the schema on the bishops, it was clear that no time could afford to be lost if Chapter V was to be included in the discussion.

Fortunately for the chapter on religious freedom, however, the Theological Commission's tardiness in revising the Constitution on the Church had provoked a crisis which was successfully broken by the intervention of one of the Council's Moderators, Cardinal Leo Suenens, archbishop of Malines-Brussels (Belgium).[15] Over the holiday of All Saints, moreover, Pope Paul VI sent a letter to Archbishop Pietro Parente (Curia), directing the Theological Commission to resume more regular and frequent meetings.[16]

Cardinal Ottaviani's opposition to the doctrine of religious freedom, of course, was long standing and well known. As pressure mounted to have Chapter V printed, Ottaviani reportedly attempted to persuade the Pope to table the subject.[17] Not only did Ottaviani fail in this attempt, but the Pope told him to convene the Theological Commission, discuss the Secretariat's draft on religious freedom, and vote on it.[18] Behind Ottaviani's failure and the Pope's directive lay a petition of the majority of bishops of the U.S., presented to the Holy Father by Cardinal Spellman, archbishop of New York, which strongly urged that the subject of religious freedom be considered at the Second Session.[19] Moreover, on November 8, Chapter IV of the schema on ecumenism, dealing with the Church's relations with the Jews, was distributed, and this increased pressure for the prompt printing of Chapter V.[20]

As a result, Cardinal Ottaviani was obliged to convene a meeting of the Theological Commission on November 11 to decide whether to grant permission to print Chapter V of the schema on ecumenism.[21] Bishop André Charue of Namur (Belgium) invited the American theologian Fr. John Courtney Murray, S.J., to speak on the subject of religious freedom. Cardinal Ottaviani did not recognize Murray and asked his neighbor, Cardinal Paul-Emile Léger, archbishop of Montreal, who was speaking. The Canadian cardinal answered without specificity: "One of the Council experts." Ottaviani's failure to recognize Murray was dramatically ironic, since Ottaviani was reportedly responsible in 1953 for restricting Murray's freedom to publish on the theology of church-state relations, a field in which Murray was a well-known scholar, and was probably a factor in "disinviting" Murray to the First Session of the Council.[22] Through the efforts of Cardinal Spellman, however, Murray had been named a conciliar *peritus* in time for the Second Session, and he was destined to play a central role in framing the eventual Declaration on Religious Freedom.[23]

On the next day, November 12, the Theological Commission met to vote the question. A subcommittee of the Commission, headed by Léger, had approved in principle the proposed draft of Chapter V by a vote of three to two and unanimously recommended its release to the Council floor. Although Ottaviani made a number of irrelevant suggestions in an effort to delay the prospect of a favorable vote, he was finally disavowed by his own fellow commissioners. The members of the Commission voted eighteen to five in favor of releasing Chapter V for conciliar consideration, with one vote invalid. The only negative votes were those cast by the ultraconservative opposition: Ottaviani, Cardinal Michael Browne (Curia), Cardinal Ermenegildo Florit (archbishop of Florence, Italy), Cardinal Rufino Santos (archbishop of Manila, the Philippines), and Parente. The text was then sent to the printers and distributed to the Council Fathers on November 19, in time for the opening discussion of the schema on ecumenism.

The first conciliar text on religious freedom, incorporated as Chapter V of the decree on ecumenism, was now in the hands of the Fathers. This text had elaborated the argument of the draft of May 30 on the right of all men to follow the dictates of an upright conscience. The draft of May 30 read simply:

Since the human person, endowed with consciousness and freedom, can only fulfill the will of God insofar as the law of God is perceived through the medium of a judgment of conscience, he cannot obtain his ultimate goal except by forming a judgment of conscience prudently and following its command faithfully. Hence the man who sincerely obeys his conscience intends to obey God Himself, although sometimes confusedly and unconsciously, and must be esteemed worthy of respect.[24]

The text distributed on November 19 repeated the above paragraph verbatim, except for the last word, where the more forceful "honor" was substituted for "respect."[25] But it also examined the argument "more deeply."[26] The result was to expand the argument by adding nineteen lines of text.[27] In every moral act, a man must observe two requirements: that of truth and that of freedom. In every moral act of the human person, he himself must personally see what the will of God demands of his freedom with the help of His grace, making use of all the channels of information, and respecting the rights of others. From the nature of things, no other individual and no other human power can substitute itself for the decision of the human person in solving the problem of moral action. Therefore, if a person arrives at an erroneous solution after applying all his efforts to see what God seeks of him in a concrete problem, no other man and no human power has "the right to act as a substitute for the erroneous conscience, in other words, to exercise coercion on it." This elaboration of the argument, of course, remained open to the question how the right of the human conscience to autonomous decision established the right not to be coerced from acting in society according to an erroneous conscience.

The conciliar text of November 19, 1963, also included for the first time notes on the development of papal teaching on religious freedom, and the notes were as long as the body of the text itself.[28] Since these notes were cited at length in the introductory report of Bishop De Smedt to the Council on behalf of the Secretariat, it will be convenient to consider them in connection with his speech.

De Smedt introduced the conciliar text to the Council on November 19, the same day as the text was distributed.[29] Debate on the whole decree on ecumenism had opened the day before, and contrary to the usual procedure, debate on the first part of the schema was interrupted on the nineteenth by the introductory report on Chapter IV by Bea and that on Chapter V by De Smedt.[30] De Smedt began his report with the observation that "very many Fathers of the Council have very insistently asked that the Council openly expose and proclaim the right of man to religious freedom."[31] Among the various reasons advanced for such a statement, De Smedt enumerated four principal ones: (1) the Church must teach and defend the right to religious freedom because there is involved a question of a truth committed to the Church's care by Christ; (2) the Church cannot remain silent on the subject of religious freedom when almost one half of mankind is denied that freedom today by atheistic materialism of various shades; (3) in all nations of the world today men adhering to different religions or no religion are called to converse peacefully in one and the same human society, and the Church must indicate the path to peaceful coexistence; and (4) many non-Catholics are embittered toward the Church, or at least suspect her of a certain Machiavellianism, because she seems to demand the free exercise of religion when Catholics are a minority in a particular nation, but denies the same freedom when Catholics are a majority. Religious freedom, in short, is too serious a problem in modern society to be omitted in a pastoral decree on ecumenism.

De Smedt took pains to distinguish the religious freedom affirmed in Chapter V from any doctrine that man is free to decide at will whether or not to embrace religion or that man is free of every obligation toward God or that all truth is relative or that man has a right to rest tranquilly in doubt. Rather, religious freedom in the conciliar text signified, positively, the right of the human person to the free exercise of religion according to the dictates of his conscience and, negatively, the right of the human person to be secure from external coercion in the personal relations with God which the conscience of man claims. Religious freedom implies the autonomy of the human person not *ab intra* (from his moral obligation in confronting the problem of religion), but *ab extra* (from impediments to following the dictates of his conscience in religious matters).

A twofold question arises at this point: (1) Can every man

claim religious freedom as a sacred right granted by God? and (2) Whether and to what extent does a duty fall on others of recognizing religious freedom? The decree on religious liberty, as a pastoral decree, intended to treat the matter especially in a practical way, and after the manner of John XXIII, attempted earnestly to remove the whole question from that world of abstractions so dear to the nineteenth century. The question is posed, therefore, about real men in real consort with other men in human society, especially in modern society.

To support the affirmation of the right of all men to religious freedom, De Smedt argued first from the nature of the act of faith. How should Catholics act toward non-Catholics precisely because of their own faith? First, all Catholics are invited by Christ to try to bring their non-Catholic brothers to the light of the gospel and the life of the Church by their prayer, penance, witness, and word. Second, they must abstain from every direct and indirect coercion; they must observe and value the right and duty of non-Catholics to follow the dictates of their sincerely formed but erroneous consciences. The reason why non-Catholics may not be coerced is based on the very nature of the act of faith. On the part of God, faith is a supernatural gift given by the Spirit to whom He wills and when He wills; on the part of man, faith is, and must be, an assent which man gives freely to God. Third, all Catholics must love and help their non-Catholic brothers sincerely and actively.

The schema at this point, De Smedt explained, took a further step and asserted that each and every man who follows his conscience in religious matters has a natural right to an authentic religious freedom. This right extends to every human person and to every religious group, provided that the person or group is following the sincere dictates of conscience. The reason why all must respect religious freedom is based on the role of conscience in mediating the divine law to the human person. From the nature of the matter, in forming judgments of conscience by which a man intends to conform himself freely to the absolute requirements of the laws of God, no other man and no other human institution can substitute for the conscience of the individual freely judging. If religious freedom is not observed, the very freedom of the human person is infringed in an important respect, in the fundamental requirement of his ordination to his supreme and ultimate goal. It is the greatest injustice to hinder a man from worshiping and obeying God according to the dictates of his conscience.

De Smedt admitted that the next step—namely, transition to the freedom of public action according to conscience—was most difficult. But he argued that religious freedom would be empty and meaningless if men could not follow the dictates of their conscience in external action, whether private and personal or public and social. Indeed, religious freedom would be empty and meaningless if human persons were hindered from constituting religious groups whose members might offer worship to God by external and communal activity and pursue a common religious way of life.

Here arose what De Smedt called "a most serious problem."[32] If the human person follows the dictates of his conscience in external action, there is danger that the rights and duties of one or more persons will be infringed. Since man is a social animal and subject to error and sin, a conflict of rights and duties cannot be altogether avoided. The right and duty to external action in accord with conscience, therefore, is not unlimited, but is subject to moderation and ordination to the common good, a task for public law in human society and belonging to governments.

Governments, however, can never act against the order of justice given by God. Indeed, Pope Paul VI, in his allocution to the Fathers of the Council at the opening of the Second Session on September 29, 1963, expressed his deep sorrow that "in certain areas religious freedom and other fundamental human rights are suppressed by principles and methods of political, racial, and anti-religious intolerance." He expressed his special sadness that "so many injuries were done to those who wish to profess their religion worthily and freely."[33]

De Smedt devoted the rest of his report, actually more than one half, to the evolution of the Church's teaching on the relation of governments to religious freedom from Popes Pius IX to John XXIII.[34] This survey was deemed important to avoid "many difficulties and confusions," i.e., objections to the schema on religious freedom on the basis of papal authority.[35] At the term of the preconciliar development, the principal document was the

encyclical *Pacem in terris* of the preceding April 11, in which
Pope John XXIII affirmed unconditionally the right of the human
person to the free exercise of religion, public as well as private,
according to the dictates of an upright conscience.

The doctrine of religious freedom, the modern term of an
evolution both in the doctrine of the dignity of the human person
and in the pastoral solicitude of the Church for the freedom of
man, developed according to two principles: the principle of
continuity and the principle of progress. According to the first
principle, the teaching of the Church and her pastoral concern
were always evident and always the same. This perennial teaching
can be summed up in the words of Pope John: "The dignity of
the human person demands that man enjoy in his activity his
own power of deliberation and freedom."[36] This doctrine, moreover, has very deep roots in Holy Scripture, which preaches that
man has been made in the image of God, from which flows the
continual pastoral concern of the Church for the genuine freedom
of man. According to the second principle, the teaching authority
of the Church adapted, exposed, and defended the true doctrine
on the dignity of the human person as particular errors and necessities demanded. By this progress, the mind of the Church was
led to examine the doctrine more deeply and to see its implications more clearly.

In a similar way, two distinctions concerning error have more
clearly developed: (1) a clearer distinction between false principles
and the institutions spawned or nourished by them; and (2) a
clearer distinction between error and the person erring in good
faith. While false ideologies must always be rejected, economic,
social, and civil institutions arising from them can contain something of value, and while errors must always be rejected, the individual in error "never loses the dignity of his person."[37]

Thus, according to De Smedt, a way was now open to understanding correctly the many papal documents of the nineteenth
century which employed language such that religious freedom
would seem to have been condemned. The clearest example is
offered in the encyclical of Pius IX *Quanta cura*, in which one
reads:

From that altogether false idea of a social regime, namely, of "nat-

uralism," they do not fear to foster the opinion fatal to the Catholic
Church and the salvation of souls, called "madness" by our predecessor of virtuous memory, Gregory XVI, that freedom of conscience and worship is undoubtedly the proper right of every man
and must be asserted and proclaimed by public law in every well-
ordered society.[38]

As is evident, that freedom of conscience is condemned because
of the ideology which the apostles of rationalism preached, relying on the principle that the individual conscience is outside all
law, freed of all norms handed down by God.[39] Also condemned is
that freedom of worship whose principle is religious indifference.[40]
Lastly, that separation of Church and state is condemned which
has its root in the rationalist view of the juridical omnipotence
of the state, according to which the Church herself must be incorporated within the monistic organism of the state and subject
to the supreme power of the state.[41]

To interpret correctly these condemnations, the constant teaching of the Church and her concern for the true dignity of the
human person and his true freedom must be discerned according
to the principle of continuity. The ultimate foundation of human
dignity is the fact that man is a creature of God, an image of
God, but not a god. From this absolute dependence of man on
God flows every right and duty of man to claim for himself and
others a genuine religious freedom. Indeed, man is subjectively
bound to worship God according to the sincere dictates of his
conscience because he depends objectively on God. Hence, other
men and even the public power must in no way prohibit a man
in religious matters from the free exercise of religion, lest his absolute dependence on God be infringed, for whatever reason. By
joining battle against the philosophical and political principles of
laicism, the Church fought with every reason for the dignity of
the human person and his true freedom. According to the principle of continuity, the Church was in full agreement on this
doctrine yesterday, as she is today, although the circumstances
were very different.

Leo XIII began an evolution of the doctrine by sharpening the
distinction between the Church, the People of God, and civil
society, the people of the earthly city. Thus he opened a path to

a new affirmation of the required and permissible autonomy which belongs to the civil order and its juridical rule. A further step was now possible according to the principle of progress, namely, to a new judgment on the so-called modern freedoms. These freedoms could be tolerated, albeit only tolerated.[42] The reason was evident. The regimes of the day in Europe which proclaimed the modern freedoms, including religious freedom, drew their inspiration consciously from the ideology of laicism. There was danger, therefore, as Leo perceived, lest the civil and political institutions of this type of commonwealth would lead to abuses which could not fail to harm the dignity of the human person and his genuine religious freedom. Pius XI moved the doctrinal and pastoral evolution to a new level. The rise of the totalitarian state had replaced the danger of the nineteenth century that a falsely conceived freedom of conscience would do injury to the dignity of the human person. The new peril was that every kind of human and civil liberty, especially religious freedom, would perish. Hence the Church began in a new way to exercise her care of defending human freedom and dignity.

Following the principle of continuity, Pius XI maintained the unchanging opposition of the Church to an antireligious laicism: "Indeed, what Pius X condemned, we too condemn; as often as there is present in 'laicity,' as they say, a sense or proposal . . . foreign to God and religion, we altogether reject such a laicity, and declare that it must be openly rejected."[43] But Pius XI observed no less the principle of progress and introduced a new distinction which was of great importance for understanding more deeply Catholic doctrine. For he distinguished between "the freedom of consciences" and the "freedom of conscience." He rejected the latter formula as "equivocal," as too associated with the laicist concept of an "absolute independence of conscience, which is absurd in view of man's creation and redemption by God." He accepted, however, the former formula and fought "the good fight with a joyful and happy soul for the freedom of consciences."[44]

Moreover, Pius XI not only fought for the religious freedom of the faithful but at the same time showed a broader pastoral concern of the Church. Pius XI developed genuinely liberal and Christian teaching to new heights by teaching that "man as a person has rights given by God, which must remain secure from every denial, privation, or impediment on the part of society."[45] And he continued unambiguously: "The believer possesses the inalienable right to profess his faith and exercise it in fitting ways. Laws which impede or make difficult the profession and exercise of this faith contradict the natural law." According to De Smedt, those who understood the circumstances of the times and the corresponding scope of the letters of Pius XI could not escape the universality of his affirmation of human rights.

Pius XII, deeply involved as a participant in the pastoral concern of his predecessor, evolved and expanded his doctrine further according to the rule of progress. In fact, the dignity of the human person was the central focus of Pius XII's thought. In this context, according to the principle of continuity, must be read a text which is important for the present subject. By enumerating "the fundamental rights of the human person," which must be recognized and cherished in every well-ordered society, he taught anew the doctrine of Pius XI and endowed it with new authority, affirming specifically "the right to the private and public worship of God, including action under the impulse of religious charity."[46] Not content to leave this doctrine on the level of theory, he drew from it the constitutional principle that there are just limits to the power of governments: "It is the chief duty of every government to safeguard and protect the inviolable rights proper to men so that each may fulfill his duties."[47]

Especially to be recalled is the doctrine of Pius XII on the limitation of the state with respect to repressing error in society: "Could it be that in certain circumstances He [God] would not even communicate the right to impede or repress what is erroneous and false? A look at things as they are gives an affirmative answer."[48] Then, after alluding to the example of divine Providence, he continued:

> Hence the affirmation that religious and moral error must always be impeded, when it is possible, because toleration of them is in itself immoral, is not valid absolutely and unconditionally. Moreover, God has not given even to human authority such an absolute and universal command in matters of faith and morality.[49]

This statement, according to the principle of progress, is of the greatest moment for the subject matter of religious freedom, especially if one recalls the former papal statements on the goals of the state.

At the end of this historical evolution, of course, came the encyclical *Pacem in terris*, the fruit of a slow process of maturation, which went on in the Church, under the light of the Holy Spirit, through the whole preceding century. The schema on religious freedom proposed to the Council had already been prepared and approved by the Central Commission and the Coordinating Commission when Pope John published *Pacem in terris*, with which, De Smedt said, the text of the Secretariat's schema agreed in every respect.

In the historical context of this doctrine, there is a progressive explication as well as continuity in the papal documents. De Smedt acknowledged that certain papal documents could be cited which sounded on their face contrary to the proposed schema. But he begged the Fathers of the Council not to make the text speak out of its historical and doctrinal context, not to make "fish swim out of water."[50]

De Smedt emphasized that the schema submitted to the Council on religious freedom was not a dogmatic treatise but a pastoral decree aimed toward men of our time. The whole world expects the decree; in universities, in national and international organizations, in Christian and non-Christian communities, in journals, and in public opinion the voice of the Church is anxiously awaited.

De Smedt expressed the hope that it would be possible to complete discussion and approve the decree before the end of the Second Session. The Secretariat promised to examine emendations suggested by the Fathers "most attentively but also most rapidly."[51]

The introductory report richly deserved the tremendous applause which it received.[52] Particularly masterful and creative were the sections on the evolution of the doctrine of religious freedom in papal teaching. But they were admittedly *ex parte* readings of history. Pius IX was not likely to have embraced religious freedom even if a De Gasperi rather than a Cavour had been the architect of the Italian *risorgimento*. Leo XIII's elaborate attempt to prescribe a blueprint for relations between Church and state was conceived as more than a dialectic directed solely against laicist errors. In fact, the aristocratic and paternal papacy of the nineteenth century never really accepted the modern concept of democracy as legitimate, much less ideal.

Moreover, the citations of Pius XI were directed only toward vindicating the rights of Catholics to religious freedom against the attempts of the totalitarian dictators to restrict it, although Nazi racism was also unequivocally condemned. Pius XII's affirmation of "the right to private and public worship of God" similarly referred in context only to the right of Catholics. Even in his speech to the Italian jurists, Pius' remarks were two edged. He did clearly indicate against the ultraconservatives that a regime of religious freedom was, in certain circumstances, not only allowed but also fully legitimate. Yet he also implied just as clearly that a regime of religious restriction was fully legitimate in other circumstances.

The introductory report's treatment of the development of papal teaching on the dignity of the human person, including religious freedom, was obviously of value for the forthcoming debate; it showed that the history of the question was more complex than the literal-minded conservative opposition wished to admit. Indeed, the introductory report did more than that. It showed strong elements of continuity between the proposed schema and papal teaching before John XXIII. But what the introductory report did not admit was that the proposed schema might be really inconsistent with some previous papal teaching. The latter was not only possible, since no definition of faith was involved, but very probable in view of the historical record. In any event, for reasons of theological and diplomatic caution, the introductory report strove to outline an uninterrupted development of doctrine toward the affirmation of religious freedom. It made a strong case for the continuity of doctrine and at least challenged the conservative opposition on its own ground.

It was now late in the Second Session, however, and there was great anxiety, especially on the part of the American bishops, whether Chapter V would be acted upon before the close of the session. A large majority was eager for a test vote on religious freedom, but a sizable, vocal, and influential minority was anxious to debate the issue at length in an effort to persuade their brothers to revise radically, if not abandon altogether, the relevant chapter.

Failing that, the dissenting minority hoped for victory by delay. Moreover, the opposition to the decree on religious freedom was strengthened by the fact that Chapter V followed the equally controversial Chapter IV (on the Jews), which also required debate.

In the opening debate on the ecumenism schema as a whole, on Monday, November 18, Cardinal Gabriel Tappouni, Syrian patriarch of Antioch, objected specifically to the inclusion of Chapters IV and V as "inopportune" in a schema on ecumenism, since ecumenism related only to the unity of Christians.[53] Cardinal José Benjamin de Arriba y Castro, archbishop of Tarragona (Spain), warned of the danger of proselytism implicit in ecumenism and declared bluntly that only the Catholic Church had the right and duty to evangelize.[54] But Cardinal Joseph Ritter, archbishop of St. Louis, embraced the whole schema, and especially Chapter V, in the name of eight American bishops.[55] Without a declaration on religious freedom, no real dialogue with non-Catholics would be possible. The declaration should proceed on the solid theological principles of the absolute freedom of the act of faith, the inviolability of the human conscience, and the incompetence of civil authority in religious matters.

On Tuesday, November 19, Cardinal Léger led off the interventions of the day, after the long introductory reports of Bea and De Smedt.[56] Although approving the schema as a whole, he thought that Chapters IV and V should not be included. Religious freedom was an important subject and should constitute its own schema.

On Wednesday, November 20, general debate on the ecumenism schema as a whole continued for the third day. Cardinal Albert Meyer, archbishop of Chicago, speaking for many American bishops, approved the whole schema and expressed his particular pleasure that Chapters IV and V were included.[57] He urged that the whole schema be accepted as a basis for discussion.

Cardinal Florit suggested on Thursday, November 21, that religious freedom be considered in connection with schema seventeen (on the presence of the Church in the modern world).[58] For him, the key issue was whether a person has a natural right to diffuse error even in good faith. Bishop Juan Hervás y Benet, prelate nullius of Ciudad Real (Spain), also thought that religious freedom belonged properly with schema seventeen, and that its inclusion in the schema on ecumenism would encourage "propaganda, liberalism, and existentialism."[59]

At this point, the Moderators put an end to the general discussion of the schema on ecumenism, which was already in its fourth day, and proceeded to hold an immediate vote on the acceptance of the first three chapters as a basis for further discussion.[60] The reservations expressed by many Fathers of the Council on Chapters IV and V and the likelihood of prolonged debate in connection with them determined the Moderators to limit the vote to the first three chapters and postpone consideration of Chapters IV and V to a later date—a "few days," in the assuring but mistaken words of the Secretary-General. Moreover, since the questions of Jewish-Christian relations and religious freedom were closely related to acceptance of the main argument of Chapters I–III, which dealt with the formal concern of ecumenism, namely, the union of Christians, approval of the first three chapters would facilitate approval of Chapters IV and V. In any event, the vote on accepting the first three chapters of the schema on ecumenism as the basis for discussion revealed a lopsided majority: 1,996 for; 86 against. The Secretariat had won a clear victory, although the time for action on religious freedom this session was rapidly evaporating.

Despite the vote of the preceding day, three speakers were heard on Friday, November 22, on the subject of the ecumenism schema as a whole. Among these, Bishop José Pont y Gol of Segorbe (Spain) urged that the subject of religious liberty be postponed until the beginning of the next session.[61] Although he agreed with the majority on the importance of the subject, he wanted to give the minority more time in the interest of peace.

In the discussion of the first three chapters of the schema on ecumenism in the succeeding days, several speakers included references to religious freedom. On Monday, November 25, Cardinal José Bueno y Monreal, archbishop of Seville (Spain), insisted on the dangers of proselytism: proselytism must not be permitted in countries, like Spain, where the gospel has been preached for many centuries.[62] On Tuesday, November 26, in discussing Chapter I, Bishop Rafael González Moralejo, auxiliary of Valencia (Spain), proposed that Chapter V, on religious freedom, be placed at the very beginning of the schema on ecumenism.[63] Later that day, Bishop Stephen A. Leven, auxiliary of San Antonio (Texas), remarked *ad hominem* that some Fathers of the Council "speak as if the whole doctrine of the freedom of conscience due every man, so clearly stated in *Pacem in terris,* were offensive to pious ears; they prefer to censure the errors of non-Catholics whom they have never seen than instruct their own people."[64] On Wednesday, November 27, Bishop Paul Joseph Schmitt of Metz (France) declared that a statement on religious freedom was indispensable.[65] On the next to the last day of debate, Friday, November 29, as hopes for action on Chapters IV and V at the Second Session dimmed, Bishop Charles Helmsing of Kansas City (Missouri) suggested at the end of his talk, almost as an aside, an immediate vote on the last chapters of the schema on ecumenism. His proposal was greeted by applause, but not by any action on the part of the Moderators.[66]

The unstructured and repetitious debate on Chapters I–III had occupied the Council for seven days; there was now no time to debate Chapters IV and V. From the start of the session, the closing date had been scheduled for December 4, and December 3 was to be devoted to commemorating the fourth centenary of the closing of the Council of Trent.[67] Had the Moderators and Pope so chosen, of course, a vote on accepting Chapters IV and V "on principle" could have been taken in adequate time before the end of the Second Session, but the American and other bishops failed to pressure for a preliminary vote.[68] Indeed, the Pope had irrevocably decided to allow a postponement of a vote, and this word was communicated to the American bishops over the weekend of November 29.[69]

On Monday, December 2, the last working meeting of the Second Session, Bea summed up the debate on ecumenism.[70] He regretted that there had been no time to discuss Chapters IV and V in particular but cited the ancient saying that what is put off is not put away. In order that his words on the intention of the Secretariat be unambiguous, he repeated them for emphasis. However, he indicated that the delay, though regrettable, was of value to the Fathers of the Council for reflection and for emendations of the texts before the next session. He urged that suggestions be sent to the Secretariat not later than the middle of February 1964.

The Second Session of the Council closed on Wednesday, December 4, 1962.[71] The schema on religious freedom had yet to be debated formally on the floor or given any preliminary vote. The conservation opposition had succeeded in its tactic of delay for two sessions now. The key question on this subject, as on others, was whether the majority could organize itself effectively to overcome the determined efforts of the minority.

Notes

1. Rynne, *Letters from Vatican City*, p. 130.
2. "Note sur le schéma . . ." p. 2.
3. Rynne, *op. cit.*, pp. 214–35.
4. John XXIII, *Pacem in terris*, AAS, LV (1963), pp. 257–304.
5. "Note," p. 2.
6. "Decretum pastorale de libertate religiosa," May 16, 1963. (Duplicated by the Secretariat, the Murray files.)
7. *Ibid.*
8. "Note," p. 2.
9. "Decretum pastorale de libertate religiosa," May 30, 1963, pp. 3–4. (Duplicated by the Secretariat, the Murray files.)
10. "Note," p. 2.
11. *Ibid.*
12. *Ibid.*
13. *Ibid.*
14. Xavier Rynne, *The Second Session* (New York: Farrar, Straus and Co., 1964), pp. 39 and 191.
15. *Ibid.*, pp. 163–65.
16. *Ibid.*, pp. 171–72.
17. *Ibid.*, p. 191.
18. *Ibid.*, pp. 191–92.
19. *Ibid.*, p. 192.
20. *Ibid.*
21. For an account of the Theological Commission's meetings, see Rynne, *op. cit.*, pp. 192–93.
22. *Ibid.*, p. 192.
23. *Ibid.*
24. "Decretum," p. 3.
25. *Schema decreti de oecumenismo, caput* V (Rome: Vatican Polyglot Press, 1963), p. 4.
26. *Ibid.*

27. *Ibid.*, p. 5.
28. *Ibid.*, pp. 7–11.
29. *Relatio super schema Decreti de oecumenismo, caput* V (Rome: Vatican Polyglot Press, 1963), pp. 27–36.
30. Rynne, *op. cit.*, p. 217.
31. *Relatio*, p. 27.
32. *Ibid.*, p. 30.
33. Paul VI, *Allocution at the Opening of the Second Session of the Second Vatican Council*, AAS, LV (1963), pp. 855–56.
34. *Relatio*, pp. 31–36.
35. *Ibid.*, p. 31.
36. *Ibid.*, p. 32; cf. *Pacem in terris, loc. cit.*, p. 265.
37. *Ibid.*; cf. *Pacem in terris, loc. cit.*, pp. 299–300.
38. *Ibid.*, pp. 32–33; cf. Pius IX, *Quanta cura*, AAS, III (1867). p. 162.
39. *Ibid.*, p. 33; cf. Pius IX, *Syllabus, prop. 3*, ASS, III (1867), p. 168.
40: *Ibid.*; cf. Pius IX, *Syllabus, prop. 15, loc. cit.*, p. 170.
41. *Ibid.*; cf. Pius IX, *Syllabus, prop. 39, loc. cit.*, p. 172.
42. *Ibid.*, pp. 33–34; cf. Leo XIII, *Libertas praestantissimum*, ASS, XX (1887–88), pp. 609–10.
43. *Ibid.*, p. 34; cf. Pius XI, *Maximam gravissimamque*, AAS, XVI (1924), p. 10.
44. *Ibid.*; cf. Pius XI, *Non abbiamo bisogna*, AAS, XXIII (1931), pp. 301–02.
45. *Ibid.*, p. 35; cf. Pius XI, *Mit brennender Sorge*, AAS, XXIX (1937), p. 159.
46. *Ibid.*; cf. Pius XII, *Nuntius radiophonicus*, December 24, 1942, AAS, XXXV (1943), p. 19.
47. *Ibid.*; cf. Pius XII *Nuntius radiophonicus*, June 1, 1941, AAS, XXXIII (1941), p. 200.
48. *Ibid.*; cf. Pius XII, *Ci riesce*, AAS, XLV (1953), pp. 798–99.
49. *Ibid.*
50. *Relatio*, p. 36.
51. *Ibid.*
52. Murray, in collaboration with Hamer, had considerable influence on this introductory report. He did not, however, influence or approve the schema's reliance on the arguments for religious freedom from the right to follow conscience and the nature of the act of faith. Moreover, Murray objected to expressing the limits on religious freedom by the formula of the common good. Murray's principal influence was on the lengthy discussion of the doctrinal development of religious freedom, and he wrote the corresponding notes appended to Chapter V.
53. Rynne, p. 235; *La Documentation Catholique*, January 5, 1964, col. 38.
54. Rynne, p. 238; *Documentation*, col. 35.
55. Rynne, pp. 236–37; *Documentation*, col. 36. Submitted as written

intervention G, 8. (Mimeographed by the Secretariat, the Murray files.)

56. Rynne, p. 240; *Documentation*, col. 39; G, 7.
57. Rynne, p. 244; *Documentation*, col. 44; G, 37.
58. Rynne, pp. 248–49; *Documentation*, col. 51.
59. Rynne, p. 249; *Documentation*, cols. 52–53; G, 63.
60. Rynne, p. 248.
61. Rynne, p. 283; *Documentation*, col. 54; G, 12.
62. Rynne, p. 264; *Documentation*, January 19, 1964, col. 117.
63. Rynne, pp. 265–66; *Documentation*, January 5, 1964, cols. 65–66.
64. Rynne, pp. 266–67; *Documentation*, *ibid.*; G, 75.
65. Rynne, p. 287; *Documentation*, January 19, 1964, col. 126.
66. Rynne, p. 271; *Documentation*, cols. 144–45.
67. Rynne, p. 291.
68. *Ibid.*, p. 272.
69. *Ibid.*
70. *Ibid.*, pp. 277–78; *Documentation*, cols. 150–52.
71. Rynne, p. 291.

IV

The Second Text

RESPONDING TO THE INVITATION of Cardinal Bea, no fewer than 380 written observations and emendations were sent to the Secretary-General and examined by the Secretariat.[1] Of the 152 interventions submitted on Chapter V as a whole, American bishops were the authors of more than a third. With the exception of those of Cardinal Albert Meyer, archbishop of Chicago, the American interventions were generally designed to indicate approval of a conciliar statement on religious freedom rather than to advance, or even enter, the argument. The bishops of Spain offered the next largest number of interventions after the Americans, one fifth of the total; their interventions were lengthy, detailed, and very much concerned with the argument.

The Conference of African Bishops submitted an entirely new draft on religious freedom, as did Bishop Léon Elchinger, coadjutor of Strasbourg (France).[2] The French bishops generally approved the argument of the text presented at the Second Session of the Council, although Bishop Charles de Provenchères of Aix-en-Provence indicated the main difficulties with the argument from a friendly point of view.[3] Very few Italian bishops intervened, and even fewer members of the Curia. The silence of the chief conservative spokesmen on the Theological Commission was striking. No doubt they calculated that the Spanish bishops would state their case well and receive a better hearing than they. (The reaction of the Council Fathers to the Theological Commission's first draft on the Church clearly indicated the reception that the conservative curial officials could expect from the Council.)[4]

Many of the interventions were concerned with relatively minor questions of style or wording. The question whether a statement on religious freedom was appropriately a chapter of the schema on ecumenism recurred repeatedly. A second question frequently raised was procedural on its face but in fact substantive; objection to the title ("On Religious Freedom") was usually motivated by opposition to the principle of religious freedom itself.

The interventions of major interest centered on either the validity of the principle or the arguments supporting it in the proposed text. Obviously, the conservative minority was obliged to attack both. But even some of those friendly to the principle of religious freedom were unhappy with aspects of the arguments advanced to support it.

The ideology of the conservative opposition to the principle of religious freedom followed a familiar pattern. The essentials of the position can be stated quite simply: society no less than the individual must praise, reverence, and serve God; since the Catholic Church is the one true Church in the divine economy of salvation, the "Catholic" state must, under ideal conditions, protect its citizens from religious error by the prescription of public law and the coercion of public power. Therefore, the "Catholic" state cannot accept as a matter of principle the right of all individuals and groups to the freedom of religious exercise. As a matter of practice, however, even the "Catholic" state, under certain circumstances, can accept a regime of legal tolerance for the religious exercise of all individuals and groups.

According to most of the Spanish interventions, the principle of religious freedom implied that the conscience of man is absolutely autonomous and thus independent of the law of God; that one religion is as good as another; and that Catholic worship and the Christian gospel are of no unique value to human society.[5] In theory the conservative opponents of religious freedom admitted the right and duty of the individual to follow the dictates of a sincerely formed conscience, even when mistaken. But the conservatives were concerned with the public arena where the exercise of individual conscience affects society. They proposed the principle that the "Catholic" state, under ideal conditions, should repress the public worship of non-Catholics and the propagation of non-Catholic religious beliefs. Error has no rights against the truth, and the person in error has no right to harm society by propagating his error.

Bishop Antonio Pildáin y Zapiáin of the Canary Islands (Spain) cast the conservative opposition to the principle of religious freedom in a sarcastic form untypical of his conservative brothers but dramatically illustrative of how they understood the issue. He proposed the following additions to the conciliar endorsement of religious freedom:

> *Our Council, therefore, solemnly teaches and proclaims* the right of every person so to conduct himself in the external exercise of his liberty that he may speak and do anything publicly . . . , although the commandments of God and the Church prohibit such doctrines and actions. . . . Such a right . . . has an altogether inalienable and inviolable foundation, *notwithstanding everything to the contrary which Leo XIII taught.* . . . This holy Vatican synod, therefore, declares that the dictates of one's own conscience, even in the external forum, prevail against the commandments of God and the precepts of the Church, that a man has a right . . . to leave the Catholic faith and religion, to embrace another religion, and . . . to practice divorce, birth control, and polygamy. . . .[6]
>
> *This sacrosanct Vatican synod solemnly declares* that such religious freedom belongs to . . . religions contradicting the Catholic religion. *The Catholic Church, therefore,* which is the only Church founded by Christ, . . . *now solemnly teaches* that other churches and religions have a right from nature, and thus from God, to profess that they are true religions and that the Catholic Church is, therefore, false and its religion in error. . . .[7]
>
> And although more than ninety modern religions, . . . founded by individual persons, agree without dissent both in denying the divinity of Christ and in rejecting the authority of the Church, this Church teaches solemnly through the Second Vatican Council that all these founders, and any other persons who . . . wish to found new religions impugning the divinity of Christ and the authority of the Church, enjoy the full right to do so.[8]

Sarcasm aside, the conservative argument rested on the identification of the state with human society. The conservatives were not wrong to argue that if the Catholic Church enjoys a unique role in God's plan to sanctify the world, the Church contributes a unique value to human society, and human society as a consequence should cherish that value. But the question at issue was whether the state is competent to judge religious matters at all, whether the state is competent to repress the public worship and propagation of non-Catholic religions.

The goal of society, as politically organized, is to secure conditions in which citizens may lead more fully human lives. The state is not synonymous with human society, but rather is the particular subsidiary organization whose special purpose looks to the good of the whole society. There is within the body politic a whole range of responsible organizations—familial, economic, scientific, and cultural—with partial tasks respecting the good of the whole society. These organizations indeed protect and advance the good of the whole society, but the state alone has this as its *specific* function. As the rational expression and specific instrument of organized society, the state is the highest subsidiary of the body politic. Since the state does derive its authority from below, from the citizens and their responsible organizations, it is limited according to the principle of subsidiarity: the state should do for its citizens only what its citizens by themselves or through their responsible organizations cannot conveniently do for themselves. With respect to civil liberties, this means as much freedom for the citizen and his responsible organizations as possible, and only as much restraint by the state as necessary. (The latter principle would be explicitly applied to the question of religious freedom in the final Declaration.)[9]

There are, moreover, limits other than those necessarily imposed on the state by the derivation of its authority from below. Of particular importance for religious freedom is the fact that the state is utterly incompetent with respect to the aspirations of man which transcend the order of justice. Political authority can establish an order of rights and obligations with respect to the harmonious organization of society, but it cannot actuate the higher aspirations of man for love and communion with his fellows. Nor can political authority actuate the highest aspiration of man for love and communion with God. As the state is without power to legislate the natural order of human love, since its authority is directed solely toward the order of justice, so, *a fortiori*, the state is without power to legislate the supernatural order of divine love. No man, and no human institution, has the right to propose, define, or interpret the call of God. The role of the state is rather to establish the order of justice in which God's plans may be freely fulfilled, to provide the natural conditions in which man's salvation can be freely accomplished.

Coadjutor archbishop Philip Pocock of Toronto, speaking in the name of the bishops of Canada, urged that the statement on religious freedom say openly that public authority is not permitted to restrict the prerogative of citizens to embrace the religion of their choice, that public authority is not permitted to deny to religious assemblies the prerogative of forming civil corporations and the right to possess property and determine freely their internal government, and that civil authority is not permitted to prohibit religious societies the right to profess their religion publicly, provided that the rights of others are secured and the common good protected.[10] He immediately added that the "common good" should not be identified with a national culture but rather regards the fundamental rights of human life and dignity. These points, Popock concluded, should be declared expressly in the text.

Similarly, Angelo Jelmini, apostolic administrator of Lugano, urged in the name of the bishops of Switzerland that it does not pertain to the state, by reason of the common good, to temper and order the rights of religion. Religious freedom is a freedom due to religion as such. To determine religious values in no way pertains to the state under the rubric of the common good.[11]

The conservatives' confusion of state and society was historically conditioned: their concept of human society was entirely paternal. In fact, so historically conditioned by the paternal concept of society was one of them, Bishop Anastasio Granados, auxiliary of Toledo (Spain), that he felt no discomfort in citing a radio address of *el Caudillo* to explain the "truly Catholic doctrine" of the confessional state.[12] To be charitable, this approach was poor theological method; to be exact, it was tainted with caesaropapism.

Since paternal society maximizes the role of authority, conservatives were understandably unperceptive of the limits to that authority. In a paternal society "the few" specify and direct the body politic toward social goals which "the many" are by supposition incapable of determining or achieving for themselves.

The problem posed by the principle of religious freedom for this peculiar function of government in a paternal society is obvious. How can rulers in a monistic, paternal, and Catholic society accept the principle of religious freedom without implying hostility to the Church? In such a society subjects are accustomed to look to their rulers for guidance in all that concerns the goals of community aspiration and action; they might easily take a regime of religious freedom to imply the indifference of the rulers to the truth or relevance of the Catholic religion for society. Indeed they might assume that the rulers endorsed a purely individual, invisible, and subjective religion as the supreme social good in preference to the social, visible, and objective claims of the Church, or perhaps even that the rulers wished to establish material, natural, and secular values without reference to those which are spiritual, supernatural, and transcendent. Even after the Council adopted the Declaration on Religious Freedom, rulers of paternally structured Catholic societies would face a delicate task in establishing a regime of religious freedom clearly dissociated in the minds of their subjects from a philosophy of religious indifference, subjectivism, or naturalism.

Moreover, religious freedom poses a problem for paternal societies on the level of political process. Since decisions in paternal societies are made by "the few," free speech, free assembly, and free press are not required as means for the functioning of the political process. In fact, indiscriminate extension of such freedoms could threaten the entire system. Another corollary of the paternal political process affects religious freedom. Religious freedom implies religious pluralism, and religious pluralism, especially because of the transcendency of religious values, threatens the unity of a paternally organized body politic. An immature society by supposition requires paternal government because "the many" are unable to specify amicably and discriminately the good of the whole body politic. Under such conditions, pluralism of culture, especially of religion, accentuates differences, fragments the body politic, and hinders "the few" from specifying the good of the whole and "the many" from accepting the specifications. Thus the strictly political implications of the paternal pattern of social organization will complicate acceptance of the principle of religious freedom.

It is important to note that the first conciliar text on religious freedom did not meet the issue of distinguishing state from society. Of course, its affirmation of religious freedom was unequivocal, but its argument did not deal effectively with the social context. The argument from the right to follow conscience moved from the world of the human subject to the world of human subjects living in an objective order of society. On the other hand, the conservative argument moved in exactly the opposite direction, beginning with the common good of the objective order of society and ending in the denial of the principle of religious freedom. Without an explicit delimitation of public power in contradistinction to the broader goals of human society, the conservative logic was hard to answer. The first conciliar text on religious freedom did not attempt such a delimitation and, in fact, appeared to accept the identity of state and society by appealing to the common good as the moral source of the state's power to limit the exercise of religious freedom.

In a similar vein, conservatives also argued against the principle of religious freedom on the ground that truth alone has rights, and that error can be only tolerated.[13] Indeed, as late as 1953, Pius XII had spoken of tolerating error, not of a right to religious freedom.[14] This language can be understood in the objective sense that no human authority can positively sanction error or evil, but it is altogether inadequate to express the concept of religious freedom. First, only physical and moral persons are the proper subjects of rights. Even in cases of witnesses in judicial proceedings and teachers, it is not truth which has rights, but it is courts and pupils who have the right to expect the conscientious effort of witnesses and teachers to communicate what is seen as true.[15] Second, a regime of religious freedom by no means implies that a government positively affirms that false religions are equal to those which are true. In a regime of religious freedom public law acknowledges only that no one is to be compelled to act against his conscience, or to be restrained from acting according to his conscience, in religious matters.[16] Third, only a competent authority can "tolerate" evil, and the state is not such an authority with respect to religious freedom. God indeed can only tolerate evil, and falsehood in religious matters is certainly an evil. But it is not the function, much less the duty, of the state to extirpate religious error. Nor is immunity from coercion in religious matters an evil to be repressed. Rather, because of the dignity of the human person, religious freedom is itself a common good to be fostered and protected by the state.[17]

Friend and foe of the principle of religious liberty alike had trouble with the attempt to base the principle on the right and duty of the human person to follow the dictates of a sincere conscience. Conservatives argued that the transition from the subjective, personal order to the objective, social order was illicit.[18] In effect, they accused the text of juridical Cartesianism: as Descartes was accused of attempting to argue from the world of thought to the world of matter, so the first conciliar text on religious freedom was accused of seeking by a similar geometric mode of argument to move from the subjective world of indivdual conscience to the objective world of social interaction. The text's argument attempted to prove not only the right of the individual not to be compelled to act against his conscience but also his right not to be hindered from acting according to his own conscience.

The conservatives were not alone in their criticism of this argument advanced by the conciliar text. Bishop de Provenchères, though a friend of the principle of religious freedom, thought that it was good to affirm the moral rights of the erroneous conscience, but that such an affirmation ought not to constitute the basis of the argument for civil freedom of religion.[19] Indeed, who will judge the good faith of the individual conscience? Fearing that such a too subjectivist treatment of religious freedom would more threaten than secure the freedom of the person, he offered three objective bases for the civil freedom of religion: the transcendent dignity of the human person, the irreversible fact of pluralism, and the participation of all persons in the political life of society. Similarly, the new text proposed by the Conference of African Bishops and authored by Fr. Guy de Broglie, S.J., a professor of the Gregorian University, sought to avoid "many grave equivocations" in the proposed conciliar text; according to the African text, some affirmations of the conciliar text favored subjectivism, and others endangered the true freedom of the human person.[20] The African text significantly omitted the argument from the right and duty of the person to follow the dictates of a sincere conscience.

The proposed conciliar text would have committed the Council to a particular foundation of religious freedom on which there was no clear consensus. Was it the task of the Council to endorse a philosophical argument in favor of religious freedom or rather to endorse unequivocally the principle itself? If the purpose of a declaration on religious freedom was pastoral, then a controversial philosophical argument was unnecessary; if the particular argument failed, or evoked no clear consensus, then its incorporation as the foundation of the conciliar Declaration on Religious Freedom was insufficient.

Related to the objections against basing the principle of religious freedom on the right and duty to follow the dictates of a sincere conscience were the complaints that the first conciliar text laid insufficient emphasis on the rights of religious groups to function in society. In this respect, Cardinal Meyer made a significant contribution to the debate by distinguishing clearly four elements in the concept of religious freedom.[21] First, there is freedom of conscience, religious freedom in the strictest sense, which is the right of an individual to immunity from all external coercion in embracing a religious faith. Second, there is the freedom of religious action, which includes the rights of public worship and proclamation of one's faith and their implications for the social and political community. Third, there is the freedom of religious association for religious and moral goals. Fourth, there is the freedom of religious groups, which is the right of religious communities to immunity from every external coercion in defining their doctrine and faith, in establishing their internal discipline, and in determining all means which are necessary or useful for their religious goals.

The last three freedoms are of a mixed order; they presuppose the social context of man. Moreover, these three freedoms are associated with civil liberties which are more general. The freedom of religious action is connected with the more general right of man to act in society according to his own counsel; the right to associate with others in religious matters is connected with the more general right of association for worthy purposes; and the right of religious institutions and corporations is connected with the more general right of associations to govern themselves.

As to the argument for religious freedom from the nature of

the act of faith, many friends of religious freedom, as well as most foes, saw that such an argument proved the right of the human person not to be coerced against his conscience but did not necessarily prove a right not to be restrained from acting according to conscience. In fact, the conciliar text itself indicated awareness of the difficulty by devoting its main attention to the argument from the right and duty to follow conscience. One expert of the Council called the text's analysis of the act of faith "insufficient, scholastic, and useless."[22]

The second major area of concern with the first conciliar text was its treatment of the limits on the exercise of religious freedom. The "common good" of the body politic covered very broad ground and implicitly accepted the identity of the good of society with the end of the state. No doubt the authors of the first conciliar text intended a narrower scope. But, as the Roman maxim observed, what the lawmaker intends is not necessarily what the law effects; the lawmaker enacts the law he writes, not the law he may think that he is writing. Friends of religious freedom, therefore, properly expressed their concern with the language and concept of the "common good" as the basis of limitations on the exercise of religious freedom.

Indeed, the conservative opposition cited many aspects of the common good against the principle of religious freedom. Three interrelated problems worried the conservatives. The first was fear of proselytism. If religious freedom were normative, religious error could be propagated by slander and other unworthy means.[23] Second, religious freedom would expose the uninstructed masses to loss of the Catholic faith.[24] Third, religious freedom would hurt the cultural unity of a Catholic nation.[25] As is sufficiently patent, all of these objections are founded on the paternal view of society typical of Hispanic civilization. Although these appeals to the common good were directed against any declaration in favor of religious freedom, it is not hard to imagine that opponents of religious freedom could have made a similar appeal to justify limitations on religious exercise had the first conciliar text been adopted.

Spanish bishops were also concerned about the effect that acceptance of the principle of religious freedom would have on legal establishment of the Church in Spain as the religion of the nation.

The classic model of legal establishment involved three elements: (1) the public profession of the Catholic religion as the one and only religion of the state; (2) the financial support of the Catholic Church; and (3) the use of the coercive power of the state to prevent the propagation of non-Catholic religions. The first conciliar text on religious freedom explicitly repudiated the third element, and it also modified the second, at least to the extent of implying that all religions must share proportionately. But the first conciliar text did not explicitly touch the first and primary element of legal establishment. Unfortunately, the Spanish interventions did not observe these distinctions.

The third major bone of conservative contention centered on papal teaching. Most observers recognized that the conservatives could argue a good case from various statements of the nineteenth-century papacy, and that even the statements of Pius XI and Pius XII were at best two edged. But John XXIII's dictum on religious freedom in *Pacem in terris* did pose a special problem for those trying to argue that religious freedom was absolutely contrary to Catholic teaching. In the face of this dictum, the conservatives mustered a whole range of arguments.

Bishop Pablo Gúrpide Beope of Bilbao (Spain) did not shrink from asserting openly in one place that John's statement on religious liberty was outside of, and contrary to, Catholic tradition![26] While such a forthright denial would solve the conservative's problem of internal consistency, it shattered the force of his appeal to past papal teaching in the matter of religious freedom.

Other conservative arguments, therefore, proceeded more circumspectly. One denied the relevance of John's statement to the conciliar text on religious freedom.[27] According to this interpretation, John's affirmation of the right of the human person to honor God according to the "right norm of his conscience" (*ad rectam conscientiae suae normam*) and to profess his religion privately and publicly referred only to the right of Catholics. They argued that the "right norm of conscience" meant a "correct," and not simply an "upright," conscience. They appealed to the citations of Lactantius and Leo XIII immediately following John's affirmation to support their contention; in the case of both authors cited by John, they argued plausibly, there was no question of the rights of non-Catholics.[28]

This conservative argument, however, was subject to rebuttal. *Pacem in terris* was addressed to all men, and the rights enumerated concerned all men. It was strained to suppose that John would address the encyclical to all men and then claim only the right of Catholics to religious freedom, or that he would abruptly insert into his enumeration of the rights of all men a right proper to Catholics alone. Nor did the conservative argument agree with the spirit of John's pontificate or the reception which the world accorded the encyclical. Lastly, the conservative argument did not recognize the distinctive use of the term "upright conscience" (*conscientia recta*) in the manuals of moral theology. There, as opposed to the usage of Saint Thomas, the "upright conscience" (*conscientia recta*) was customarily distinguished from the "upright and correct conscience" (*conscientia recta et vera*).[29] If the citations of Lactantius and Leo XIII did not support a broad affirmation of religious freedom, they remain perfectly intelligible in terms of the curial style of papal encyclicals.

One further argument remained in the conservative arsenal. They could and did argue that the relevant text in *Pacem in terris* affirmed only the right of the person to the public profession of his religion.[30] This affirmation failed to mention a right of the person to the propagation of his religion, and the conservatives argued that the omission was significant. The Pope, they argued, intended to restrict the right of the person to private and public worship; he did not intend to claim a right to propagate publicly non-Catholic religions. In reply to this argument, one must note that the relevant text in *Pacem in terris* affirmed religious freedom only briefly and in general terms, and that the text referred to the right to *profess* religion publicly, and not simply to a right to *worship* publicly. The text did not, however, spell out how far the right to the public profession of religion extended. That was presumably the task of the conciliar declaration on religious freedom, and no conservative argument could obscure the fact that *Pacem in terris* was in line with such a declaration.

Interestingly, the reported draft of a law on the rights of non-Catholics considered by the Spanish government after publication of *Pacem in terris* assumed the narrow construction just indicated.[31] While that draft acknowledged the right of non-Catholics to immunity from coercion and discrimination, the right to practice their religion in public as well as in private, and the legal status of their churches, seminaries, schools, and liturgical publishing firms, proselytism was expressly forbidden. ("Proselytism" here apparently had the broad sense of any effort to gain converts by public preaching, propaganda, or canvassing.)

To bolster their argument from papal teaching, the conservative opposition cited the concordats which the Holy See had concluded with many countries from the time of Leo XIII.[32] But concordats were the most historically conditioned of any papal action and, indeed, were principally concerned with relations between the Church and a particular government rather than the problem of religious freedom as such.

A plenary session of the Secretariat weighed all these interventions at Aricca, Italy, from February 27 to March 7, 1964.[33] As a result of this scrutiny, the Secretariat produced a new text on religious freedom, which was presented to the Council at the beginning of the Third Session, on September 23, 1964, now as a separate declaration appended to the schema on ecumenism rather than a chapter of the schema proper.[34]

Since an explanation of the term "religious freedom" was considered altogether necessary to prevent confusion and false conclusions, a new paragraph was introduced at the beginning of the redaction indicating what the term meant and what it did not mean in the context of the Declaration.[35] The explanation of "religious freedom" began with a description of man's divine vocation. Formed in the image of God and called to association with Him, man has the duty and the privilege of following His will in religious matters according to dictates of his conscience. "Thus arises the right to religious freedom in society, by virtue of which men may exercise their religion privately and publicly, and no coercion may prohibit its exercise." This religious freedom requires that the necessary conditions in human society be promoted whereby all men, as individuals and members of religious groups, can fulfill freely and completely their divine vocation.

The text's so-called explanation of religious freedom was in fact a schematic and not too covert argument. After describing man's divine vocation, the new paragraph explicitly drew the conclusion ("thus") that man has a right to religious freedom in society. Conceding that man's divine vocation establishes a right not to be coerced to act against conscience, there remains the familiar question whether it establishes a right not to be restrained from acting according to conscience. At the level of "exploration," the new paragraph sought to write into the text a microcosm of the argument for religious freedom from the right and duty to follow conscience.

Lest the description of religious freedom be misinterpreted in a laicist sense, the text went on to explain that man is in no way emancipated from the power of God by the principle of religious freedom.[36] Man cannot value equally the true and the false, nor is he free of obligations toward God, nor may he shirk the duty of forming his conscience sincerely, nor may he determine at will whether and in what religion he wishes to serve God. Thus, the text was at pains to distinguish freedom in relation to God and freedom in relation to men. The scope of the Declaration concerned relations among men as individuals and members of religious groups and among men as citizens in relation to those who govern their commonwealth. In his oral report to the Council on September 23, 1964, Bishop De Smedt called religious freedom a formally juridical notion involving a right founded in the nature of the human person which all must respect and which must be acknowledged in fundamental law (the constitution and legal guarantees) so that it becomes a civil right. Its recognition, protection, and promotion must be pledged by society generally and especially by governments.[37]

The text then repeated the argument of its predecessor from the nature of the act of faith.[38] The Church has the duty to announce the gospel to all men, and the faithful were exhorted to lead men to the light of the gospel by their prayer, word, and example. They should lovingly, prudently, and patiently deal with men who are in error concerning the faith. But, because of the very nature of the act of faith, "every direct and indirect force" must be avoided and rejected. The disavowal of force was an elaboration from the words of the first conciliar text. There religious freedom was equated with immunity "from every external force," but here the text demanded abstention from the use of indirect as well as direct force.

The text then turned full attention to its main argument,[39] which had been already schematized in the introductory para-

graph of "explanation." The Church asserted that religious freedom must be respected not only by Christians and for Christians,
but also by all men and for all men and religious groups in human
society. The divine vocation, which opens and prescribes for man
the path toward God and salvation, constitutes the highest dignity
of the human person. "Therefore, the freedom to follow this
vocation in social life without any imposition or threat of force
constitutes the highest good proper to every man and the foundation of other freedoms." "Thus," religious freedom must be respected by every man as a true and strict right of those with whom
he lives. According to the new text, the exercise of religious freedom was not only deducible from man's divine vocation but
even constituted the highest good and foundation of other freedoms. The text thus took on the additional burden of asserting
a "preferred position" for religious freedom among other freedoms.
In view of the opposition to the general argument for religious
freedom from the right to follow conscience, this was certainly
a brave, if unnecessary, counterattack.

Although the objective law of God is the norm of man's vocation, he can obey the will of God only insofar as he perceives the
divine law in the dictates of his own conscience, and he can
obtain his ultimate goal only by forming prudently a judgment
of conscience and following faithfully its dictate. Whoever sincerely obeys his conscience obeys God, although sometimes confusedly and unwittingly, and must be esteemed worthy of honor.
Here the text drew a conclusion not so clearly expressed in the
first conciliar text: if anyone following the dictate of a sincere
conscience falls into error, no man and no human power has a
right to induce him to act against the dictate of his conscience.

From this affirmation of the right not to be coerced to act
against conscience, the text moved to affirm the right not to be
restrained from acting according to conscience—in effect, but not
in these words. Since religious freedom would be deprived of an
essential element and become meaningless if it could not be
exercised publicly, the text affirmed not only freedom of thought
and freedom of public worship but also the true and proper right
of the human person to observe and witness to his private and
public duties toward God and man. He has the right to order
his whole life according to the requirements of his religion in

matters concerning the family, education, culture, society, charity, and other human activities.

This affirmation, of course, focused immediately the problem of limits to the freedom of religious exercise. According to the new text, the exercise of rights in religious matters is limited because of the social nature of man; it cannot be permitted to harm the essential dignity of the human person or make human society impossible. But the exercise of religious freedom may be limited only insofar as it gravely contradicts the "end of society," which is present in the complex of conditions of social life by which men are able to develop themselves more fully and more readily and at the same time observe faithfully the inalienable rights given by God to men in common.[40]

The text sought to make more explicit the precise nature of the limits which might be imposed on the freedom of religious exercise. To avoid the criticism voiced about the breadth of the term "common good," the new text offered as a rubric the "end of society." The substitute, however, was subject to exactly the same objection as the original. What was the "end of society" but the "common good"? As long as the guide for the limits to the freedom of religious exercise was the end or good of society, the conservative opposition could easily argue that the propagation of religious error was against that end or good. The fundamental question was not what was in itself good for human society, but what was the precise competence of the state. The new text did not really face this question any more than its predecessor had, despite the change of vocabulary.

After offering the "end of society" as the norm to determine the limits of the freedom of religious exercise, the text applied the limits to the question of proselytism.[41] (The term "proselytism" was here used in contradistinction to "witness" and implied the use of unworthy or dishonorable means of propagating religion, e.g., slander, libel, deceit, bribes, threats). If religious freedom is put to perverse uses which clearly harm personal dignity and the rights of others, governments may reasonably prevent them according to the rules of prudence. This application was made to meet the objection that religious freedom could be used as an opportunity to slander the Church or entice the uneducated from the Church by deceit, bribes, or threats. While the text's application of the limits on the freedom of religious exercise to proselytism was generally acceptable in principle, it was open to a practical objection: Who would determine when "personal dignity" was offended by missionary work? The text's rejection of proselytism raised a new problem of definition.

The text then condemned discrimination among citizens on the basis of religious affiliation.[42] Governments may not require the profession of any religion as a condition of participation in national life, nor may they penalize citizens for religious reasons. Religious freedom is violated by physical punishment in the name of religion, the deprivation of material goods, the denial of equality or nationality, and the refusal of access to the courts or the exercise of fundamental rights.

Government must also safeguard and promote the right of the person to freedom in religious matters.[43] For it is the responsibility of the commonwealth not only to recognize and respect the rights of the person but also to render their exercise easier and prevent harm to those exercising their rights.

The second text responded to the criticism that the first text laid insufficient stress on the freedom of religious groups by devoting an entire section to this aspect of religious freedom.[44] Religious groups are formed by the free decision of persons under the impulse of conscience and required by the social nature of man. They have the right, therefore, to direct themselves according to their own regulations, offer public worship to God, aid their members in the exercise of their religious life, and promote institutions for ordering the activities of their members according to their religious principles. This right belongs not only to the Catholic Church but also to other religious groups. They may zealously propagate or announce their religion by worthy methods, but they must avoid a "proselytism" which uses improper methods. They may not be prevented from proposing accounts of their religion in order to persuade listeners to join their community.

The concluding paragraph on the right of all religious groups to freedom of exercise struck a new note.[45] For the first time, a conciliar text on religious freedom dealt explicitly with the constitutional question of the state's competence in religious matters, although judging by its position in the text, in contrast to the centrality of the argument from conscience, one may assume that the paragraph was not considered critical by the drafters of the text. The paragraph stated that governments have no direct capacity or competence to determine or moderate the relations of citizens with their Creator and Savior; governments may not subordinate religious bodies to the temporal goals of the commonwealth. But the more civil society supplies favorable conditions for developing religious life the more will it enjoy the goods which flow from the fidelity of men to their divine vocation. Despite the fact that the text did not explain or make clear what it meant by "direct" competence or what were the "favorable conditions" which society was encouraged to supply, the text's affirmation was a welcome addition. Unfortunately, however, it was not given a more central position in the text.

The closing paragraphs emphasized the need for religious freedom especially at the present time.[46] Men of diverse culture and religion are today drawn into ever closer relations; there is an ever growing consciousness of personal responsibility; and the juridical structures of the modern commonwealth are not suited to pass judgment on religious matters. As a result, the peaceful coexistence of the whole human family today demands religious freedom.

The second conciliar text on religious freedom was now before the Fathers. It was not substantially different from the first conciliar text, and for that reason, it was likely to evoke the same objections. But at least the Council could now specifically debate the subject.

Notes

1. *Relatio [oralis] super declarationem de libertate religiosa schematis decreti de oecumenismo* (Rome: Vatican Polyglot Press, 1964), p. 3. These interventions were mimeographed by the Secretariat, and copies are in the Murray files.
2. Interventions G, 17 and 46.
3. G, 27.
4. Rynne, *Letters from Vatican City*, pp. 214–32.
5. See, for example, G, 42 and 43 (Bishop Gúrpide Beope of Bilbao).

6. G-4, 12.
7. G-4, 16.
8. G-5, 12.
9. Declaration on Religious Freedom, Art. 7. Appendix I, p. 193.
10. G, 23.
11. G, 82.
12. G, 72.
13. See, for example, G, 42 and 43.
14. Pius XII, Ci riesce, AAS, XLV (1953).
15. This distinction is noted in "Relatio, pars altera," Schema declarationis de libertate religiosa [textus re-emendatus] (Rome: Vatican Polyglot Press, 1965), pp. 49–50.
16. This distinction is noted in "Relatio," Schema declarationis de libertate religiosa [textus emendatus] (Rome: Vatican Polyglot Press, 1964), pp. 39–40.
17. This distinction is noted in "Relatio" [textus re-emendatus], pp. 48–49.
18. See, for example, G, 14 (Archbishop Lefebvre).
19. G, 27.
20. G, 17.
21. G, 26.
22. Quoted by Cardinal Larraona, G-3, 2.
23. See, for example, G, 79 (Cardinal Larraona).
24. See G, 44 (Bishop Gúrpide Beope of Bilbao).
25. Ibid.
26. G, 42.
27. Ibid.
28. Cf. Lactantius, Divinarum Institutionum, Bk. 4, Ch. 28, 2, Patrologia Latina, Vol. VI, p. 535; Leo XIII, Libertas praestantissimum, ASS, XX (1887–88), p. 608.
29. See, for example, Franz Hürth, S.J., and Pedro Abellán, S.J., De principiis, de vitutibus et praeceptis (Rome: Gregorian University Press, 1948), Vol. I, pp. 141–42. One should also note that the main architect of Pacem in terris, Msgr. Pietro Pavan, participated actively in drafting the Declaration on Religious Freedom from the third text forward and collaborated closely with Murray. For a statement of his views on the subject, see Libertà religiosa e publici poteri (Milan: Editrici Ancora, 1965). On the specific question of interpreting the dictum on religious freedom in Pacem in terris, Pavan claims that John did not commit himself. He was aware of the division of theological opinion on religious freedom but wanted to allow time for further study. Op. cit., p. 357. Nevertheless, the thrust of the whole encyclical favored a liberal interpretation of the dictum.
30. See, for example, G, 42.
31. See America, October 24, 1964, p. 471.
32. See, for example, G, 120 (Archbishop Muñoyerro).

33. "Relatio circa rationem qua schema elaboratum est," *Schema decreti de oecumenismo: declaratio altera de Judaeis et non christianis* (Rome: Vatican Polyglot Press, 1964), p. 11 (51).

34. *Schema decreti de oecumenismo: declaratio prior de libertate religiosa* (Rome: Vatican Polyglot Press, 1964), pp. 29–38. For the date, cf. Xavier Rynne, *The Third Session* (New York: Farrar, Straus and Giroux, 1964, 1965), p. 24. On April 18, 1964, the Coordinating Commission had expressed the opinion that the theme of religious freedom should be put to the Council as a separate document. See Pavan, "The Declaration on Religious Freedom," *Information Documentation on the Conciliar Church,* Doss. LXVI–XXVI (November 30, 1966), p. 1.

35. *Declaratio prior,* p. 29.

36. *Ibid.*

37. *Relatio [oralis],* p. 4.

38. *Declaratio prior,* pp. 29–30.

39. *Ibid.,* pp. 30–31.

40. *Ibid.,* p. 31.

41. *Ibid.*

42. *Ibid.,* pp. 31–32.

43. *Ibid.,* p. 32.

44. *Ibid.,* pp. 32–33.

45. *Ibid.,* p. 33.

46. *Ibid.*

V

The Council Debates
Religious Freedom

DEBATE ON THE PROPOSED Declaration on Religious Freedom appended to the schema on ecumenism opened on Wednesday, September 23, 1964, after the introductory report of Bishop De Smedt.[1] Cardinal Ernesto Ruffini, archbishop of Palermo (Italy), the first speaker, endorsed the conservative position on religious freedom; he emphasized the difference between freedom and tolerance and defended legal establishment of the Catholic religion.[2] In a similar vein, Cardinal Fernando Quiroga y Palacios, archbishop of Santiago de Compostela (Spain), complained that the text exposed the faithful to grave perils and that the text stressed novelty to the detriment of tradition.[3] He urged that the text be entirely revised and entrusted for this purpose to a new mixed commission which would have the help of experts able to appreciate the gravity of the problem.

The conservative temper of the debate was changed at this point by the interventions of several liberal cardinals. Cardinal Léger endorsed the Declaration but did not think that the text offered a sufficiently broad foundation for the principle of religious freedom.[4] The text's argument supposed belief in God, but it is necessary to show that religious freedom is a value for all, for the nonbeliever as well as for the believer. Hence, it is necessary to show that religious freedom is a claim of man in the exercise of his reason, and that every restraint on that freedom is a restraint on human nature.

Next, Cardinal Richard Cushing, archbishop of Boston, spoke in the name of almost all the bishops of the United States.[5] Although the Declaration needed changes here or there, Cushing expressed the desire that such changes make the Declaration stronger rather than weaker. According to Cushing, the freedom which the Church had always claimed for herself and her members she would now claim in the Declaration on Religious Freedom for other churches and their members, indeed for every human person. He proposed four reasons for this affirmation of religious freedom, citing by way of summary the principle of Pope John in *Pacem in terris* that every well ordered society is founded on truth, justice, love, and freedom. First, equal and universal freedom of religion is demanded by that fundamental truth according to which all men are of equal dignity insofar as they are human persons, equally endowed with the same human rights, among which Pope John numbered the right to religious freedom. Second, religious freedom is demanded by justice, because all citizens equally enjoy the same civil rights, among which the right to religious freedom is first. Third, religious freedom is demanded by love, because nothing more violently disturbs the unity and friendship of citizens than coercion or discrimination for religious reasons. Fourth, religious freedom is demanded by the very principle of civil liberty, because, as Lord Acton said, "freedom is the highest political end" of organized society and indeed a necessary means of attaining the higher goals of the human person.

Cardinal Bueno y Monreal resumed the conservative attack on the Declaration.[6] According to the Cardinal, the text was guilty of two equivocations: it moved unjustifiably from the order of truth to the political order and from the individual to the social level. Error has no rights, and the state may prevent the dissemination of error to protect the rights of citizens. But, for political reasons, it is necessary to see what can be accorded to error in order to insure peace.

Cardinal Meyer spoke next and generally approved the text, especially because all men were waiting to see the Church's approval of the principle of religious freedom.[7] Moreover, the Declaration would help men to understand better that religion does not consist in exterior actions but in interior adhesion to the will of God. Lastly, it would facilitate the dialogue with separated

Christians. Cardinal Ritter also approved the text but thought the presentation too restrained; it must show better that religious freedom is an aspect of human freedom, and that it is founded on human nature.[8] On the other hand, there is a question here of a declaration which ought to expose and propose an affirmation of religious freedom but not to elaborate a proof. The present schema offers arguments which can stir interminable discussions; it would be better to suppress these arguments and make the text simpler. Above all, one must consider the substance of the Declaration and distinguish it from the arguments; the Moderators could allow the two elements to be voted separately. (The Moderators did not act upon the Cardinal's suggestion.)

Cardinal Raul Silva Henriquez, archbishop of Santiago (Chile), in the name of fifty-eight bishops of Latin America, warmly approved the text, especially as an independent declaration.[9] The Cardinal hailed the text's affirmation of religious freedom and its denial of the competence of civil powers to determine the relations of their citizens with God. In these respects, the text resembled the declaration of the U.N. on religious freedom.[10] A proclamation of religious freedom by the Church is very important not only for Christians but for all men; it is particularly important for the evangelization of Latin America, which has need of being rechristianized because of the modern development of ideas on the individual and the common good. The Cardinal ended his remarks with a condemnation of "proselytism."

Cardinal Ottaviani broke the public curial silence on the Secretariat's schema on religious freedom.[11] The schema, he thought, makes clear the general principle always preached by the Church that no one is to be compelled to embrace the Catholic religion, but exaggerates when it suggests that the person sincerely following an erroneous conscience is "worthy of honor"; such a person is worthy only of tolerance, or at most of respect. Then Ottaviani catalogued a list of the schema's defects: the text does not take account of the problems which concern non-Christian religions or atheism; the text lacks an explicit affirmation that the genuine right to religious freedom belongs objectively only to those adhering to the true religion; the text does not affirm that the Church's freedom is unlimited; the text does not qualify the right to follow conscience by the condition that the conscience is not contrary to divine law; the text does not reconcile the general assertion of the right to follow one's own conscience with the admitted right of society to limit that right for social reasons; the text's assertion that the commonwealth is incompetent to judge truth concerning religious matters contradicts the solemn affirmation of Leo XIII; the text's affirmation that every religion has the right of propagation would result in damage to those nations in which the Catholic religion is generally professed by the citizens; and the admonition against "proselytism" might be turned to condemn the work of Catholic missionaries. Thus spake the Pro-Secretary of the Holy Office.

The last speaker of the day was Bishop Smiljan Cekada of Skopje (Yugoslavia)[12] who said an affirmation of religious freedom was necessary because, in the present day, philosophical and social systems claim an infallibility for themselves. Nazism was one such system, and today there is atheistic Marxism. The Council has a great pastoral responsibility and should address itself directly to the United Nations to ask that the right to religious freedom be proclaimed and that the application of the right be defined. The Bishop did not indicate any awareness that the United Nations had already spoken on the subject, or that there was any way of enforcing the U.N. declaration on religious freedom when member states were unwilling to use force.

On the second day of debate, Thursday, September 24, Cardinal Franziskus König, archbishop of Vienna, also voiced concern for religious freedom behind the Iron Curtain.[13] The Council should not pass over in silence the tragic fact that there are today peoples for whom there exists no real religious freedom, and countries where governments work to promote atheism. Freedom of religious worship exists, but the religious education of the young is impeded or even forbidden. In these countries, citizens are divided into two classes, to only one of which complete freedom is granted. This way of acting sins against tolerance, the search for truth, the common good, and the dignity of the human person. The Council must reflect attentively on the way in which, speaking in the name of all who believe in God, it can influence world opinion in order that these anomalies cease, obtain the separation of atheism and the state, and affirm peace. The Cardinal was warmly applauded.

Eight conservative spokesmen followed the Archbishop of Vienna. Cardinal Browne, vice president of the Theological Commission, led off by calling the Declaration unacceptable.[14] It was evident to him that the rights of the correct conscience are not the same as those of the erroneous conscience. Archbishop Parente also found much in the text to object to.[15] There were involved in the text many extremely delicate and complex questions of theology, philosophy, jurisprudence, history, and sociology; these ought to be treated separately and more precisely. In the present text, besides affirmations admitted by all, there are others which, far from meeting the consent of all specialists, could incite very diverse reactions in a number of countries. It was not necessary for the Council to enter such a forest; therefore, as Cardinal Ritter suggested, the text should be corrected so as to affirm only what is sure. The reformed Declaration should build on principles concerning the dignity of man, freedom of conscience, the right of the Church to preach the gospel, the right of all to practice their religion, and the duty of the state to respect every religion. The rest should be left to the disputation of theologians, philosophers, and sociologists.

Archbishop Pedro Cantero Cuadrado of Saragossa (Spain) thought the text equivocal on the social nature of religious freedom and inadequate in expressing a distinction between religious freedom and freedom of conscience.[16] Bishop Juan Abasolo y Lecue of Vijayapuram (India) repeated the arguments that the rights of man flow from his duties toward God, that the sincere but erroneous conscience does not have the same rights as the conscience which coincides with objective truth, and that only the latter conscience has absolute rights in its external manifestations.[17] Archbishop Enrico Nicodemo of Bari (Italy) insisted that the text make clear the irreconcilable opposition between truth and error.[18] Only truth has the objective right to diffusion, and religious freedom is founded on only a subjective right to follow one's conscience. The Declaration should define the obligations of the faithful to their religious authority and the obligations of all to the natural law.

Bishop José Lopez Ortiz of Tuy-Vigo (Spain) was concerned about the passage in the text disclaiming the competence of the state in religious matters.[19] The state can declare itself Catholic and, in doing so, only submits to the commandments of God. Indeed, numerous documents of the magisterium treat of the duties of the state toward religion and the Church. Bishop Antonio de Castro Mayer of Campos (Brazil) accused the text of equating the true religion with those which are false.[20] Only the true religion has the right to be professed, and the human dignity cannot be protected, much less promoted, by the diffusion of error. Auxiliary Bishop Giovanni Canestri of Rome also attacked the text strongly for equivocations and imprecision. At one painful point, Canestri declared that a priest converting to Protestantism has no right to religious freedom because he cannot be in good faith and can be acting only from motives of gain, ambition, or pride.[21]

Bishop Johannes Pohlschneider of Aachen, with the approbation of the German bishops, introduced "the school question" into the conciliar debate.[22] The Declaration should insist on freedom in the matter of the religious education of youth: although this question is studied in the schema on Christian education, the Declaration on Religious Freedom should make allusion to it. In modern society the exercise of the right of parents in education supposes that they can choose freely the schooling they desire for their children. A paragraph in the final Declaration would accede to this suggestion, albeit in rather general terms.[23]

Archbishop Marcel Lefebvre, superior general of the Congregation of the Holy Spirit, noted that freedom is not an absolute value but ordered to what is good, that internal and external acts in religious matters should be distinguished, that external acts are subject to authority, that grave consequences follow from allowing a right to act externally according to conscience, and that the Declaration involved relativism because it was not founded on the rights of the truth.[24] Archbishop Lefebvre thought that the Declaration would lose the Church respect and esteem, because she would appear to renounce her love of truth.

Fr. Joseph Buckley, superior general of the Marists, strongly endorsed a conciliar declaration on religious freedom but expressed concern that the affirmation be founded on a solid base.[25] He disapproved the idea that an erroneous conscience constitutes a divine vocation; such an idea is the last stage of an unhappy evolu-

tion in the usage of language. The adequate foundation of the
inviolability of religious freedom is rather to be found in the imperative of a conscience submissive to God's will, as far as that is
understood.

The next speaker, Bishop Ernest Primeau of Manchester (New
Hampshire) made two important contributions to the argument
for the principle of religious freedom.[26] First, he urged that freedom of conscience, an internal and personal freedom, and the
free exercise of religion, an external and social freedom, were
indissolubly connected. He deplored the attempt to deduce the
latter freedom from the former, since man is not an individual
in one moment and only socially oriented in a second moment.
According to the true metaphysics of the human person, human
existence is essentially social and historical; in one and the same
moment the human person is both an individual and an individual
related to others. From this it follows that it is in no way legitimate
to allow a man freedom of conscience and at the same time deny
him the free exercise of religion; both pertain with equal claim
to the dignity and integrity of the human person. Any attempt to
separate these two freedoms would be some type of Kantianism,
a separation of the juridical order from the moral order. If it is
clearly understood that the free exercise of religion is not some
logical inference from the freedom of conscience, it will be clear
that the doctrine of religious freedom involves no illegitimate
transition from the subjective order of conscience to the objective
order of rights. The true concept of religious freedom is understood through a simple analysis of the human person himself, who
is one subject of one right embracing both freedom of conscience
and the free exercise of religion.

The second question raised by Bishop Primeau concerned the
sense in which religious freedom is a true and strict right. A right
is a moral power, but "moral power" can be taken in two senses.
There is a moral power to do something, and there is a moral
power to demand that others not do something. Religious freedom
is a true right in the latter sense, that there is a true juridical immunity from any legal or social force in matters of religion. In
this sense, the Declaration proclaims the right of all men and all
churches to religious freedom in society. But in no sense does the

Declaration proclaim that all men and all churches have the same command to spread their doctrine and worship, which would endorse religious indifferentism.

Bishop Anton Nierman of Groningen, in the name of the bishops of Holland, thought that the principle of religious freedom embodied in the Declaration ought to be applied to the revision of canon law in what concerns "mixed marriages," so that the conscience of the non-Catholic party would be fully taken into consideration.[27]

Bishop Angelo Temino Saiz of Orense (Spain) attacked the idea that all religions and all religious groups have the same rights.[28] According to Temino, this is equivalent to religious indifferentism on the social or public level and cannot be reconciled with the teaching of the First Vatican Council. While civil powers cannot direct the relations of citizens with their Creator, they can recognize the truth of the Catholic religion in the same way as they judge matters of public morality. When a nation is almost entirely Catholic, the Church obtains a certain security by concordats with civil authority. Thus public manifestations of other religions, which would harm the faithful, are avoided.

Bishop Michael Klepacz of Lodz, in the name of the bishops of Poland, thought that the foundation of religious freedom was the rational nature of man, who is created free.[29] From that comes his dignity and certain important consequences: all men are free to practice the religion of their choice; all men have the right to propagate their religion by worthy means; and all men must seek the true religion. On the basis of these principles, it is necessary to affirm that no human power has the right to prevent a man from professing his religion publicly or to impose a philosophical creed on him by force or trickery. Religious freedom is also founded on the principle of justice, which obliges individuals, society, and the state.

Archbishop Marcel Dubois of Besançon (France), while approving the text generally, complained that it was clothed in too philosophical and juridical a form.[30] He urged that it be given a religious foundation worthy of the Council, drawn from Scripture and the Fathers of the Church, notably Saint Augustine. The last speaker of the day, Bishop Granados, argued that the right to propagate religious truth and error indifferently is a novelty in the teaching of the Church.[31] The traditional doctrine teaches the right of truth and tolerance for error according to the exigencies of the common good. The Declaration makes no distinction between the internal forum of conscience and the relation of man to others in society. In conclusion, he urged caution in establishing the theological foundation of the Declaration and asked that other experts or the Theological Commission itself come to the "fraternal aid" of the Secretariat.

On Friday, September 25, the debate on religious freedom resumed for the third day. Cardinal Francesco Roberti (Curia) opened the day with a suggestion that the Declaration take account of the distinction between "freedom of conscience" and "freedom of consciences."[32] The Church rejects the former because not all religious doctrines are equal, but the Church admits the latter, in the sense that no one can have a religious doctrine imposed on him in any way. According to Cardinal Roberti, this was a formula accceptable to all.

Archbishop Denis Hurley of Durban (South Africa) took up the establishment question.[33] Discrimination on the basis of religious belief as a condition for participation in the social life of a nation is always forbidden, but application of the principle is difficult when there exists a union of Church and state. The state seems then to assume charge of public religious worship, a charge proper to the Church. (Archbishop Hurley would admit the duty of the state to foster religion directly if the Church were not charged with that office.) Moreover, the Church can better exercise influence when she is free in her activities and without obligation to make continual appeal to the support or subsidies of the state. This does not exclude particular accommodations between the Church and the state, as in the case of state support of religiously affiliated schools.

Bishop Ubaldo Cibrián Fernández, prelate nullius of Corocoro (Bolivia), altogether rejected the Declaration.[34] He accused the Declaration of involving false principles, of proceeding too philosophically and rationally, of ignoring and weakening the teaching of the magisterium, and of confusing the absolute value of moral principles with their practical application. Archbishop Frederick Melendro, exiled from Anking (China), did not think that the time was ripe for a conciliar declaration on religious freedom.[35]

Moreover, the Declaration subordinates the objective order to a subjective norm, and the divine law makes an obligation of the objectively true religion. The Church ought not to contradict positions previously taken.

Archbishop Karol Wojtyla of Cracow (Poland) thought that the Declaration was attempting to fulfill two purposes, one ecumenical and the other concerned with the observation of religious freedom in the social order.[36] In the case of the first purpose, the connection between freedom and truth should be underlined. Freedom is for the sake of truth, and this relation is of great moment for the ecumenical movement, which seeks union in truth. As to the civic sense of religious freedom, it is necessary that the human person be seen in the real sublimity of his rational nature and religion be seen as the highest perfection of that nature. The secular arm cannot inject itself into the relation of man to God because religion itself by its very nature transcends everything secular. Indeed, the right to the free exercise of religion is connected with those rights of the person which concern truth, i.e., the right to know, to teach, and to communicate. The Second Vatican Council, therefore, must bravely and effectively affirm this religious freedom.

Archbishop Gabriel Garrone of Toulouse (France) spoke on the historical evolution of the Church's teaching on religious freedom.[37] To avoid the appearance of contradiction, an explanation of the continuity between the present doctrine and that of the past should be added to the text. The conditions of human society have undergone great change. The concept of the state is not the same as in the Middle Ages or even the last century; the power of the state is today restricted by the legally recognized freedom of persons. Indeed, the common good cannot be defined today only in relation to a particular nation; it must include relations to the whole world. Further, society is generally pluralist today in matters of religious belief. Lastly, and of most importance, with the progressive growth in understanding the gospel, respect for the human person is today more clearly perceived as fundamental.

In the nineteenth century the Church felt obliged to condemn those aspects of liberalism which were most dangerous from the objective point of view. Today the Church considers more closely and concretely the rights of the human person. In the past the Church did indeed act in a way different from that prescribed in the present Declaration. But the historical context must be understood if the past is to be judged correctly and not in the light of the present. The Church does not hesitate to confess and regret that she has erred in the past from human weakness.

Bishop Hoa Nguyên-van Hiên, bishop of Dalat (Vietnam) thought the Declaration on Religious Freedom of great moment not only for relations among Christians but also for areas in which Christians constitute a small minority.[38] The Declaration should make clearer at the outset, however, that it is not concerned with the relations between man and God but between men. Bishop Nguyên-van Hiên then laid down two principles for religious freedom: the divine vocation of men culminating in Christ and His Church and the corresponding right and duty to respond freely to this divine vocation. From these principles, two corollaries were drawn: man is not free from the ordination of divine Providence, and others must aid, not hinder, man's free response to God's ordination. Specifically, neither the Church nor civil society should mutilate any cultural patrimony among the nations to which Christ is announced.

Archbishop Karl Alter of Cincinnati spoke in the name of many bishops of the United States.[39] On September 17, the bishops considered and almost to a man approved generally the text of the Declaration. The Declaration affirms not any kind of freedom but precisely the right of the human person to immunity in religious matters from every external force induced by the public or any other power. In no way does the Declaration affirm the right of the human person to teach error or do evil. Today, almost everywhere, citizens claim for themselves the right to judge religious matters and deny the competence of the state therein. According to Alter's rather limited argument, this development was merited because democracies follow the decision of the majority, and the truth of the Church's doctrine and the value of her discipline should not be subject to a majority vote. Alter also affirmed the absolute right of the Church to religious freedom. In conclusion, he accepted the validity of the arguments in the text from the nature of the act of faith and the rational nature of man. He admitted, however, that there are other valid arguments from the nature of the modern constitutions of many nations, from the incompetence of governments in religious matters, from the need of peaceful relations among citizens of different religious beliefs, and from the example of our Lord.

Fr. Aniceto Fernandez, O.P., master general of the Dominicans, was critical of the text.[40] He thought it inopportune to insert the Declaration in the schema on ecumenism because the Declaration concerns all men and not only Christians; the fundamental principle of the Declaration is of a subjective order, and the rights of conscience are so exalted that Christian doctrine is cast in a shadow; affirmations about the "divine vocation" of following conscience can involve grave confusion between the natural and supernatural orders; the equality of the rights of the Church and all other religions to propagate their respective doctrines is unacceptable; and the freedom of the Church is presented as an exigence of the conscience of the faithful and not of the Church's divine rights. These difficulties, and others as grave, he thought, called for a total revision of the Declaration.

Bishop Cornelius Lucey of Cork and Ross (Ireland) pointed out that the proposed Declaration on Religious Freedom did not seem to affirm the freedom of the nonbeliever or admit that there are atheists in good faith.[41] Although no one has a right "in the objective moral order" to profess or propagate a false religion or atheism, there exists a "subjective moral order" in which men of good will have a right to follow the dictates of their conscience. Hence religious freedom must be understood in a negative sense as a right not to be coerced by others or hindered from exercising free choice in religious matters. This freedom is limited by the demands of the public peace and the rights of others. As to the state, it is not the defender or promoter of any form of religion or irreligion. Rather, the state is required to grant and protect the freedom of all those religions which its citizens wish to profess and practice peacefully. The state, however, may favor a particular religion or establish a particular religion as the religion of the state, provided that the freedom of other religions is observed.

Since the last speaker of the day, Auxiliary Bishop Carlo Colombo of Milan (Italy), had been the private theologian of Pope Paul at the First Session, his words were attentively listened to.[42] He stressed the necessity that the Declaration affirm religious freedom in terms of doctrinal principles which hold for all times and places. According to Colombo, there are three principles on which the Catholic doctrine of religious freedom in civil society is founded, two of natural order and one of the supernatural order. First, every man has a natural right to seek truth, especially in religious and moral matters, and this involves the freedom to investigate, communicate, and explain the truth as each finds it, or thinks that he has found it. The second principle is that each man is obliged to follow the dictates of a certain conscience. Third, the free and supernatural character of the act of faith withdraws relations between man and God from the judgment of the state. From these principles, he argued, it follows that the state must guarantee religious freedom. To avoid the dangers of subjectivism and relativism, however, Colombo urged that two other points be vigorously asserted: the serious obligation of every man to seek truth, and the value of revealed truth as an essential element of the common good in human society. The relation between revealed truth and the common good, he admitted, is very delicate, because revealed truth cannot be communicated by political means. The duty of the state is rather to protect the religious freedom of all citizens and of the Church.

After this intervention, one of the Moderators, Cardinal Sue-nens, proposed a standing vote to close the debate on religious freedom.[43] (The decision to close debate was apparently made the evening before, when the Moderators saw the Pope.) The motion was carried overwhelmingly, and the debate was closed early enough on Friday to permit Cardinal Bea to introduce the next subject on the Council's agenda, the Declaration on the Jews, before he departed on Saturday to return a relic of Saint Andrew to the Orthodox Church of Greece, some five hundred years after the last Byzantine emperor had entrusted it to Pope Pius II to keep it from falling into the hands of the invading Turks.

Of the fifteen scheduled speakers cut off by the cloture, six were Americans and eleven favorable to the Declaration on Religious Freedom. By contrast, nineteen of the speakers actually heard in the three days of debate were basically opposed to the Declaration. A false impression was thereby created that the conservative opposition constituted a very sizable minority. The disproportion given to the conservatives in the conciliar debate was only partially redressed by allowing four speakers in favor of the Declaration on Monday, September 28. All four spoke in the name of many other bishops.

Archbishop John Heenan of Westminster (England) intervened in the name of the hierarchy of England and Wales, many bishops of Scotland, Ireland, Australia, and New Zealand, as well as certain bishops of France and Belgium.[44] In the sixteenth century, he observed, there were violent persecutions of Catholics in England (and of Protestants under Mary Tudor). By the end of the century, Protestants had triumphed, and the Church almost ceased to exist in Great Britain. But the Catholic Emancipation Act of 1829 restored to Catholics most, if not all, of their civil rights. Today, although the Church of England is the established church, a complete freedom of religion is guaranteed to citizens of other religions. For example, the state gives substantial aid to Catholic schools, and the Catholic schools enjoy the same rights and privileges as those of the Church of England. As to the limits on religious freedom, Heenan thought that external exercise of religion should be restricted only when necessary to safeguard the public order.

Bishop Adrian Ddungu of Masaka (Uganda), in the name of sixty bishops of Africa, urged the necessity of adopting the Declaration to safeguard the life and prosperity of the Church, especially in Africa.[45] In the newly independent states of Africa, recognition of religious freedom is of great moment because restrictions have been frequently placed on religious freedom, especially in the sphere of education. In Africa there are influences at work which seek to impose materialism or a non-Christian religion on individuals and groups by force. If in Christian states the Christian religion should be defended and the freedom of other religions restricted, then in non-Christian states freedom for the Christian religion should be equally restricted.

Bishop John Wright of Pittsburgh was concerned with the relations between religious freedom and the common good.[46] Although propagation of error disturbs the common good, the denial of religious freedom also, and more seriously, hurts the common good because the common good of its very nature positively requires and presumes such freedom and its recognition by the civil power as an integral and essential element. The common good, as Jacques Maritain observed, is not only the accumulation of material benefits but also includes as an essential element the greatest possible development of the human person. Hence it follows that the common good, as ethical and moral, requires and presumes a freely accepted religious faith; the necessity of freedom from coercion in religious matters also follows from the requirements of justice. But religious freedom is compatible with a regime favoring a particular religion for historical reasons, as in England. The last speaker of the day and of the opening conciliar debate was Archbishop Jéan Zoa of Yaoundé (Cameroons), who in the name of seventy bishops of Africa urged that the Declaration on Religious Freedom be universal in its mode of affirmation, doctrinal in its foundation, and necessary in its content.[47]

In addition to the opinions expressed in the public debate, many Fathers wrote their observations to the Secretariat. All together, the total number of oral and written interventions after the introduction of the second text reached over 140.[48] From this mass of material, several significant comments emerged.

Much comment was focused on the relation of freedom to truth. The Declaration was accused of omitting the positive aspect of freedom, its ordination to truth. Actually, this criticism misconceived the basic character of the order of rights about which the Declaration was speaking. As a political right, religious freedom is concerned with man's freedom from coercion, not with the use to which man should put this freedom.

Related to the attempt to link "freedom from" to "freedom to" was the argument for religious freedom introduced by Colombo and echoed by Auxiliary Bishop Alfred Ancel of Lyons (France).[49] According to this argument, a man has the right to search for truth and communicate the truth he has found, or thinks he has found. Therefore, he has a right to religious freedom. There are several difficulties with the argument if it is too simply stated. The fact that a person has a right to *search* for truth would not necessarily of itself give him a right to *communicate* what he thinks is true but which is in fact false. (It is, for example, no defense in a libel or slander action for an individual to claim that he thought a statement true.) Much less would the right to search for truth give a right to communicate what is known to be false. Nor would the right to search for truth of itself give a man complacent in the possession of what he thinks is true the right to communicate his religious views, whether true or false.

Of course, the argument could be made in a more sophisticated way within a social and political context. One could argue that a man has a right and duty to search for truth, that search for truth is necessarily a social enterprise involving communication and exchange, and that the state must promote conditions favorable to the enterprise. Therefore, within the limits of public order, the state may not impede the investigation or communication of ideas, including religious ideas, and every man, whether communicating truth or error, whether in good faith or bad, whether searching for truth or complacent, has the corresponding right to immunity from coercion in all that concerns the order of truth and religious truth in particular. The state's competence, in fact, is limited to the order of action.

Certainly simpler was the argument for religious freedom voiced by Primeau from an analysis of the human person himself, who, as individual and member of society, can claim both freedom of conscience and the freedom of religious exercise on the basis of his rational and free nature. This argument avoids the pitfalls of the argument from the subjective order of conscience to the objective order of rights in society. Other bishops echoed Primeau's point of view less eloquently.

On the limits to religious freedom, Archbishop Patrick O'Boyle of Washington, D.C., made a significant contribution, and it is much to be regretted that the premature termination of the floor discussion on Friday, September 25, deprived the whole Council of his words.[50] But the Secretariat did read his words, and his concept of the limits to religious freedom would appear in subsequent drafts of the Declaration. At the outset, he rejected summarily a theological norm—namely, the truth or falsity of religious belief—for the limits to religious freedom, because governments are incompetent to judge the truth or falsity of any religion.

Likewise, he rejected summarily an ethical norm, namely, the sincerity of conscience, because governments are incompetent to make the requisite inquiry. This argument needs explanation and at least one qualification. Because the state is concerned with public action, not private virtue, it is generally incompetent to judge conscience. Although governments have a legitimate interest in the state of an individual's conscience when there is question of a crime, or fraud is an issue in a civil suit, the argument for the state's incompetence to judge conscience has special force, as applied to the limits on the exercise of religious freedom. First, the state is incompetent to judge the religious norms by which conscience is formed. Second, inquiry into the sincerity of conscience in the exercise of religious belief would as a practical matter involve the reasonableness, and ultimately the truth, of religious belief itself. Third, even if courts could successfully determine sincerity of conscience in religious exercise without touching the truth of belief itself, this would not solve the problem of limits to religious freedom: many sincerely motivated public actions must be restricted, and another norm is accordingly required to judge the legitimacy of such restrictions.

O'Boyle next asked whether governments can rightfully repress religious manifestations opposed to the common good of society. Answering the question in the negative, O'Boyle introduced for the first time into the conciliar discussion on religious freedom the distinction between society and state or, as Pius XII expressed it, between the total social life of man and the juridical order over which governments have charge. Consequent to this distinction, O'Boyle introduced a further distinction between the whole common good of society and that limited part of the common good of society which is committed to governments to protect and promote by the coercive force of law.

This limited part of the common good committed to the state O'Boyle called the public order. It includes three goods: (1) a political good, the preservation of public peace; (2) a moral good, the safeguarding of public morality; and (3) a juridical good, the protection of human and civil rights due equally to all citizens. The third good requires that the rights of citizens be reconciled peacefully and justly when conflict arises. (Unfortunately, O'Boyle did not make clear that his remarks on the limitation of the power of the state to necessities of the public order were directed exclusively to questions of personal freedom and not to economic or social questions.)

With the help of these distinctions, O'Boyle was able to set down what he called a juridical norm for the use of coercive power by the state in religious matters: governments can legitimately limit the exercise of religion in society only if the public order, according to its political, moral, and juridical elements, so requires. In other words, the exercise of religion in society is immune from interference by the coercive power of the state unless a public manifestation of religion gravely harms the public order, whether by disturbing public peace or violating public morality or invading the rights of others. As a corollary to this analysis, O'Boyle objected to the text's expression of the limits to religious freedom in terms of the "end of society," because the "end of society" and the "end of the state" are not coextensive.

Archbishop Eugene D'Souza of Nagpur (India) read the text's condemnation of "proselytism" with some fear.[51] Of course, a proselytism involving unworthy means of propagating religious belief is worthy of condemnation, but the difficulty is in judging what is a worthy or an unworthy means. He was especially fearful that the Declaration's condemnation of "proselytism" would boomerang against the Church in mission countries.

The paragraph denying the "direct capacity and competence" of the state in religious matters was the most controversial of the additions to the second conciliar text on religious freedom. The Spaniards were particularly exercised about the paragraph and saw in the denial of the state's competence a repudiation of legal establishment. Although this was not the intention of the text, it was an implication which the text did not disavow. On the other side, several Fathers of the Council were apprehensive because the text denied only an undefined "direct capacity and competence" of the state in religious matters. Bishop de Provenchères even called for an outright repudiation by the Church of any privileged position.[52] The relation of legal establishment to the affirmation of religious freedom would continue to plague the Council's attempt to draft the Declaration and would receive explicit attention in the last three texts.

The constitution of a state, of course, could simply declare as a matter of fact that a particular religion was the religion of an overwhelming majority of its citizens. But legal establishment does more; it gives special legal recognition to a particular religion. Hence the conservative question arises forcefully: If the state has no competence in religious matters, can it legitimately recognize one religion as the religion of the state? To be sure, if religious freedom is guaranteed to all individuals and groups, and no special subsidies are given to a particular religion, legal establishment has no material consequence other than as an element of social prestige presumably beneficial to the established religion. On principle, however, legal establishment remains difficult to reconcile with an affirmation of the state's incompetence in religious matters.

Although legal establishment historically concerned only the establishment of a particular religion or religions over others, it can be understood today in a broader sense to include any preference of religious belief over disbelief. If the state has no competence in religious matters, is it competent to grant general and proportionately equal subsidies to the religious activities of all faiths? Indeed, may a state prefer religious belief in any way? The equality due to all citizens in a democracy clearly militates against any general financial support or even any legally institutionalized preference of religion, but it is less certain that preference of religion is altogether beyond the competence of the state. Since the existence of God and the value of acknowledging Him do not necessarily depend on any special revelation, it can be argued that the state may legitimately encourage belief in, and homage to, God. Even the United States, which is committed by the First Amendment to the principle of governmental neutrality between religion and nonreligion, unquestionably prefers religious belief over disbelief in minor ways, e.g., inscribing "In God we trust" on coins, offering prayers before sessions of Congress. Some commentators even think that it is impossible for the state to be neutral between religious belief and disbelief; to be "neutral," they argue, would effectively favor disbelief.

An affirmation of the state's incompetence in matters of religion also raises questions concerning cooperation between the state and religious groups. If the state is incompetent in religious matters, can it legitimately cooperate with religious activities or institutions? This question is related to the preceding question, of the preference of religion over nonreligion. But the state can accommodate religious activities in circumstances implying no preference for them and aid religiously oriented institutions performing secular functions without laying any claim to competence

in religious matters. Thus, for example, despite a specific constitutional prohibition against "an establishment of religion," the
United States government maintains chaplains for those whom
the government itself has removed from access to the religious
facilities of civilian communities and aids the construction of
hospitals operated under religious auspices. Indeed, failure to cooperate in some circumstances could even discriminate against
religious belief. Of necessity, secular and religious concerns overlap
in organized society, and separation of church and state does not
imply the hostility of the state to religious concerns. It is in this
context that the call of Bishop Pohlschneider for genuine freedom
of choice in education must be understood.

The second text on religious freedom had now been debated by
the Fathers of the Council. It remained for the Secretariat to revise the text, and that the Secretariat would do in a radical way.

Notes

1. See Rynne, *The Third Session*, p. 24.
2. Subsequently submitted as written intervention GG, 30 (mimeographed by the Secretariat, the Murray files).
3. GG, 52.
4. GG, 45.
5. GG, 50.
6. GG, 47.
7. GG, 48.
8. GG, 49.
9. GG, 31.
10. The United Nations adopted a Universal Declaration of Human
    Rights on December 10, 1948. Article 18 of that Declaration ac-
    knowledges the right of every person to freedom of religion, includ-
    ing the freedom to change his religion and the freedom to manifest
    his religion, in public and private, by instruction, practices, wor-
    ship, and observances. On December 7, 1962, the General Assembly
    charged the Commission of Human Rights with the task of draft-
    ing an international convention on the elimination of religious
    intolerance. That project is still in the preparatory stage. Both the
    relevant provisions of the Universal Declaration and the prelimi-
    nary draft of the projected convention can be found in *Vatican II:*

La liberté religieuse, eds. Hamer and Congar, Annexe IV, pp. 264–73.

11. GG, 46.
12. GG, 51.
13. GG, 32.
14. GG, 27.
15. GG, 85.
16. GG, 34.
17. GG, 28.
18. GG, 29.
19. GG, 33.
20. GG, 36.
21. See *Le Monde,* September 26, 1964, p. 8, and *La Documentation Catholique,* October 18, 1964, col. 1320. Antoine Wenger, however, gives a different account; *Vatican II: chronique de la 3ème session* (Paris: Éditions du Centurion, 1965), pp. 323–24, n. 6. According to Wenger, Canestri remarked in the course of an argument against basing religious freedom on the dictates of conscience: "Now take the case of a priest who becomes a Protestant . . . for reasons of money. . . . He would have a right to religious freedom, but that freedom does not rest on his religious convictions." Canestri himself submitted no written intervention.
22. GG, 37.
23. Declaration on Religious Freedom, Art. 5, Appendix I, p. 191.
24. GG, 35.
25. GG, 39.
26. GG, 44. The striking similarity of Primeau's intervention to Murray's thought is no accident; Murray was consulted by many American bishops.
27. GG, 43.
28. GG, 38.
29. GG, 40.
30. GG, 14.
31. GG, 41.
32. See *La Documentation Catholique,* October 18, 1964, col. 1324; Roberti submitted no written intervention.
33. *Documentation,* cols. 1324–25; Hurley submitted no written intervention.
34. GG, 61.
35. *Documentation,* col. 1325; Melendro submitted no written intervention.
36. GG, 59.
37. GG, 70.
38. GG, 58.
39. GG, 55.
40. GG, 69.
41. GG, 54.

42. GG, 94
43. Rynne, *op. cit.*, p. 30.
44. See *Documentation*, cols. 1329–30; Heenan submitted no written intervention.
45. GG, 91.
46. GG, 84.
47. GG, 88.
48. See "Relatio de animadversionibus Patrum" *Schema declarationis de libertate religiosa [textus emendatus]* (Rome: Vatican Polyglot Press, 1964), p. 32.
49. GG, 94 and 76.
50. GG, 67. The similarity of O'Boyle's intervention (like that of Primeau's) to Murray's thought should be noted.
51. GG, 53.
52. GG, 15.

VI

The Third Text

THE SECRETARIAT BEGAN WORK to revise the text on religious freedom immediately, and De Smedt commissioned Murray as "first
scribe" to compose a new version which would include both his
own ideas and as much as possible of the original text.[1] A subcommission of the Secretariat, consisting of De Smedt, Murray,
and Msgr. Pietro Pavan, a conciliar expert whose views coincided
closely with Murray's, with the assistance of Willebrands and
Hamer, was proceeding smoothly with the work of revising the
text on religious freedom until the evening of Friday, October 9,
when Cardinal Bea revealed to the Secretariat that he had received two letters from Archbishop Pericle Felici, secretary-general
of the Council.[2]

The second letter announced that the President of the Council's
Coordinating Commission, Cardinal Cicognani, had decided at
the request of the Pope to have the Declaration on Religious
Freedom examined and revised by a mixed commission. (The
first, which does not directly concern the present study, asked
that the Declaration on the Jews be affixed to the Constitution
on the Church.) Four members were named to the mixed commission: Cardinal Browne, Fr. Fernandez, Archbishop Lefebvre,
and Bishop Colombo. Bea read the letter to the Secretariat without comment and wrote immediately to the Secretary of the
Council. Admitting his readiness to follow the requests of the
Pope, Bea asked several questions: Who would preside over the

mixed commission? Who would name its members? Who would present the text to the Council? Events rapidly bypassed the context of Bea's letter, and it never received a reply.[3]

The genesis of the Felici letter is now better understood than it was in the days immediately following its receipt by Bea. According to normal curial practice, the Pope ordinarily expresses his intentions to the principal members of his administration without detailing to them the means by which they are to be achieved. In the instant case, the Pope wanted to conciliate the opposition to the Declaration on Religious Freedom and to reach a broad consensus by some form of dialogue. It is not known in what precise terms the Pope expressed his intention, and the affair is complicated by the presence of an intermediary between the Pope and Felici, namely, Cardinal Cicognani, who had a daily audience with the Pope and was Felici's immediate superior.

In any case, Felici did not take on himself the initiative to form the mixed commission. Indeed, the name of Archbishop Marcel Lefebvre on the list of the membership of the mixed commission may have been the result of confusing him with another Council Father of the same name.[4] The Secretary-General asked one of his undersecretaries, Archbishop Casimiro Morcillo González of Madrid (Spain), to suggest names from among the most characteristic critics of the proposed Declaration. This the undersecretary, whose impartial performance of his duties is well known, did honestly. Certainly Browne, Fernandez, and Colombo represented articulate opposition to, or an independent viewpoint on, the Secretariat's text on religious freedom. Lefebvre, on the other hand, belonged to no conciliar commission and had not notably influenced the debate on religious freedom. According to one report, Felici hesitated when the name of Lefebvre was mentioned and designated him only when he was assured, mistakenly, that the proposed nominee was not the irreconcilable Lefebvre who addressed the Council on September 24. The "other" Lefebvre was presumably the liberal Cardinal Joseph Lefebvre, archbishop of Bourges (France), who had said nothing on the subject of religious freedom, and whose choice would have been itself a mystery.

Whatever the origin of the membership of the mixed commission named in the letter, its effect as constituted was clear enough: three of the four (all except Colombo) were irreconcilably opposed to the principle of religious freedom. Although the exact power of the mixed commission was not clear, it seemed to withdraw the Declaration from the jurisdiction of the Secretariat and submit it to the new organ. Given the announced composition of the mixed commission, the minority appeared to gain a veto power that their numbers did not warrant. (The minority, as events would show, was far from the one-third required to negative proposed schemata.) This veto power was hardly likely to promote the dialogue apparently desired by the Pope. In fact, no dialogue with the conservative opposition was really possible at all.

Moreover, the proposed mixed commission was not formed according to the rules of the Council.[5] Perhaps no aspect of the Felici letter more irked the liberal majority than the apparent disregard of "due process of law." Article 58, paragraph 2, of the Council rules provided that the Moderators should remit schemata to their proper commissions for revision when the Council Fathers so indicated. If a schema belonged to two commissions, then an *ad hoc* mixed commission was to be set up jointly from the membership of the two commissions involved. This rule was violated on three counts: (1) the Declaration on Religious Freedom belonged exclusively to the Secretariat; (2) the mixed commission was not assigned by the Moderators; (3) the proposed mixed commission, as named in the letter, was not composed jointly. Even on the supposition that the Theological Commission had an interest in the Declaration on Religious Freedom, which at this date it did not, the Secretariat was not represented at all. Indeed, Lefebvre was not a member of any conciliar commission.

As rumors of the Felici letter spread through Rome, ten cardinals assembled at the home of Cardinal Josef Frings, archbishop of Cologne (Germany) on Saturday afternoon, October 10, and drafted a letter of protest and petition to the Pope.[6] The letter began by expressing the "great sorrow" of the signitories at the news that the Declaration was to be entrusted to a mixed commission of which three of the four designated members were opposed to the orientation of the Council on the subject. The signatories complained specifically of the violation of the rules of the Council. If a mixed commission was necessary, it should be formed from the existing conciliar commissions, as provided in Article 58, paragraph 2.

Nine of the cardinals present signed the letter: Bernard Alfrink, archbishop of Utrecht (Netherlands), Julius Döpfner, archbishop of Munich (Germany), Frings, König, Lefebvre, Léger, Meyer, Ritter, and Silva Henriquez. The tenth, Cardinal Bea, wrote personally to Pope Paul as president of the Secretariat on the subject of the two Felici letters. To these nine signatures were added those of Juan Landazuri-Ricketts, archbishop of Lima (Peru), Cardinals Maurice Feltin, archbishop of Paris (France), Giacomo Lercaro, archbishop of Bologna (Italy), Achilles Liénart, (archbishop of Lille (France), José Quintero, archbishop of Caracas (Venezuela), Paul Richaud, archbishop of Bordeaux (France), Laurean Rugambwa, archbishop of Bukoba (Tanzania), and Suenens.[7] The latter, absent in Brussels, gave his agreement by phone and hastily returned to Rome to sign the letter Monday morning.

The letter of the seventeen cardinals was brought to the Pope Monday morning, October 12. Although no written, official reply was made to the letter of the cardinals, the affair was effectively terminated at the long audience of the Pope with Frings on Tuesday, October 13.[8] The Pope assured Frings that the Declaration on Religious Freedom would remain under the jurisdiction of the Secretariat, although it would be examined by a joint committee composed of representatives of the Secretariat and the Theological Commission. This face-saving solution was formalized on October 16, when the Pope directed Cardinal Cicognani to write letters to Cardinals Bea and Ottaviani asking each to nominate ten members of their respective commissions to a consultative committee to examine the text on religious freedom.[9] This time the Secretary-General was charged only with the delivery of the letter to Bea. The Pope then chose ten of these twenty, five from each list, to constitute the joint committee. Four of the five members representing the Theological Commission were Cardinal Browne, Archbishop Colombo, Archbishop Parente, and Bishop Georges Pelletier of Trois-Rivières (Canada).[10]

There were two essential differences between the mixed commission originally proposed in the Felici letter and the joint committee directed by the Pope. First, the Declaration on Religious

Freedom now clearly remained under the jurisdiction of the Secretariat, and the joint committee had only the power to make suggestions. Second, the membership of the joint committee was drawn exclusively from the Secretariat and the Theological Commission. Thus Archbishop Lefebvre was eliminated, and Article 58, paragraph 2, of the Council rules safeguarded. Indeed only one of the original three intransigents remained on the joint committee, Cardinal Browne. (Bishop Colombo, of course, was also a carryover from the original list, but he was very much in favor of the principle of religious freedom.)

In the meantime, the Secretariat had continued its work of revising the text of the Declaration. Although De Smedt had not originally accepted Murray's political and legal approach, the thirty bishops of the Secretariat now unanimously accepted on October 24 a draft by Murray, the fifth discussed since September 28.[11] This text was presented for examination to the joint committee established by the papal directive of October 16.[12] A single session on October 27 sufficed to gain the approval of four members representing the Theological Commission that nothing in the text was against faith and morals; only one judged that the text's doctrine could not be admitted. After this session De Smedt submitted a new, abbreviated text (a little over two double-spaced typewritten pages), which attempted to affirm religious freedom without elaborate argument.[13] On October 29 De Smedt's draft was rejected, and Frs. Hamer and Murray were asked to write introductory reports for the approved text.[14] The purpose of Murray's report was to answer the principal objections against the Declaration on Religious Freedom.

When the reports were ready, and the text revised on minor points, everything was set for their printing. But the Secretariat was instructed by Cicognani, president of the Coordinating Commission, presumably at the request of the Pope, to submit the text to the Theological Commission for its approval (*nihil obstat*).[15] The Theological Commission met on November 9 and approved the text.[16] Of the twenty-eight present, twelve approved the text without reservation, nine approved with reservation, six disapproved, and one abstained. According to the new conciliar text's introductory report, this vote was interpreted to mean that more than two thirds of the members of the Theological Commission approved the text. Some of the majority, however, made observations, which were transmitted in writing to the Secretariat. The latter weighed these observations on November 10 and accommodated them to the extent to which they were compatible with the approved text.[17] The definitive text was sent to the printers on November 11.[18] As the end of the Third Session was approaching, however, the Vatican printing office was swamped with work, and the text on religious freedom was not printed until November 16. On November 17 the text was distributed to the Fathers, and on November 19 De Smedt read the introductory report on the text.[19]

The third conciliar text, the *textus emandatus*, was a full-fledged declaration, no longer an awkward appendix to the schema on ecumenism. It began by noting the growing modern consciousness of the dignity of the human person. Men today demand civil liberties so that they can live a life in society worthy of man. Hence they demand a juridical limitation of the public power in order to protect personal freedom, including religious freedom. Religious freedom means immunity from coercion on the part of men or any human power, not only in the formation of conscience but also in the free exercise of religion. Moreover, the latter aspect of religious freedom involves two aspects: no one may be compelled to act against his conscience or hindered from acting according to his conscience within limits determined by moral and juridical norms. Thus religious freedom is defined in juridical terms and does not imply that man is free to determine whether or how he should serve God without respect to the order of truth or the will of God.[20]

At this point, the text developed a long thesis on the historical origins of the Church's teaching on religious freedom.[21] Largely repeating the lines of the first introductory report, the text defended the nineteenth-century papal condemnations of religious freedom as products of a polemic against laicism and the divorce of governments from regard for moral imperatives. As times changed, however, the Church's doctrine grew. The Church affirmed the rights of man against the ideology of totalitarianism and brought the subject of religious freedom to a new stage. Today it is a question of observing and protecting the dignity of the human person and of thus effectively defending his rights, first among which is his right to be free from coercion in religious matters, especially on the part of the public power.

With terms thus defined and history so interpreted, the Declaration moved to affirm the principle of religious freedom.[22] The Declaration first affirmed that the Church was the one true Church founded by Christ. Then the Declaration claimed that there was nothing in the Catholic teaching about the one true religion opposed to the principle of human freedom in society. The Declaration affirmed that the contemporary juridical regime of religious freedom, founded on the principles of human reason, is in itself worthy and truly necessary to guard the personal and civil dignity of the human person in modern society. It affirmed further that religious freedom in the sense described is a true right, founded on the very dignity of the human person, which all men and all religious bodies can legitimately claim for themselves.

Only after this clear affirmation did the second chapter of the new text advance five interrelated arguments for the principle of religious freedom.[23] The first argument based the principle on the social nature of man. If an interior, personal freedom of man in religious matters is admitted, the free exercise of religion in human society should not be denied; the connection between interior freedom and its social manifestation is altogether indissoluble. Although this argument was primarily directed against a rigid dichotomy of the internal order of conscience and the external order of society, it also sought to establish the principle of religious freedom from the integrity of the human person. Implicitly, the argument appealed to the dignity of man and the corresponding limitation on the competence of the state.

The second argument, taken from Colombo and Ancel, was based on the right and duty of men to seek truth. Seeking truth, and adhering to truth when found, depends on free investigation and personal assent. Moreover, since man is by nature social, he seeks and finds truth by instruction and communication with his fellow men, whereby they explain to one another the truth that they have found, or think they have found. Hence, in matters of religious truth, no one should be impeded from explaining his beliefs.

As noted in the previous chapter,[24] this argument must be developed in a social and political context if it is to be convincing.

Because search for truth is a social enterprise and part of the common good, the state must promote the freedom which is necessary for that search. It is only in this context and within the limits of public order that *every* man, whether communicating truth or error, whether in good faith or bad, whether searching for truth or not, may claim a right to immunity from coercion in all expression that concerns the order of truth and religious truth in particular. The argument thus framed is based on the dignity of the rational person and the corresponding limitation on the competence of the state in matters of religious truth and the order of truth generally. The state may and does judge whether actions are good or bad for the secular goals committed to its care, but it is incompetent to undertake the general function of judging whether propositions are true or false.

The third argument was based on the nature of religion. By its nature, the exercise of religion consists primarily in the altogether free interior acts by which a man directly orders himself to God. These internal acts, because of the social nature of man, flow over into external acts. Hence a man has a right to immunity from legal or social coercion in the public exercise of his religious beliefs. This argument is very close to the first argument and, like that argument, implicitly appeals to the dignity of the human person, especially in his relations with God.

The fourth argument was based on the role of conscience in the moral life of man. Although the argument immediately drew as a conclusion from the right and duty to follow conscience "the absolute moral principle," that no one should be compelled to act against his conscience, it approached more circumspectly the right to act in society according to conscience. To sustain the latter right, it appealed not only to the right to follow one's conscience but also to the growth in modern times of the consciousness of human dignity, personal and civil. Contemporary consciousness of human dignity demands that no one be hindered in human society, especially by the public power, from acting in religious matters according to his conscience, provided that the public order, which constitutes an essential part of the common good, is safeguarded. This demand is altogether consonant with reason and worthy of man. Thus the fourth argument invoked openly the dignity of the human person to support the right to act in society according to conscience.

The last argument for religious freedom was explicitly based on the concept of limited government. Religious acts, by which men privately and publicly order themselves to God, transcend the temporal and earthly order of things. Hence man is not subject in these acts to the power of government, whose competence is limited to the temporal and earthly order by its very finality, and whose power to make laws extends only to exterior acts. Therefore governments, which cannot judge internal religious acts, likewise cannot coerce or impede the public exercise of religion, provided that the exigencies of the public order are protected. The rule to be followed in this matter is: as much freedom as possible, only as much restraint as necessary. The public power would altogether exceed its limits if it in any way mingled in the care of souls.

Of all the five arguments advanced in the new text, the last alone was cast entirely in a political and legal context. Indeed, the fifth argument alone explicitly followed the juridical frame of conceptual reference elaborated in the first chapter of the new text. But the other arguments were at least correlative to this argument; all five arguments ultimately rested on two closely linked concepts: the dignity of the human person and the incompetence of the state in matters of religious truth. With this explicit and implicit emphasis on the political and legal context of religious freedom, there could be no question about who had the right or whether it reached the external, social order. All men, in good faith or bad, have a right to freedom of conscience and to the free exercise of religion in society.

As indicated in the fifth argument, the right to the free exercise of religion in human society is not without limits.[25] The first norm for these limits is the moral principle of personal responsibility toward others. In exercising one's own rights, one must take account of the rights of other persons and of one's duties toward others, with whom one must act justly and humanely. Moreover, civil society has the right to protect itself against abuses perpetrated in the name of religious freedom.

It belongs especially to governments to offer protection of this kind according to juridical norms constituted by the exigencies of the public order. The public order is that essential part of the common good committed to governments for protection. According to these juridical norms, the exercise of religion in society should be immune from the coercive intervention of the state unless it gravely harms the public order by disturbing public peace, violating public morality, or invading the rights of others. The text's treatment of the limits to the freedom of religious exercise, incorporating O'Boyle's intervention, constituted a significant advance over the preceding two texts. The grounds for limiting religious freedom were narrowed and better defined. In the place of a broad and ill-defined concept of the "common good" or "end of society," the new text substituted the narrow and relatively well-defined concept of the public order.

The third chapter of the new text dealt with the practical consequences of the principle of religious freedom.[26] Since every government has a special duty to safeguard the inviolable rights of man, it should undertake the effective protection and care of religious freedom by just laws. Similarly, governments must protect the equality of all citizens against legal discrimination for religious reasons. It is wrong for governments to impose on citizens by force or fear the profession or rejection of any religion. It is even more against the will of God and the sacred rights of the person and the family of nations to use force to destroy or restrict religion itself. The right of the human person to religious freedom should be recognized and effectively protected by juridical safeguards in all nations of the world. Indeed, "the more society supports conditions favorable to the spread of truth and to the development of religious life the more will it enjoy the goods which accrue from the fidelity of men to God and His will."

The latter call on society to support conditions favorable to religious belief raised the whole panoply of questions associated with religious establishment. Was the text inviting the general establishment of religious belief over disbelief? Was the text approving general subsidies to religious activities or institutions? Was the text endorsing the cooperation of governments with religious activities in particular areas of overlapping concern? Was the text contemplating aid to religious institutions performng secular functions? Interpretation of this sentence is further com-

plicated by its address to "society," while the context indicates
that governmental action is signified. At any rate, it is clear that
the text was calling for something more than the guarantee of
religious freedom.

The implications of religious freedom for religious bodies were
then spelled out: religious bodies are of right entitled to independence and autonomy in regulating themselves according to
their own rules, in honoring God by public worship, in helping
their members to practice their religious life, in supporting them
by teaching, and in promoting institutions in which their members
cooperate to order their lives according to their religious principles.[27] Likewise, religious bodies have a right not to be impeded
by legal means or the administrative action of the state from
selecting and educating their own ministers, from communicating
with religious authorities in other parts of the world, or from
acquiring and using material goods. Religious bodies also have a
right not to be impeded from teaching and bearing witness publicly to their faith by spoken and written word. In spreading religious faith and introducing religious practices, however, "every
type of action must be avoided which may seem to savor of coercion or of unworthy or unbecoming persuasion, especially when
there is a question of children or the uneducated." Lastly, religious
groups can freely show the singular value of religious truth in
ordering human society and directing all human activity.

This section on the freedom of religious groups was fuller than
the corresponding treatment in the preceding texts. Specifically,
the new text applied the principle of religious freedom to the right
of groups to select and train their ministry, to communicate with
religious authorities in other lands, to acquire and use property,
and to apply their religious values to the social order and all areas
of human activity. Although the new text avoided using the term
"proselytism" when condemning the propagation of religious belief by unworthy means, the condemnation itself was explicit
enough and broadly worded. In view of the fact that this paragraph would be incorporated in successive texts, some of the
language is unfortunate. To say that "every type of action must be
avoided which may seem to savor of coercion or of unworthy or
unbecoming persuasion" is to offer a pretext for the abuse of

religious freedom to public authorities so disposed. Of course, the text laid the injunction on religious groups and did not speak explicitly of the state's police power.

Where the previous text affirmed summarily the right of men to order their lives according to the requirements of their religion in matters of family and education, the new text spoke more specifically of the right of parents to determine the way of giving religious instruction to their children.[28] Indeed, governments must recognize the right of parents to choose schools and other means of education for their children with full freedom; unjust burdens must not restrict parents' freedom of choice in the education of their children. This paragraph on the "school question" was added in response to the interventions of Pohlschneider and other Council Fathers, but it did not attempt to determine in concrete cases what constituted the condemned "unjust" burdens on freedom of parental choice in education. The new text then introduced an affirmation that the human person has a right not to be impeded from joining or leaving a religious body and echoed the previous text in asserting the right of men to establish groups or associations for religious, educational, cultural, social, and charitable purposes.

Chapter IV of the new text explained the doctrine of religious freedom in the light of revelation.[29] First the text pointed out that in Catholic tradition the freedom of the Church is a fundamental principle of the relations which ought to obtain between the Church and the civil order of human life.[30] The Church claims for herself freedom in human society and before every public power because she is a spiritual authority constituted by Christ and charged by divine command with the duty of preaching the gospel to the whole world and every creature. She likewise claims freedom for herself because she is a divinely commissioned society of men, each and every one of whom enjoys in society the right of living according to the Christian precepts of reason and conscience.

Where a contemporary regime of religious freedom is in force, the Church herself obtains a stable condition in law and fact and full freedom to follow the divine mission committed to her by the mandate of Christ.[31] Moreover, Christians enjoy the civil right not to be impeded from leading their life according to the principles of the Catholic faith. Thus there is an agreement between the freedom which the Church claims for herself by the mandate of Christ and the religious freedom which the Church requires for all men and groups as a true right evident to the light of reason. The text in this way clearly distinguished two grounds, supernatural and natural, on the basis of which the Church claims freedom for herself in contrast to the single, natural ground on the basis of which the Church affirmed the principle of religious freedom for all men and all other religious groups. But the object or content of the freedom claimed by the Church for herself is exactly the same as the freedom claimed by the Church for other religious communities.

Congruous theological arguments, however, were not omitted. First, the text appealed to the fundamental Catholic doctrine that a man must exercise true responsibility in accepting faith, and that no one may be compelled to embrace the Catholic faith.[32] By its very nature, the act of Christian faith is a free act. Man, redeemed by Christ and called to adoption as a son of God through Jesus Christ, cannot adhere to God revealing Himself unless the Father draws him, and he offers a reasonable and free response to God's invitation. Hence the more genuine is faith the more free and personal it is. Any type of coercion in religious mattters is contrary to the nature of Christian faith. In a regime of religious freedom, conditions exist in which the demands of Catholic doctrine in this matter are observed. The text thus made no attempt to argue to a plenary religious freedom, including the freedom not to be coerced from acting in accord with one's religious beliefs, from the freedom required for the act of faith, the freedom not to be coerced into acting against one's judgment about religious truths. Rather, it was satisfied to show that the broader freedom protected the narrower.

A second theological argument claimed deep roots in the word of God for the contemporary concept of religious freedom. The text introduced here an entirely new section on the relation of that juridical concept to the mind of Christ and the Apostles.[33] Of course, the freedom which Christ preached was the freedom by which man is freed from sin and ordered to God the Father through Jesus Christ His Son. But the right to religious freedom in society is founded on the dignity of the human person, which

Christ always respected in leading men to the perfect freedom of the sons of God.

Meek and humble of heart, Jesus drew disciples gently and never compelled them to follow Him. Although He worked miracles so that His hearers would be led to believe in His word, He refused time and time again to work prodigies by which men would be somehow compelled to assent. Indeed, Satan proposed prodigies of this sort to Christ when tempting Him, and many Jews likewise sought such signs, all of which Jesus refused. He rebuked the disciples James and John for suggesting violent retribution on the Samaritans who would not receive them. Christ was always that perfect Servant of Yahweh who did not break a bruised reed or quench a smoking wick; He came to serve and to offer witness to the truth, which in the end He showed pre-eminently by shedding His own blood.

What Christ did and taught, the Apostles followed. From the very beginning of the Church, the disciples of Christ worked to convert men to God not by coercive action or by unworthy artifices, but by the power of the word of God. Following the example of meekness and moderation of Christ, the Apostles preached the word of God with full confidence in the divine power of this word to destroy the powers opposed to God and bring men to the faith and service of Christ. The Church, therefore, acts today according to the mind of Christ and His principles when, with the growth among men of the consciousness of their own dignity, she defends and fosters the regime of religious freedom in virtue of her pastoral concern for human freedom.

The new text repeated its predecessor's exposition of the duty of the Church and all Christians to preach the truth with due respect for the human person. It added, however, an instruction to the faithful to attend diligently to the teaching of the Church in forming their consciences. By the will of God the Catholic Church has the duty to explain and teach authentically the truth which is Christ and at the same time to declare and confirm by its authority the principles of the moral order which flow from human nature itself.

Introducing the conclusion, the text noted two contrasting facts about religious freedom in the modern world.[34] First, men of every culture today desire to be able to profess freely their religion in public and private. Indeed, religious freedom is now declared a civil right in most constitutions. Second, there are regimes in which, although their constitutions recognize a right to offer worship to God, governments themselves attempt to wean citizens from the profession of religion and make life very difficult and even dangerous for religious bodies. Hailing the former fact and deploring the latter condition, the text urged the faithful and all men to consider very attentively how necessary religious freedom is in the present condition of human life. For it is manifest that peoples are becoming more and more one, that men of diverse cultures and religions are bound together by closer relations, and that the consciousness of personal responsibility is increasing. For peaceful relations among men, therefore, it is altogether necessary that religious freedom be protected by effective juridical safeguards and that the highest rights and duties of men to lead their religious lives freely in society be observed.

The third text was significantly different from the first two texts. First, "conscience" was used broadly to mean any conviction on matters of ultimate concern, whether religious or not. Second, the state of conscience, *i.e.*, its sincerity or insincerity, was made irrelevant to the principle of religious freedom; man was held to maintain a right to immunity from coercion in religious matters because of his inalienable dignity as a free, rational agent. Third, the object or content of religious freedom was negative, a freedom from coercion. Fourth, the text carefully distinguished two levels of religious freedom: (1) the freedom not to be coerced into acting against conscience; and (2) the freedom not to be hindered from acting according to conscience. As the text indicated, it is the latter freedom which poses critically the question of limits.[35] Fifth, the text attempted to define more precisely the limits of religious exercise by the concept of public order. Lastly, the text distinguished the freedom demanded by the dignity of the human person, a natural right accessible to reason, from the freedom demanded by the mission of the Church, a supernatural right derived from the word of God.

While the new text sought to meet the main difficulties raised against the preceding texts, it invited new lines of attack by both advocates and opponents of the principle of religious freedom. Some friends would accuse the text of too political and legal a cast. Some would complain specifically that the text was not theological enough, that the appeal to Scripture was too muffled. Many would call the treatment of the historical question too apologetic and too simplistic. For their part, in addition to their other, long-standing objections, opponents of any affirmation of the principle of religious freedom would fasten on the implication of the text's denial of competence to the state in religious matters for the question of legal establishment.

As indicated above, the *textus emendatus* was not distributed to the Council Fathers until Tuesday, November 17.[36] The Secretary-General announced at the beginning of that day's session that a vote on the Declaration would take place Thursday, November 19, and he indicated at the end of the session that there would be four votes on the individual parts of the text by *placet* (approval) and *nonplacet* (disapproval) and then a vote on the text as a whole, at which time votes *placet juxta modum* (approval with reservation) could be cast.[37] This was now the last week of the Third Session of the Council, and there was no possibility that the Declaration on Religious Freedom would obtain final approval before the session ended. But there seemed to be every reason to expect a first vote, after which only modifications of detail would remain to be worked out before and during the next session.

At the end of the next day's meeting, the Secretary-General announced in the name of the President (Cardinal Eugène Tisserant of the Curia) and the Moderators that there would be a preliminary vote to determine whether the Council wished to proceed to the scheduled votes on the Declaration on Religious Freedom.[38] The President and Moderators decided on this action because "numerous" Fathers had asked the Council presidency for a delay, conformable to Article 30, paragraph 2, and Article 35 of the Council rules, in order to study the Declaration before voting, especially because the text distributed only the day before was essentially a new text. The petition in question carried around two hundred signatures, mostly Italians and all opposed to the Declaration.[39] Only twenty-five of the eighty Spanish bishops and one Spanish cardinal (Larraona) signed the petition.[40]

The measure thus taken by the Council Presidents and the Moderators was restrained; it allowed the Council itself to decide the merits of the opposition's plea for time. In fact, the chances of postponement were small. The overwhelming majority of the Fathers supported the Declaration on Religious Freedom, and the vote allowed the expression of reservation and the prospect of a new construction of the text during the intersession.

Since the opposition was also well aware of how small were the chances of a vote approving its petition, it continued to press for a postponement without any vote by the Council. The next day (November 19), the day scheduled for the votes on the Declaration, began placidly enough with the continuation of debate on the Declaration on Christian Education. At around eleven o'clock, Archbishop Dino Staffa (Curia), one of the leading signers of the petition for delay, approached the Secretary-General, who motioned him to Cardinal Tisserant, seated at the middle of the Council Presidents' table.[41] After he and Staffa had exchanged words briefly, Tisserant consulted the other Presidents on either side, but not the Moderators. Then he made a brusque announcement that provoked the wildest episode of the Council. Some Fathers had complained, he reported, that they would not have enough time before the scheduled votes to study the text, which the Secretariat's introductory report acknowledged to have a new structure and a new content. It appeared to the Council Presidents that this question of procedure could not be decided by a vote of the Council. Therefore there would be no vote on the Declaration on Religious Freedom in this session of the Council, although the introductory report would be read. Fathers who had observations to make on the text were advised to submit them to the Secretary-General before January 31, 1965.[42]

There was some short-lived applause of the decision by those who had sought the postponement, but the wave of protest that swept the Council indicated clearly what the overwhelming majority thought of the decision.[43] One of the Presidents, Cardinal Meyer, usually a calm and smiling figure, lost his composure. Banging his fist on the table, Meyer turned to his neighbor, Cardinal Ruffini, to ask whether he knew of the decision announced by Tisserant in the name of the Council Presidents. Ruffini replied with a satisfied smile. Then Meyer went to find Tisserant, whom he asked for an explanation. Unsatisfied, Meyer left Tisserant and went to the side of the tribunal near the Confession of Saint Peter, where a rapidly growing circle of bishops, experts, and theologians formed around him. Meyer, who sat at one end of the table, apparently had not heard, or at least had not understood, the postponement which Tisserant had proposed to the Council Presidents. In any event, with the liberal Cardinal Liénart absent, the scales of the twelve-man Council presidency, rather tightly balanced between conservatives and liberals, were tipped in favor of the petition for postponement.[44] One fact which Tisserant had not mentioned was that the Administrative Tribunal of the Council, under the presidency of Cardinal Roberti, had met twice the day before and agreed with the petition of the opposition.[45]

The informal way in which Tisserant polled the members of the Council presidency certainly was a procedure unequal to the seriousness of the matter. Moreover, two days were rather adequate to study a text of fewer than four thousand words, especially when the proposed vote admitted expressions of reservation with a view to reconstructing the text before the next session of the Council. But the proposed text was a new text, twice as long as its predecessor, and nearly 80 per cent original; it differed substantially from its precedessor in structure, conception of the problem, and arguments advanced. The decision of the Council Presidents was in itself defensible. What really irked the majority and provoked the tumult was the brusque way in which the decision was so obviously arrived at and the long history of the majority's frustration at the hands of the minority. After all the delays that the opposition had imposed on the Secretariat's efforts to present a text on religious freedom to the Council before the end of the Second Session and all the attempts of the opposition to prevent the Council from considering the two texts subsequently presented to it, the majority found it unseemly for the opposition now to complain that they lacked time to study the new text.

The circle around Meyer hit upon the idea of a petition to the Pope for a reversal of the decision announced by Tisserant.[46] Written by hand, the petition begged "urgently, very urgently, most urgently," that a vote on religious freedom be held before the end of the session so that the aspiration of the world, Christian and non-Christian, might not be disappointed. Copies were circulated and signatures collected by bishops moving through the tiers of seats. Four hundred and forty one signatures were collected before the session ended.[47] During the afternoon, after the original petition had been presented to the Pope, additional signatures swelled the total to well over one thousand.

All the tumult, of course, had rather drowned out the last speakers on the Declaration on Christian Education. Then Bishop De Smedt rose to give the introductory report on the new text of the Declaration on Religious Freedom.[48] He was forced to add one word to the first sentence of the printed report: "The text which we do *not* present today for your approval. . . ." Heard with rapt attention, De Smedt was applauded frequently and vigorously. Indeed, four bursts of applause interrupted a single line. At the end, he lowered his voice and described the history of the proposed text, to which the session of November 19 was adding a new chapter. When he had concluded his report, wild applause, the longest and most sustained of the Council, was accorded his speech. Some of the bishops even stood up in order to clap more vigorously, and two Moderators openly joined the cheering forbidden by rules. Cardinal Döpfner, the Moderator of the day, made no attempt to stop the sustained applause. In any event, he was powerless to control this display of enthusiasm. Thwarted of a vote, the bishops gleefully indicated their approval of the principle of religious freedom by their voices and their hands. Only at length, after several unsuccessful attempts to speak, was Döpfner able to thank De Smedt for his report.

At the end of the morning's session, Cardinals Meyer, Ritter, and Léger brought the petition asking for a vote on religious freedom to the Pope.[49] Although they were without appointment, the Pope received them and listened to their complaint. However, the Pope informed them that the decision announced by Tisserant was according to the Council rules. He promised them that the Declaration on Religious Freedom would be, if possible, the first order of business in the Fourth Session.

Later in the afternoon the cardinals present in Rome attended a meeting with the Pope which had been scheduled before the morning drama.[50] Cardinal Frings seized the occasion to bring up the subject of the morning's postponement of the vote on religious freedom and asked the Holy Father to allow a vote before the end of the session. Cardinal Suenens, admitting a basis for the decision in the Council rules, deplored its psychological effect. But the Pope's decision on the petition for a vote, already expressed verbally to Meyer, Ritter, and Léger, was formally communicated to the Council the next day, Friday, November 20, by Cardinal Tisserant.[51] After these words and the general silence which followed, broken by a light scatter of applause, the Council resumed its regular schedule. The episode thus ended with a whimper.

After four years of preparation, three sessions of the Council, three conciliar texts, and two public debates, the Declaration on Religious Freedom had yet to be put to a vote by the Council.[52] Yet the conservatives' doom was sealed. They had failed in their attempt to wrest control of the Declaration from the jurisdiction of the Secretariat, and they had so aroused public opinion by the Felici letter and especially the Tisserant action that the Council could not sidetrack the Declaration in the Fourth Session without being condemned as a failure by all non-Catholics and most Catholics.

Notes

1. See Wenger, *Vatican II chronique de la 3ème session*, p. 337.
2. For various accounts of the Felici affair see Henri Fesquet, *Le Monde*, October 13, 1964, p. 1; October 14, p. 1; October 17, p. 12; October 29, p. 8; René Laurentin, *L'enjou du Concile: Bilan de la 3ème session* (Paris: Éditions du Seuil, 1965), pp. 136–44; Robert Rouquette, S.J., "Le Concile: Le deuxième mois de la 3ème session," *Études*, December 1964, pp. 716–22. Rynne, *The Third Session*, pp. 63–68; Wenger, *op. cit.*, pp. 333–38. Rouquette gives the most authoritative account of the genesis of the affair.
3. Rouquette, pp. 718–19.
4. Rouquette, p. 720.
5. Rouquette, p. 721.
6. *Le Monde*, October 17, 1964, p. 12. The Cardinals' letter was communicated to the press by one of the signatories; see Rouquette, p. 720.
7. The participation of Lercaro and Feltin is only probable; see Laurentin, p. 140.

8. Laurentin, p. 140.
9. See "Relatio," *Schema declarationis de libertate religiosa [textus emendatus]* (Rome: Vatican Polyglot Press, 1964), p. 30.
10. Rouquette, p. 722. Rouquette also hesitantly names Fr. Anastasio del Sacratissimo Rosario, O.C.D., superior general of the Discalced Carmelites, but Murray denies that the latter was a member of the joint committee.
11. Laurentin, p. 142.
12. Rouquette, p. 722.
13. A copy of De Smedt's text, with notation of its rejection, is in the Murray files.
14. Wenger, p. 339.
15. "Relatio," p. 30.
16. Rouquette, p. 722.
17. "Relatio," p. 30.
18. "Relatio," p. 31.
19. "Relatio," *Schema declarationis de libertate religiosa [textus re-emendatus]* (Rome: Vatican Polyglot Press, 1965), p. 27.
20. *Textus emendatus*, pp. 3–4.
21. *Ibid.*, pp. 4–5.
22. *Ibid.*, p. 6.
23. *Ibid.*, pp. 7–9.
24. *Supra*, pp. 87–88.
25. *Textus emendatus*, p. 9.
26. *Ibid.*, p. 10.
27. *Ibid.*, pp. 11–12.
28. *Ibid.*, p. 12.
29. *Ibid.*, pp. 12–17.
30. *Ibid.*, pp. 12–13.
31. *Ibid.*, p. 13.
32. *Ibid.*, pp. 13–14.
33. *Ibid.*, pp. 14–15. Murray was substantially assisted in drafting this section by Frs. Stanislaus Lyonnet, S.J., and Francis McCool, S.J., both scholars of the Pontifical Biblical Institute of Rome. They drew much inspiration from Joseph Leclerc, *Histoire de la tolérance au siècle de la Réforme* (Auber: Paris, 1955), I, pp. 56–58. Fr. Pierre Benoit, O.P., director of the École Biblique de Jérusalem, assisted in later revisions of the section. See Yves M.-J. Congar, O.P., "Avertissement," *Vatican II: La liberté religieuse*, eds. Hamer and Congar, p. 11, n. 1.
34. *Ibid.*, pp. 17–18.
35. For a critique of the *textus emendatus'* absolutization of the freedom not to be coerced into acting against conscience, see Chapter VII, *infra*, pp. 123–124.
36. *Supra*, p. 100.
37. Wenger, p. 340.
38. "Relatio" *[textus re-emendatus]*, pp. 27–28.

39. Rouquette "Le Concile: Les derniers jours de la 3ème session," *Études*, January 1965, p. 113.
40. Wenger, p. 342, n. 6.
41. Rynne, p. 257.
42. "Relatio" [*textus re-emendatus*], p. 28.
43. Rynne, pp. 258–60; Wenger, p. 343.
44. *Le Monde*, November 21, 1964, p. 7.
45. Wenger, p. 342. According to Pavan, the Pope had the Administrative Tribunal review Tisserant's action as a result of the tumult of November 19 and the petition of protest which followed. The Tribunal upheld Tisserant. See Pavan, "The Declaration on Religious Freedom," *Information Documentation on the Conciliar Church*, Doss. LXVI–XXVI (November 30, 1966), p. 7.
46. Rouquette, p. 113.
47. See Giovanni Caprile, *La Civiltà Cattolica*, February 13, 1965, p. 328.
48. Wenger, p. 345; Laurentin, p. 276; Rynne, p. 260.
49. *Le Monde*, November 21, 1964, p. 7.
50. Rynne, p. 261.
51. Rouquette, pp. 113–114; "Relatio" [*textus re-emendatus*], p. 28.
52. A first, abbreviated debate took place in the general discussion of the schema on ecumenism at the end of the Second Session. See Chapter III, *supra*, pp. 47–50.

VII

The Fourth Text

FROM THE CLOSE OF THE THIRD SESSION on November 21, 1964, until February 17, 1965, 218 written interventions on the *textus emendatus* of the Declaration on Religious Freedom were submitted through the office of the Secretary General to the Secretariat for Christian Unity.[1] These comments were examined by experts of the Secretariat, who met in Bishop Willebrands' residence at the foot of Monte Mario, Italy, from the eighteenth to the twenty-eighth of February, and proposals for revising the text were noted.[2]

The third conciliar text was generally better received than its two predecessors. Not surprisingly, the constitution-minded American bishops strongly supported the new draft.[3] The Dutch bishops and Cardinal Silva Henriquez of Chile also indicated preference for the new text over the older ones.[4] But many French bishops objected to the juridical structure of the *textus emendatus*. Bishop Elchinger, writing in the name of seven bishops of eastern France, thought that it was indispensable to remain faithful to the classic conciliar method of beginning with a doctrinal exposition; in restricting the liberty of the person at the start to a civil right, the schema was said to lack a solid base.[5] A definition, both philosophical and theological, of free will and moral freedom should be placed at the beginning of the schema, after which the juridical consequences for religious freedom should be drawn from the Christian doctrine of freedom. Bishop Jean Sauvage of Annecy

(France), in collaboration with many bishops and theologians of France and Belgium, also thought it indispensable to begin with what Scripture says of religious freedom instead of arguments of the rational order, and Archbishop Dubois repeated his call for a more theological foundation of religious freedom on Scripture and the Fathers of the Church, especially Saint Augustine.[6]

For obvious reasons, this line of analysis was frequently, if somewhat too facilely, called the "French" view. The difference in method and argument between the *textus emendatus* and the "French" view was profound. Only after defending the principle of religious freedom on rational grounds did the *textus emendatus* approach consideration of religious freedom in the light of revelation. There was no attempt to demonstrate exegetically or theologically that man has a right to religious freedom. Rather, the text attempted to show how the contemporary, technical, and juridical concept has roots in the written word of God, and how well it accords with such revealed truths as the doctrines on the freedom of the act of faith and the freedom of the Church.

The "French" view, however, proposed another method. The French critics of the text would first expose the scriptural and patristic doctrine on the freedom of man and then support that exposition by arguments from reason. In their view, the Council ought to speak out of the treasury of Catholic teaching in conciliar speech and style, not by arguing but by proclaiming the truth on the freedom of man from the deeper riches of Holy Scripture.

There were many objections against the method and argument proposed by the French critics. In a schema on religious freedom, the particular question is not the general freedom of man or the freedom of the sons of God, although it is connected with these. Moreover, since the Council wanted to be heard by all men throughout the world when it spoke on religious freedom and not only by the Christian faithful, it was obliged to recognize that most men today understand the question best as one formally juridical, political, and ethical, a question to be solved by rational arguments confirmed by experience.

Although the scriptural doctrine on the dignity of man and his freedom by God's grace is for the believer deeper than that which is open to reason, a great difference between the scriptural doctrine and the contemporary concept of religious freedom is evident. Civil freedom may be demanded by the freedom proclaimed in the word of God, but it cannot be deduced in any strictly logical way from the latter as a juridical consequence. Rather, the connection between the two freedoms is better understood by means of historical experience than by any merely logical argument, by the leavening influence of the gospel among men and its fruit through the centuries. The difficulty of proving a strict right to immunity from coercion in propagating a false religion from the New Testament's spirit of love and peace did not escape the notice of the conservative opposition. Bishop Laureano Castán Lacoma of Sigüenza-Guadalajara (Spain) raised this specific objection even against the argument of concordance between the teaching of the gospel and the modern concept of religious freedom advanced in the *textus emendatus*.[7]

A group of conservative opponents of the principle of religious freedom, organized as the International Assembly of Bishops (or International Group of Fathers), submitted two lengthy interventions. The first was an elaborate attack on the *textus emendatus*, following the classic lines of the conservative argument on religious freedom.[8] The second, however, was a more subtle elaboration of a whole new text, following the structure of the text it was designed to replace.[9] Instead of expressing the conservative thesis, it chose ambiguity to blunt the affirmation of religious freedom. Thus, for example, it affirmed the principle of religious freedom, but subjected it to the limitation of the social norms of an ordered common life. The conservatives were able in this way to approve the freedom of non-Catholics to public worship and mask their disapproval of the freedom of non-Catholics to propagate their religion.

The third text's treatment of the nineteenth-century "historical question" was heavily attacked.[10] A few bishops thought the historical prospectus should be expanded to cover more than the nineteenth century. Others thought that the historical prospectus should be left to a footnote. But most critics urged that it be suppressed altogether. There were many reasons advanced against the text: a disquisition on the history of the nineteenth-century papacy's reaction to liberalism was out of place in a conciliar declaration on religious freedom; defense of the Syllabus of

Errors at the very outset of the Declaration would hardly facilitate the desire of the Council to put the minds of non-Catholics at rest on the attitude of the Church on religious freedom; the historical question was vastly more complex than the text suggested; and the text was too apologetic, implying that the nineteenth-century papacy was itself without fault in the matter of religious freedom. As a result of this criticism, treatment of the nineteenth-century "historical question" was eliminated from succeeding drafts of the Declaration.

Conservatives raised the usual question of the confessional state. One Spanish bishop, Eugenio Britia of Santander, insisted that the legal establishment of the Catholic religion was not only compatible with religious freedom, but also generally obligatory.[11] Another Spanish bishop, Luis Alonso Muñoyerro, military vicar, defended Spain as a "Catholic island" in a pluralist world and a distinct favor from God.[12] Two Colombian bishops, Pedro Rivera Mejia of Socorro y San Gil and Héctor Rueda Hernández of Bucaramanga, made a more moderate and practical suggestion, which was accepted and modified in succeeding texts of the Declaration.[13] To lessen resistance to the schema, they argued, it would be wise to incorporate into the text an explicit admission, such as that made in the introductory report to the *textus emendatus*, that the principle of religious freedom does not forbid the legal establishment of the Catholic religion.

One intervention, in the course of rejecting the argument for religious freedom from the right and duty to seek truth, added the observation that Catholics have no obligation to seek truth![14] This static concept of faith was at the heart of the conservative attitude on religious freedom and most other issues of the Second Vatican Council: the Church had nothing to learn. As a consequence, conservatives would admit no development of doctrine and no growth in understanding the meaning of God's revelation.

Several missionary bishops, including Bishop Edward Mason, vicar apostolic of El Obeid (Sudan), were worried lest the text's admission that religious freedom might be restricted for reasons of public order could serve as a pretext for the abuse of that freedom.[15] Since they conceded the principle that public peace might require restriction of the free exercise of religion, however, they were really asking words to do more than they have the power to do. No formula can prevent the abuse of governmental power and violation of freedom; only the responsibility of governments and the vigilance of citizens can insure freedom against abuse.

An Italian bishop, Enrico Compagnone of Anagni, complained that the Latin of the text often smacked of transliteration from a "certain modern language."[16] Since the identity of the principal author of the text was rather well known, there was little doubt about which modern language Compagnone had in mind. Perhaps this was an indirect attack on what many Latins regarded as an American effort to write the First Amendment and Anglo-Saxon jurisprudence into Church doctrine. At any rate, other Italian and Spanish bishops also criticized the Latin style of the text, thus asserting their mastery of the Church's official language even when their custody of the Church's orthodoxy was being successfully challenged.

When the experts completed their study of the interventions, they reported to the Secretariat, and at a plenary session at Ariccia from February 28 to March 6, 1965, the Secretariat revised the *textus emendatus*.[17] The resulting text, the *textus re-emendatus*, was sent at the beginning of April to Cardinal Ottaviani, president of the Theological Commission, and transmitted by him to the members of this commission.[18] From these Fathers, the Secretariat received seventeen suggestions, which experts and members of the Secretariat examined at Rome from May 2, and accordingly made a number of modifications.[19] Finally, with the revised text completed on May 11, 1965, the Coordinating Commission decided to send it and the introductory report to the Fathers of the Council.[20] This was done the following month.[21]

The introduction and summary declaration of the principle of religious freedom in the *textus re-emendatus* was less than half the length of the introduction and summary in the preceding text.[22] This was largely the result of omitting the difficult and complex question of the historical evolution of the Church's teaching on religious freedom, which was left to theologians. Also omitted were references to the contemporary limitation of governmental power and the contemporary constitutional guarantee of religious freedom. Since language about the political and juridical structure of modern society seemed to many too historically conditioned and too legalistic, especially at the beginning of a conciliar statement, it was eliminated from the introduction and initial affirmation of religious freedom.

The dignity of the human person, of which modern man is more and more conscious, demands that man follow his own counsel and freedom, moved by consciousness of his duty rather than by force. Noting these desires of men, the Church sees how conformed they are to truth and justice. At the same time, the Church examines her treasury of doctrine and draws from it what serves to confirm the just desires of men. Thus the right to religious freedom is founded on the dignity of the human person as evidenced by reason and especially by the revealed word of God. The new text in this way introduced at the outset the relation of religious freedom to revelation which it would develop in the third section.

"Religious freedom" was again defined as "immunity from coercion," such that in religious matters no one should be forced to act against his conscience or hindered from acting according to his conscience, in private or in public, within due limits. Moreover, the right to religious freedom must be recognized in the constitutional structure of society as a civil right which all men and all religious bodies can rightly claim.

The summary declaration then concluded with the admonition that the affirmation of religious freedom did not imply freedom from the will of God, religious indifference, or religious subjectivism. Specifically, the new text strongly insisted that the principle of religious freedom left intact the Catholic doctrine on the one true religion and the one Church of Christ.

In the second chapter, the new text investigated the arguments from reason for the principle of religious freedom.[23] The fivefold division of the arguments in the *textus emendatus* was altered to fit the two aspects of religious freedom described in the first chapter. First, arguments were advanced to show that no one should be constrained to act against his conscience; second, arguments were advanced to show that no one should be restrained, within due limits, from acting according to his conscience.

As to the first aspect of religious freedom, since man perceives and recognizes the dictates of God's law through the medium of conscience, he is held to follow his conscience faithfully in all his activity. Moreover, man has the right and the duty to seek truth in religious matters, and this search is made by instruction and communication. There is, therefore, a solemn moral principle that forbids anyone from being compelled to act against his conscience.

In the *textus emendatus,* the "solemn moral principle" just cited was called absolute. But the *textus re-emendatus* omitted that qualification. The reason for the change was the recognition that there are a number of cases where governments apparently force citizens with good cause to do things that their consciences forbid. Although it is against the religious convictions of some sects, the state often insists on the medical care of children, transfusions for pregnant mothers in danger of death from loss of blood, and vaccination. In the first two examples cited, the state acts as *parens patriae* in the interest of minors; in the third case, the state acts to protect public health. It might be argued that in these cases no one is compelled to act against his conscience, but only to allow someone else to do something. Or it might be argued that civil, not religious, acts are involved in these cases. These arguments, however, are difficult to sustain, since most observers would describe the cases as forcing citizens to submit to things that their consciences forbid as matters of genuine religious conviction.

Actually, the third text's attempt to absolutize the right not to be coerced to act against conscience was based on two important differences between a dictate of conscience which forbids an action and a dictate of conscience which commands an action. In the typical case, the former is more unconditional for the circumstances for which it is enunciated than the latter. This is due, at least in part, to the greater specificity of negative precepts. Moreover, inaction by citizens for reasons of conscience is less likely to conflict with the rights of others or the public interest than action according to conscience. The right to immunity from coercion to act against conscience, therefore, ought to be broader than the right to act according to conscience, both because of the structure of conscience itself and the relation of the dictates of conscience to the social context. Since these points were unnecessary to a conciliar affirmation of religious freedom, however, the *textus re-emendatus* simply dropped altogether the qualification "absolute" to describe the right not to be coerced to act against conscience.

Next, the text advanced arguments in favor of the right not to be coerced from acting according to conscience. The first argument advanced applied the social nature of man to acts of religion. Although the exercise of religion consists primarily in the internal acts by which man orders himself directly to God, the social nature of man demands that man manifest socially his internal acts of religion by external acts which he shares with others. The second argument was based on the incompetence of the state in religious matters. In the light of the dignity of the person and his rights, the competence of the state is restricted to the terrestrial and temporal order, so that men can tend with greater liberty to their ultimate end according to their own conscience. Governments would exceed their limits if they mixed in those things which are concerned with the relations of men to God.

The *textus re-emendatus* accepted the same limits to religious freedom as had the *textus emendatus*.[24] The first norm is the moral principle of personal and social responsibility: all men and social groups must take account of the rights of others. The second norm is juridical: public order requires preservation of public peace, protection of public morality, and the peaceful conciliation and effective safeguarding of equal rights for all citizens. For the rest, the rule of law must be observed according to which a man has a right to as much freedom as possible and may be restricted only when and as necessity requires.

To many conservatives, and even to some liberals, the concept of public order seemed to constrict too narrowly the general power of the state. The charge by the conservatives, and the fear of the liberals, was that the concept of public order reduced the state to the role of a corner policeman after the fashion of nineteenth-century liberalism. The result, of course, would be to deny the legitimacy of welfare legislation. Conscious of this criticism, the second introductory report of the *textus re-emendatus* defended the limiting concept of public order as proper for matters involving religious freedom and protested that the schema was not concerned with social questions.[25] The right of the state to restrict personal freedom is qualitatively more limited than its right to redress the distribution of property, and the text's limitation of the power of the state to restrict the freedom of religious exercise to the necessities of the public order reflected the pre-eminent value of personal freedom, not the political philosophy of the Manchester school of economics.

In the course of its argument against interpreting the limiting concept of public order in matters of religious freedom as an implicit adoption of *laissez-faire* political theory, the second report also claimed that the schema "touched briefly" the question of state subsidies for religious activities.[26] So brief and so light was the touch, in fact, that it left no clear impression at all. As had the *textus emendatus*, the new text vaguely commended to governments that they supply conditions favorable to fostering the religious life of the people. Since the issue of aid to religious activities and institutions is tied to the establishment question rather than directly to the question of religious freedom, the *textus reemendatus* was content to "touch briefly" the whole subject in this vague way.

In drawing practical consequences from this affirmation of religious freedom, the text followed closely its predecessor.[27] But, affirming the duty of the state to safeguard effectively the religious freedom of all citizens, the text added an important statement: it categorically denied that a regime of religious freedom prevented special recognition of one religious body in the constitutional organization of the state where peculiar historical circumstances obtain.[28] This categorical admission of the legitimacy of legal establishment, softened to a hypothetical mode in the two succeeding texts, was obviously designed to appease the conservative opposition and make the Declaration less objectionable to the devotees of the "Catholic" state. As the coming debate and interventions would show, this addition would not appease the opposition and would, in fact, worry many liberal supporters.

The text then applied the principle of religious freedom to religious bodies and the family, following the previous text almost verbatim.[29] On the "school question," the text added one sentence: the civil power violates the right of parents if it imposes a single system of education, from which all religious formation is excluded.[30] Although no names were mentioned, the text clearly had the state-controlled school systems of Communist nations in mind.

By more than four new paragraphs in the third chapter, the

textus re-emendatus expanded on the roots of religious freedom in divine revelation, where the dignity of the human person in its fullness was first manifested.[31] The text began its search for these roots in the Old Testament. God created man in His own image and left him in the hands of his own counsel. Moreover, He invited him to adhere to Him freely in a sacred covenant. Through the prophets, He little by little made clear that each man must personally turn to Him, and He promised a new covenant in which He would write His law in man's mind and heart. Then, in the fullness of time, He sent His own Son, who gave the commandment of love to His disciples, and He poured His Spirit and love in their hearts, by which they were constituted sons of God and called to freedom. Jesus specifically distinguished the things of God from the things of Caesar so that the Christian faithful might obey both in good conscience.

The Church through the centuries guarded and handed down all these truths. She instructed the faithful for greater freedom of spirit, and she cultivated the genuine sense of obedience in them. She resisted the oppression of secular powers, and she fought for the freedom of her sacred ministry. Finally, although there were some who acted in a way opposed to the spirit of the Gospels, yet the teaching of the Church always remained unshakable that no one should be compelled to embrace the faith. The ferment of the Gospels also worked for a long time in the minds of men and helped to bring it about that a wider recognition was accorded in the course of time to the principle that the immunity of men from coercion in religious matters must be observed in society.

Indeed, God calls men to serve Him but does not coerce them. He takes account of the dignity of the human person He has created, who must follow his own counsel and enjoy his own freedom. This was most manifest in Christ Jesus, in whom God revealed Himself and His ways as in the perfect human exemplar. Then the text traced the example of Christ and the Apostles, following closely the words of the previous text.

Succeeding paragraphs also repeated closely the *textus emendatus* on the freedom required for the act of faith, the freedom which the Church may claim by reason of her divine mandate, the duty of the Church to preach the gospel, the duty of the faithful to form their consciences in obedience to the teaching of the Church, and the duty of exercising love, prudence, and patience with men in error or ignorance concerning the faith.[32]

The fourth and concluding section added two paragraphs, which revealed more about the bishops' concern with authority in the Church than the question of religious freedom in political society.[33] Not a few, the text warned, seem to think that they may reject all subordination and make little of all obedience in the name of freedom. But religious freedom ought to serve men to achieve more fully that noble freedom to which they are called by God. All are warned, therefore, especially those who have the duty of educating others, to strive to train men to be obedient to legitimate authority and to respect genuine freedom. Men, who ought to judge things in the light of truth by their own counsel, ought also to act with a sense of responsibility and strive to follow what is true and just in collaborating freely with others.

During the summer of 1965, Fr. Guy de Broglie, S.J., prepared a lengthy critique of the text to be submitted to the Council in September.[34] As those of a long-time professor at the Gregorian University, and of one of the Church's leading theologians, de Broglie's words circulated with great authority, especially among the French bishops. (In fact, de Broglie was the author of the substitute draft on religious freedom submitted by the French-speaking African bishops after the Second Session.[35]) De Broglie sent a copy of his remarks to Murray, and the latter wrote a detailed reply, which also circulated among the French bishops, thanks to the dossier prepared by Bishop Sauvage.[36]

Among the many points raised by de Broglie was the definition of religious freedom. He objected to the appeal to "conscience" in the introductory definition of the first section and wished to substitute the following: "Religious freedom consists in freedom from coercion in professing and following the positive or negative opinions in religious matters which a man wishes to hold." Three reasons for the change were advanced: (1) as a matter of fact, the opinions and actions of men in religious matters are often guided by motives other than the strict dictates of religious or moral conscience; (2) rights should be defined in terms of their object, not in terms of the subjective motivation in their exercise; and (3) a definition of religious freedom in terms of conscience neglects the case of the atheist and agnostic.

In answer, Murray claimed that the word "conscience," as used in the introductory section, meant simply one's freely chosen opinion and was equivalent to the substitute formula proposed. In this sense, the atheist or agnostic can be said to act according to "conscience." Indeed, atheists and agnostics opposed to war have sought classification and consequent exemption from military service, or at least combat duty, precisely as "conscientious objectors."

Murray further claimed that the schema already defined religious freedom in terms of its object, namely, immunity from coercion. It by no means asserted, he argued, that the object of the right to religious freedom is the following of the dictates of one's conscience, or that the foundation of the right is found in the subjective sincerity of conscience. Precisely in this respect, both the *textus emendatus* and the *textus re-emendatus* were said to depart from the lines of the first two conciliar texts. To say that the object of the right to religious freedom is the profession and practice of such religious or irreligious opinions as one chooses to hold is erroneous and invites serious speculative difficulties. On the other hand, one can claim the right to immunity from coercion in the profession and practice of such opinions as one chooses to hold in religious matters on the basis of the dignity of the human person.

As for the problem of atheism, Murray claimed that the schema was concerned only with the constitutional-political dimension. The schema accordingly affirmed two points: (1) the atheist as citizen should be guaranteed his freedom from coercion as well as should the believer; and (2) militant atheism has no right to use the coercive apparatus of government to destroy or restrict religious freedom. Beyond this the schema did not purport to go.

De Broglie also attempted to reshape the argument from reason for religious freedom. According to him, the right to religious freedom consists of two essential elements: (1) the absolute right of a man to full freedom as to his internal religious assents or dissents; and (2) the consequent freedom to conform his speech and conduct to his inner convictions. Murray objected to this argument because he claimed that it presented the external freedom of religious exercise as a conclusion from the internal freedom of religious assent. Thus, according to Murray, de Broglie fell back into the position he wished to condemn, *i.e.*, that the object of the right to religious freedom in society is the interior persuasion that one possesses. So formulated, the argument is also incapable of offering a justification for any limits to the exercise of religious freedom in society.

Murray argued that the schema, on the other hand, was based from the outset on the social nature of man and the consequent social nature of religion: the essential sociality of man's freedom in religious matters is constituent of man's dignity as a person and may not be restricted unless government can prove a necessity of the public order. Correlatively, the power of the state is limited to the service of man's secular concerns, and its coercive power may not be used to restrain the freedom of the human person in the pursuit of higher goals.

One curious aspect of de Broglie's observations was his endorsement of legal establishment. Although he was anxious to guarantee the religious freedom of the atheist, he was unprepared to accept the propriety of the religiously neutral state. De Broglie was Frenchman enough to defend *la liberté* and patrician enough to hold fast to the principle of *noblesse oblige*.

The dossier of Bishop Sauvage was printed by the Conciliar Secretariat of the French episcopacy on August 31; it not only clearly juxtaposed the positions of de Broglie and Murray but also analyzed the more general question of the structure of the Declaration, on which the "French" and "American" schools disagreed. Since Sauvage's conclusions were generally favorable to the *textus re-emendatus* and Murray's explanation of it, the result of the dossier's distribution to the French bishops was to make the new text more acceptable to them.[37]

The stage was now fully set for the fourth and last session of the Vatican Council. After the turmoil of the last days of the Third Session and the pledges of the Pope and Tisserant, there was no reason to doubt that religious freedom would be the first order of business at the Fourth Session. This would mean another debate and a first vote on what was now the fourth text submitted by the Secretariat to the Council.

Notes

1. "Relatio" [*textus re-emendatus*], p. 28.
2. *Ibid.* Willebrands was consecrated bishop July 4, 1964.
3. See L. Gen., 4, 7–11, 55, 59–62, 64–74. (Mimeographed by the Secretariat, the Murray files.)
4. L. Gen., 43; L. Gen., 38.
5. L. Gen., 5.
6. L. Gen., 49; L. Gen., 28.
7. L. Gen., 25.
8. L. Gen., 79.
9. L. Gen., 80.
10. L. Gen., 10, 13, 18, 75; L-2, 1, 2, 3, 29, 43.
11. L. Gen., 42.
12. L. Gen., 52.
13. L. Gen., 48.
14. L-4, 10 (Cardinal Bueno y Monreal).
15. L. Gen., 22.
16. L. Gen., 57.
17. "Relatio," p. 28.
18. *Ibid.*
19. *Ibid.*
20. *Ibid.*, p. 29.
21. *Ibid.*, p. 31.
22. *Textus re-emendatus*, pp. 5–6.
23. *Ibid.*, pp. 7–9.
24. *Ibid.*, pp. 9–10.
25. "Relatio, pars altera" [*textus re-emendatus*], p. 52.
26. *Ibid.* Cf. *textus*, p. 11.
27. *Textus*, pp. 10–12.
28. *Ibid.*, p. 11.
29. *Ibid.*, pp. 11–12.
30. *Ibid.*, p. 12.
31. *Ibid.*, pp. 13–16.
32. *Ibid.*, pp. 16–18.
33. *Ibid.*, pp. 19–20.
34. Mimeographed, the Murray files.
35. *Supra*, Ch. IV, p. 60; on de Broglie's authorship, see Antoine Wenger, *Vatican II; chronique de la 2ème session* (Paris: Éditions du Centurion, 1964), pp. 186–87, n. 6.
36. Copy of the personal letter, the Murray files; dossier, August 31, 1965, mimeographed by the Secrétariat conciliaire de l'Épiscopat français, the Murray files.
37. A sympathetic explanation of the fourth text by Fr. Yves Congar,

O.P., a *peritus* of the Secretariat and convert to the Murray-Pavan approach, was also influential with the French bishops. See *La déclaration sur la liberté religieuse*, "Études et documents" [private series of studies and documents for the French bishops]; Paris: Secrétariat conciliaire de l'Épiscopat français, June 14, 1965). See also Congar's "Le bloc notes," *Information Catholique*, October 1, 1965, pp. 3–4.

VIII

Final Debate and First Vote

THE EXPECTATIONS OF THE SECRETARIAT were not disappointed. On Wednesday, September 15, 1965, the day after the Pope solemnly opened the Fourth Session of the Council, the Declaration on Religious Freedom became the first order of business.[1] After the introductory report of Bishop De Smedt, who stressed the limited aspect of the problem of freedom with which the Declaration was concerned, namely, the human and civil right of individuals and groups to be free from coercion in religious matters, Cardinal Spellman led off the debate with a strong endorsement of the *textus re-emendatus*. He was particularly pleased that the text founded its doctrine on the dignity of the human person and avoided ambiguous appeals to "freedom of conscience."[2]

Cardinal Frings also endorsed the schema on religious freedom, but made a number of recommendations.[3] The initial declaration of the first section should include treatment of the limits of religious freedom, its protection, the freedom of religious bodies, and the freedom of families. The arguments from reason should be suppressed, because such exposition belongs to theologians and philosophers rather than to a council. The recommendation that the state provide conditions favorable to religion and the admission that the state may, for historical reasons, give special recognition to a particular religion should be omitted to avoid misunderstanding. In the section on religious freedom in the light of revelation, treatment of the roots of the doctrine in the history of salvation should be dropped; different notions of religious freedom are there confused, and what is said of the teaching and practice of the Church is not exact. Finally, the conclusion could be very much shortened.

The conservative Cardinal Ruffini then spoke, repeating the old thesis on the duty of the state to the Catholic religion.[4] Although admitting that the schema contained many excellent considerations of the "technico-juridical" order, he insisted that only the true religion has a right to freedom. He praised the articles of the U.N. Declaration of Human Rights on religious freedom for the attempt to favor peace among men of different beliefs but found them tainted with religious indifferentism.[5] The public authorities have an obligation to render God the worship due to Him and, as far as possible, to favor (the Catholic) religion. Besides, no one can deny that (the Catholic) religion confers many benefits on society. (The first benefit named by Ruffini was that of chastity!) It is not sufficient to affirm that, in certain peculiar historical circumstances, the state can give special juridical recognition to a religious body; such an affirmation does not explain adequately the concordats which the Holy See has signed with different states.

Another conservative, Cardinal Giuseppi Siri of Genoa (Italy), took a similar line.[6] Although he protested that he was not opposed to freedom, he clearly indicated that he wasn't for it either. He claimed that despite the express words of the text, the schema would permit immoral practices, even the shedding of blood, in the name of religious freedom. Since God Himself can only tolerate evil, the Council should not undertake to defend it. Moreover, the defense of religious freedom would lead to religious indifferentism. Lastly, the Cardinal asked whether the schema was in accord with the sources of theology, namely, the teaching of Popes Leo XIII, Pius XI, and Pius XII. He anticipated the answer to his own question.

A third conservative, Cardinal de Arriba y Castro, also spoke against the Declaration.[7] For him, only the Catholic Church has the duty and the right to preach the gospel, and therefore proselytism by non-Catholics among Catholics is illicit and ought to be prevented. The Council ought to be careful not to decree the ruin of Catholicism in nations where it is the only religion; the problem ought to be entrusted to national episcopal conferences, which could, with the approbation of the Holy See, apply the principles of the Declaration more easily to different situations. But the Cardinal admitted that the right of non-Catholics to private worship and the right of all not to have any religion imposed on them were indisputable.

The intervention of Cardinal Giovanni Urbani,[8] patriarch of Venice (Italy), was significant for several reasons. First, he endorsed the schema in the name of thirty-two Italian bishops. (The Pope had recently appointed him to the board of bishops of the Italian episcopate.) Second, he made three recommendations for revision of the text which were to be incorporated into succeeding texts: (1) the title should state expressly that the religious freedom in question is a civil freedom; (2) the Declaration should express the belief of the Catholic Church that there is one true religion, which the Church possesses and teaches in its fullness; and (3) the argument for religious freedom from reason should be more clearly based on objective factors connected with the dignity and integrity of the human person, specifically the right and duty of seeking truth.

Cardinal Cushing, of course, supported the schema.[9] He approved its doctrine as solidly founded on the truth of the dignity of the human person and described its object as the good of freedom from coercion. Thus, both as to its foundation and its object, the schema was based on the objective order of truth, not on an altogether subjective order. Moreover, promulgation of this doctrine is a pastoral necessity of the first rank. The gospel is not only the gospel of truth but of the freedom to which men are called by God. This freedom proceeds from the gift of grace insofar as men are made sons of God the Father and from the right of nature insofar as men are created in the image of God. In the present order of salvation, the right of man to freedom in society is, in its own way, part of his vocation to the freedom announced in the gospel.

The last speaker of the day, Cardinal Alfrink, spoke in the name of all the bishops of the Netherlands.[10] He warmly praised the schema but offered two criticisms. First, the description of religious freedom at the beginning of the Declaration was too negative. Freedom is more than the absence of constraint (a "freedom from"); it is first of all the right to adhere to values which contribute to the perfection of the human person (a "freedom to"). Second, the text's treatment of the legal establishment of a particular religion was too affirmative. Since the text could give rise to erroneous interpretations, he suggested that the passage be put in the conditional mode of statement: "If, in view of historical circumstances, special recognition is granted to a religious body in the juridical structure of the state, care must be taken that at the same time the right of all citizens and all religious bodies to freedom in religious matters is recognized and observed."

The next day Cardinal Ritter opened the debate by warmly endorsing the schema.[11] Indeed, he said, it lacked nothing, nothing except approbation without delay and timely promulgation. Charity, justice, and logic do not permit delay or refusal in approving this schema. Charity demands it because many are suffering persecution for the sake of their faith and fidelity to their consciences; justice demands it because in some Catholic nations separated brothers in Christ are suffering much for the sake of their Christian consciences; and logic demands it because, without the Declaration, much in the already promulgated Constitution on the Church and Decree on Ecumenism would have no meaning, no value, and no truth.

Cardinal Silva Henriquez offered some pastoral reasons why he approved the Declaration with joy.[12] The schema implies an affirmation of the evangelical spirit of freedom. Moreover, the economy of freedom concerns not only the accession to faith but also the preservation of faith. No coercion against the person, whether political, economic, sociological, or psychological, is a fit means of preserving the assent of faith. Lastly, from a consideration of this sense of freedom, we are brought to consider a peculiar aspect of the responsibility of the baptized on the subject of affirming the necessity of the Church. Since the baptized constitute the Church, it is they who, in their formally Christian activity, vindicate the claims of the Church. All free activity inspired by the love of Christ is thus very important in the Church.

Cardinal Paul Meouchi, Maronite patriarch of Antioch (Syria), made two interrelated observations.[13] First, the question of terminology is very important, and the text ought to be evolved from the life of man and from the depths of his spiritual experience, not in a quasi-objective mode of thought. Second, the method used in explaining the doctrine of religious freedom ought not to be theological and metaphysical but founded in experience.

Deeply conscious of the persecution of the Church behind the Iron Curtain, Cardinal Josef Slipyi of Lwow (Ukraine) strongly supported the Declaration on Religious Freedom.[14] Immunity from coercion not only belongs properly to the Church, as revelation and reason prove, but it also contributes to the safety and good of the state. When citizens are oppressed, they rightly desire to liberate themselves, and given the opportunity, they revolt. The Cardinal asked in particular that the language affirming the rights of parents in education be more striking. Finally, to avoid private interest becoming the norm of conduct in the application of the principle of religious freedom, he asked that the virtue of "nobility" of soul be cultivated.

Cardinal Lorenz Jäger of Paderborn endorsed the schema in the name of one hundred and fifty German bishops.[15] But he thought that the difficulties raised the day before by the three conservative cardinals centered on the neuralgic point of the whole discussion and should be seriously weighed. Although the *respublica Christiana* of the Middle Ages has disappeared, there are states today where nearly all citizens belong to one religion. The schema admits the legitimacy of the confessional state on condition that all citizens enjoy a genuine religious freedom based on the rights of the person. Thus the schema answers the objections formulated by the conservative spokesmen. On the other hand, the schema by no means favors indifferentism; it affirms clearly that the Catholic Church is the one true religion, and that each has a duty to seek truth and form his conscience according to God's law. Finally, religious freedom pertains to the juridical order, not the moral order. The state has no competence to judge conscience, and the problem of the erroneous conscience in bad faith does not concern the juridical order.

Although Archbishop Nicodemo accepted the schema on religious freedom, he was particularly worried about its implications for relations between the faithful and ecclesiastical authorities.[16] The Declaration ought to avoid offering any occasion for religious individualism in the Church. From the affirmations and silence of the Declaration, no one should think that further arguments can be deduced to claim a false religious freedom in the Church.

Archbishop Morcillo González found the schema totally unacceptable.[17] He admitted that considerations of religious pluralism, international relations, ecumenism, reciprocity among different religions in the exercise of their freedoms and rights, and the moral impossibility for many of finding religious truth were sufficient to justify a declaration on religious freedom. But the philosophical and scriptural arguments alleged by the schema to establish propositions deriving from a contingent situation are not valid. Man has a right to act according to his conscience, but he has first the duty to seek religious and moral truth and the right to be helped in this search. While the state has no competence in religious matters, it can hear and accept what the Church teaches. The biblical arguments invoked by the schema prove nothing, and the teaching of popes from the time of Leo XIII is ignored, despite the subtle words of the introductory report.

Bishop Stanislaus Lokuang of Taiwan (Formosa) thought the schema of the highest importance for mission lands and deserving of approval by a great consensus of the Council Fathers.[18] But he noted several obscurities to be removed. First, he proposed that the definition of religious freedom be put in a more positive form and include the obligation of seeking the true religion and the true God. Second, he thought that the schema's acceptance of the legitimacy of the legal establishment of a particular religion equated establishment of the Catholic Church and that of other religions, an equation which has no place in the theological and doctrinal order, much less in a solemn document of an ecumenical council. He also thought that this passage implied that a regime of religious neutrality was superior to a regime of special recognition of the Church, which affirmation was very inconvenient in a conciliar document.

The next speaker, Bishop Juan Velasco, O.P., of Hsiamen (China) provided something of an interlude in the debate.[19] Denouncing the schema as totally unacceptable, he complained bitterly that the authors of the schema were taking no account of the comments of the minority opposed to the principles of the Declaration. He did not explain how, within the framework of the principle of contradiction and majority decision, the authors could incorporate or accommodate such comments.

Archbishop Gregorio Modrego y Casáus of Barcelona (Spain) continued the solid Spanish opposition to the schema.[20] Religious truth is one of the goods which constitute the common good and thus within the competence of the state. On principle, therefore, the state cannot be indifferent to the truth or falsity of religious beliefs. Moreover, the cited passages of Scripture neither prove nor confirm the thesis of a natural right to full freedom in religious matters. Finally, the doctrine of the schema contradicts explicit papal teaching and teaching implicit in the concordats of the Holy See with many governments.

Coadjutor Archbishop Duraisamy Lourdusamy of Bangalor (India) was very pleased with the schema but offered several suggestions.[21] He argued, first, that man has a duty to seek truth not only because of his social nature but also because of the nature of truth itself; no individual or group acquires and exhausts the meaning of any truth. Second, the whole section on the legal establishment of a particular religion should be omitted. Special recognition cannot avoid the danger of discrimination, and this is especially true in mission lands. Third, what is said of the Church's role in the development of religious freedom ought to be dropped because it is not entirely true; the Church herself was sometimes at fault in opposing that freedom.

Archbishop Juan Aramburu of Tucumán and two of his fellow Argentine bishops complained that the reference to public peace as a limit on the exercise of religious freedom was too broad.[22] They urged that in order to avoid abuse by civil powers, the reference should be qualified to read: "the legitimate and natural public peace." They did not indicate, however, how the added words would prevent abuse any more than would the formula in the text.

Since the introductory report of Bishop de Smedt admitted that there was a great distance between the scriptural doctrine and the modern concept of religious freedom, Bishop Luigi Carli of Segni (Italy) argued that this posed a choice between adjusting the latter concept to the former doctrine or bending the former to support the latter.[23] According to Carli, the schema chose the second solution. But the texts cited from Scripture concern only psychological freedom. Moreover, the texts chosen do not adequately represent the whole of Scripture; there are words of Christ and texts of John, Paul, and James which are extremely severe on those who diffuse error or choose not to listen to the Church.

Missionary Bishop Mason urged that the Declaration give some practical directives for the efficacious promotion of religious freedom, especially in the education of youth to respect the opinion of others and the formation of statesmen to follow the policy of tolerance.[24] Governments have a duty not only to proclaim the right to religious freedom but also to take care that the right is respected. The Declaration should note more expressly that religious freedom forms an indivisible whole with other freedoms, so that if it is destroyed or infringed, others also suffer loss.

Bishop Giuseppi Marafino of Veroli (Italy) thought that the schema should affirm openly that the care of religious freedom does not free the state from conforming its laws to ethico-religious principles and favoring religion "in some way," with due respect for different religious bodies.[25] The incompetence of the civil power in religious matters does not imply indifference to religion; the state ought to esteem greatly the religious needs of the people and make its laws and administration accord with the precepts and morals of right reason.

Although Maronite Archbishop Ignace Ziadé of Beirut (Lebanon) warmly praised the schema, he made several notations.[26] First, he asked how special recognition of a particular religion in the juridical structure of the state could mean anything else but some discrimination. Second, he urged that in addition to applying the principles of the Declaration to the duties of the state to recognize the rights of parents, the schema should apply its principles to the duty of the Church to respect the rights of parents in the case of marriages between spouses of different faiths. Non-Catholic spouses should not be forced, against their consciences, to promise that their offspring will be baptized and instructed in the Catholic faith.

The last speaker of the day, Archbishop Emilio Tagle Covarrubias of Valparaiso (Chile), in the name of forty-five bishops of Latin America, sharply objected to the separation of the juridical order from the theological and moral order.[27] There can be no right which does not have its foundation in the divine order of truth and justice. Thus the juridical concept of religious freedom contained in the schema is ambiguous and contradictory; it is a species of juridical positivism.

Cardinal Thomas Cooray, O.M.I., archbishop of Colombo (Ceylon), opened the discussion of Friday, September 17. He thought that the Council should adopt the principle that every limitation of religious freedom must be based on objective truth.[28] Otherwise, he said, the way is opened for equivocations on the Catholic doctrine of the one true religion and the one Church of Christ.

Cardinal Florit insisted that there were two different rights in the matter of religious freedom: a natural right proper to all men and a supernatural right proper to those who believe in Christ.[29] Accordingly, the Cardinal proposed (1) that the Declaration should affirm at the outset the supreme and sacred right of all who profess the Christian religion to religious freedom; (2) that the Declaration should affirm the right of the Church to full freedom in religious matters at all times; (3) that the Declaration should state clearly the right of the Church to the free exercise of religion even when that exercise disturbs the religious freedom which men claim as a natural right; and (4) that the Declaration affirm openly that Christian religious freedom aspires not to a comfortable situation for the Church but to the humanly uncomfortable obligation of preaching the gospel to all men. The Council should be concerned above all with the sacred right to Christian religious freedom and leave to an international organization the task of drawing from the conciliar text a declaration on civil freedom in religious matters.

Like other bishops from lands under Communist governments, Cardinal Franjo Seper, archbishop of Zagreb (Yugoslavia), strongly supported the Declaration.[30] Religious freedom is a necessary condition for the flowering of religious life and the accomplishment of the Church's mission in the modern world. The Declaration is of great value, although one can only hope that religious freedom will be respected everywhere. At least the consciences of all men will be made sensitive to violations. But the Cardinal thought that several passages on the role of the state in relation to religious freedom ought to be revised. Since the state is without competence in religious matters, all mention of conscience should be deleted where it is a question of the role of the state. On the other hand, special recognition of one religion by the state ought to be founded on reasons which the state can judge within the limits of its proper competence: the benefit of religion in the life and welfare of the state. Governments can certainly aid religious bodies in preserving monuments of art, in educating students, and in conducting works of charity. Lastly, the text should specify that the public order which limits religious freedom must be conformed to justice.

Cardinal Heenan again urged that the Council proclaim the doctrine of religious freedom.[31] It would be absurd to affirm that truth or error has rights; only persons, not things, have rights. A man has the inviolable right to obey his conscience, provided that he does not injure the public order or the rights of others. This was the argument of the Declaration, Heenan claimed. The Declaration also considered the possibility that proselytism by fanatical sects would raise disturbances among Catholic peoples and accordingly limited the exercise of religious freedom by the necessities of the public order.

Noting the Church's suffering from religious persecution in his own country, Cardinal William Conway, archbishop of Armagh (Ireland), approved the Declaration on Religious Freedom.[32] He did, however, add two observations. First, it is necessary to affirm categorically that the state should not discriminate against religiously affiliated schools solely on account of their religious character. Second, if one asserts that the competence of the state is restricted to the things of the secular order, this could be interpreted to imply recognition of the necessity of a totally secularized public life. To avoid this danger, Conway suggested that the statement be dropped altogether.

Cardinal Ottaviani stated anew his well known opposition to the Declaration.[33] The schema ought to begin with a solemn affirmation of the rights which the Church enjoys by reason of her divine origin and mission; the true and the false are not equal and cannot enjoy the same rights. Specifically, he objected that the schema endorsed positions opposed to the common and received teaching of the Church, that the right to propagate error does not follow from the dignity of the human person, that the citations of Scripture were partisanly chosen, and that what was said of the relations of Church and state was opposed to the teaching of recent popes. In short, the Church cannot depart from traditional teaching, which is in the safe possession of public ecclesiastical law and strongly defended by popes against the assaults of liberalism, agnosticism, and atheism.

The solid ranks of Spanish opposition to the Declaration were broken by Archbishop Cantero Cuadrado.[34] Concerned with an accurate definition of terms and statement of the question, Cantero pointed out that the schema dealt with the civil right to religious freedom. The theological foundation of this right is the nature and transcendence of the religious option and the incompetence of human authority to intervene except when external acts invade the rights of society or of others. Its juridical foundation lies in man's psychological freedom and his social nature.

Archbishop Antoni Baraniak of Poznań, speaking in the name of all the bishops of Poland, joined the chorus of bishops from behind the Iron Curtain supporting the Declaration.[35] He offered, however, several corrections and additions. The schema should acknowledge the existence of institutions in the Church which oppressed religious freedom; the schema should make clear that the term "coercion" designates means of action which are unjust in themselves, not the religious education of youth or exhortation of the faithful to exercises of piety; the schema should say that the juridical norm which limits the exercise of religious freedom must be conformed to moral principles; the schema should explain that religious freedom is founded on religious truth, with the consequence that the foundation is objective for Christians and only subjective for those sincerely in error; the schema should say more clearly that governments have no right to discriminate among citizens for religious reasons; lastly, the schema should complete the paragraph on the rights of parents in education by speaking against the imposition of a positively atheistic form of education as well as one which is simply areligious.

The next three speakers endorsed the Declaration and offered various modifications. Bishop Sauvage thought that the text should speak more strongly of the social nature of the human person and affirm that the former is a constitutive part of the latter's dignity.[36] In the name of twenty bishops of Italy, Archbishop Salvadore Baldassari of Ravenna argued that religious freedom is rationally founded on the dignity of the human person, not only in itself but also in relation to the necessities of the common good in a pluralistic society, that the schema presented public order too absolutely as the limit of religious freedom, and that the Declaration should state that it denies to the state only the right to restrict religious acts, not the power of the Church in the administration of the sacraments.[37] Bishop Elchinger made three suggestions.[38] First, the Church should present herself here as the guardian of the natural law and make only brief reference to the example of Christ and the sources of revelation. Second, the Declaration should say that the principles of which there is question in the matter of religious freedom extend to all spiritual values, e.g., search for truth, cultivation of science and art. Third, the conclusion should address a fraternal invitation to all religious bodies and to all men of good will to defend and promote religious freedom.

Bishop Abilio del Campo y de la Bárcena of Calahorra y La Calzada-Logroño (Spain), however, had no kind words for the Declaration.[39] According to del Campo y de la Bárcena, the schema smacked of "naturalistic humanism," not considering the dignity of the human person in the present supernatural economy. It ignored entirely the rights of God; it drew arguments from sociological facts such as pluralism as if these could modify principles, or as if the constitutions of states could be considered sources of Catholic doctrine; it favored religious subjectivism and situational ethics; lastly, it invited the conclusion that the Christian education of youth violates freedom.

Bishop Jean Rupp of Monaco thought that the text should be limited to a few affirmations.[40] The schema is too negative and corresponds to an abstract conception of freedom, which bears the mark of the nineteenth-century mentality. It would be better to suppress altogether the arguments from reason and revelation. He proposed that the Declaration simply affirm the statement on religious freedom recently worked out by the World Council of Churches.[41]

Auxiliary Bishop Charles Maloney of Louisville (Kentucky) strongly supported the Declaration, not only for himself but in the name of all of the observers at the Council.[42] He insisted that the right to religious freedom, as a right to immunity from coercion, was not a right of error but a right of the human person. Applying the principle to the conciliar debates, Maloney argued *ad hominem* that Council Fathers in error had a right to speak because of their dignity as persons, not because of the truth or falsity of their statements.

The next two speakers were sharply critical of the schema. Custodio Alvim Pereira, archbishop of Lourenço Marques (Mozambique), claimed that freedom for the public exercise of every religion leads to religious indifferentism, and that this constituted the essential defect of the schema.[43] Society has a right to protect subjects from error; indeed, society was described by Alvim Pereira as the "master of religious worship"! Bishop Primo Gasbarri, apostolic administrator of Grosseto (Italy), accused the schema of juridical positivism because it conceded the same civil rights to truth and error.[44]

The fifth American to speak in this conciliar debate was Archbishop Paul Hallinan of Atlanta (Georgia), who, like the others, approved the text.[45] He noted that its doctrine on the limits of government in religious matters was based on the more general concept of limited government and rooted in the dignity of the human person. When a state guarantees religious freedom, it by no means professes religious indifferentism, a false neutrality, or agnosticism.

The day's debate ended with a denunciation of the schema by Segundo García de Sierra y Méndez, archbishop of Burgos (Spain).[46] Echoing his fellow countryman, del Campo y de la Bárcena, he accused the schema of "naturalistic humanism" because it equated the supernatural right of the Church to religious freedom with the natural right of others. Further, he charged the schema with religious indifferentism. He closed with the ringing admonition that the Council should not try to please modern man in those things which cannot please God.

Cardinal Lefebvre, the liberal Lefebvre, opened the debate of Monday morning, September 20.[47] Systematically and patiently, he replied to the chief objections of the conservative opposition. First, the Declaration did not favor religious indifference because it was concerned only with civil freedom and affirmed explicitly the obligation of every man to seek truth. Second, the text expressly left intact the Catholic doctrine on the one true religion.

Third, religious freedom does not mean that every type of religious propagation is permitted. Fourth, the Declaration would aid, not hurt, missionary spirit. Fifth, the principle of religious freedom does not exalt man at the expense of God, but rather permits man to obey God, who made him free. Lastly, the Declaration did not propose a doctrine contrary to tradition, because the Church today faces the problem of violence to human freedom, not the nineteenth-century problem of laicism.

From the intrepid primate of Poland, Cardinal Stefan Wyszinski, archbishop of Warsaw, came further support for the Declaration.[48] The Cardinal noted that "right," "state," and "freedom" have different meanings in Marxist ideology than in Western usage and urged that the differences be mentioned at the beginning of the Declaration.

Cardinal Santos thought that the Declaration ought to begin by affirming man's duty to worship and reverence God in both internal and external acts.[49] From this principle flow all man's rights to religious freedom. Also, he objected to speaking of non-Catholic religious bodies and their rights. Since only the Church has received from God the right as a moral person to preach the gospel, the text should speak of the rights of associations of citizens in religious matters rather than the rights of non-Catholic religious bodies as such.

A confessor of the faith, Cardinal Josef Beran, archbishop of Prague (Czechoslovakia), added his voice to those of his fellow bishops from behind the Iron Curtain in support of the Declaration.[50] Movingly, he told of the evils which flow from the deprivation of freedom and humbly confessed the faults of the Church in his country in the past. History was said to warn that the principle of religious freedom should be affirmed in clear language without any restriction.

Cardinal Owen McCann, archbishop of Cape Town (South Africa), approved the schema substantially but desired some changes.[51] First, he wanted a stronger statement that every person has the duty of conforming his conscience in religious matters to the truths revealed by God and proclaimed by the Church. Second, he found the passage admitting the legitimacy of the legal establishment of a particular religion too vague. It was necessary to indicate that there should be no obligation on citizens not affiliated with the privileged religion to contribute taxes marked for that religion. Third, it should be more clearly stated that parents exercising their freedom to choose the school for their children have a right to proportionate subsidies.

In support of the schema, Cardinal Lawrence J. Shehan, archbishop of Baltimore, spoke on the evolution of the doctrine of religious freedom from the time of Leo XIII.[52] Admitting that the doctrine of the schema was not to be found explicitly in the writings of Leo, Shehan pointed out that Leo advanced considerably beyond the teaching of the Middle Ages and post-Reformation era. The concept of tolerance was not the core of the Leonine doctrine or the irreformable teaching of the Church on religious freedom. Indeed, the concept of tolerance was predicated on rule by a prince with full power in civil matters. Nor was Leo's master idea on the public care of religion the affirmation that truth alone has rights. Rather, he was concerned to declare against the rationalists that that truth and error cannot enter the juridical order with equal title. Only in this abstract way can the dictum of Leo be rightly understood.

It was the contribution of Leo to affirm in a new way the transcendence of the Church and at the same time the independence of the secular order. But the core of the Leonine doctrine is found in the freedom of the Church, which, according to Shehan, implies the freedom of a people fulfilling the necessary conditions of personal and political maturity. Likewise, freedom of the people implicitly demands religious freedom as a juridical guarantee correlative to the constitutional limitation of government. Fighting for the freedom of the Church, Leo opened the way for the freedom of the human person, including religious freedom, which his successors developed.

In the name of eighty-two bishops of Brazil, Cardinal Agnelo Rossi, archbishop of São Paulo, praised the Declaration but asked for certain changes.[53] First, the term "religious matters" should be defined. Second, a paragraph should be added on the pastoral consequences of the Declaration, e.g., personal growth in faith, formation of the Christian consciousness of the community in apostolic action, and the sense of the Church's poverty. Third, a substantial majority of the Brazilian bishops wanted the statement on the legitimacy of the confessional state formulated in the conditional mode as Alfrink proposed.

Cardinal Browne remained steadfastly opposed to the principles of the Declaration.[54] Since the greatest dignity of man consists in his elevation to the supernatural order, the preservation of those who profess the true faith from the preaching of other religions is required. Rulers as well as subjects can discern and embrace the true religion; if the state is constituted of Catholics, rulers are obliged to recognize the protection of the true religion as the greatest good of their citizens. Moreover, diffusion of other religions in such a country is a violation of public morality opposed to the rights of Catholics and putting their faith in peril.

To Cardinal Joseph Cardijn of Belgium, with sixty years' experience in the apostolate of the Young Christian Workers, a solemn and clear proclamation of the right of all men to religious freedom seemed an urgent necessity for three reasons: (1) the Declaration would help to unify a pluralist world; (2) the Declaration would make apostolic, missionary, and ecumenical work more effective; and (3) the Declaration would have an educative value, leading men to the freedom of soul by which they are made responsible toward society and God.[55]

Archbishop Lefebvre, the conservative "mystery man" in the Felici affair of the Third Session, bitterly condemned the Declaration.[56] The introductory report described the concept of religious freedom as the term of a long evolution, which only in the eighteenth century began to be recognized. But this concept began to be recognized only outside the Church, among philosophers such as Hobbes, Locke, Rousseau, and Voltaire, who attempted to destroy the Church in the name of human reason. Since the concept of freedom cannot be defined without relation to the divine law, only the Church has a right, properly speaking, to religious freedom.

Bishop John Gran of Oslo (Norway) strongly supported the Declaration.[57] Indeed, since all freedoms are interconnected, he thought that the Declaration should more strongly exhort all to promote the climate of freedom.

Bishop Antonio Añoveros Ataún of Cádiz y Ceuta (Spain) was concerned to fix the limits of religious freedom so as to make precise the rights of minorities and majorities.[58] His first point was that although the civil power may restrict religious freedom to preserve public peace, it must be noted that this restriction is valid only for a time. His second point: a government may also restrict religious freedom to safeguard public morality, which includes spiritual as well as temporal goods. Third: the civil power may restrict religious freedom to protect legitimate rights. The Bishop made other observations: that the text should be submitted to a subcommission of experts; that the schema should be inscribed "On Civil Freedom in Religious Matters"; that it was not timely to base religious freedom only on the dignity of the human person; and that the citations from Scripture neither affirm nor prove the principle of religious freedom.

The last speaker of the day, Auxiliary Bishop Thomas Muldoon of Sydney (Australia), found the schema altogether intolerable.[59] To remedy the defects of the text, he proposed that the introduction say openly that the Declaration was concerned only with the juridical condition of men in human society, and that the subtitle be restricted to speak of the right of the person and groups to civil freedom in religious matters.

On Tuesday, September 21, Cardinal Enrico Dante of the Curia opened the fifth day of debate on religious freedom.[60] He accused the schema of relying on a very grave equivocation. It sought to establish that the Catholic religion is free to preach the gospel throughout the world in virtue of a legally established right, but this is what Catholic liberals of the last century wanted, and what French Revolutionaries affirmed in their Declaration of the Rights of Man (1789). Thus the limits on the free exercise of religion are equivocal: if the state which fixes the limits is Christian, the concept of public order has a valid meaning; if, however, the state is not Christian, these limits can be transformed into an instrument of tyranny against religion, and if the state is Communist, all expressions will take on a totally different meaning, and the limits in question will be contrary to the natural law.

Cardinal Charles Journet, theologian and professor at the major seminary of Fribourg (Switzerland), thought that the differences among the Council Fathers on the subject of religious freedom could be reduced if certain themes of the schema were underlined.[61] The human person is a member of two social orders, one temporal and the other spiritual. As to the temporal order, the human person as person transcends the whole order, although he is in one respect a part of society. Nor does the person who errs or sins lose his dignity as a person. Since society has a duty to honor God, it cannot ignore the different religious families in the state and must leave worthy praise of God to them. Above this order of natural rights, the Church has a supernatural right to preach the gospel to every creature. Lastly, although the rulers of the Church invoked the secular arm and the medieval concept of the *respublica Christiana* more than once in the past to defend the faithful, the distinction between the temporal and spiritual orders has become progressively more explicit under the influence of the gospel, and is now obvious to all.

Archbishop Adam Kozlowiecki of Lusaka (Zambia), in the name of seven other bishops of central east Africa, generally approved the schema but thought it should indicate clearly that it was affirming only the rights of a correct conscience, *i.e.*, a conscience objectively formed according to the will of God.[62] The next speaker, Coadjutor Bishop Pablo Muñoz Vega, S.J., of Quito (Ecuador), was dissatisfied with the failure of the schema to relate the natural, sociojuridical right of religious freedom to the supernatural right of religious freedom to which all men are called in Christ.[63]

After these four interventions, Cardinal Krikor Agagianian (Curia), the presiding Moderator of the day, remarked that sixty-two Fathers had thus far spoken on the religious freedom schema, and he asked the assembly to decide by a standing vote whether or not it was time to close discussion.[64] The Fathers rose almost to a man, and the Moderator yielded the floor to De Smedt, who summed up the debate. After more than four days' debate, the Moderator's proposal and the Council's approval were not altogether surprising.

There was a lapse of a few minutes before De Smedt assured the Fathers that the confrontation of opinions in the debate had been very constructive, and that all the proposals would be attentively studied.[65] In particular, attention would be focused on the social and civil meaning of religious freedom in the schema, a more positive description of its content, the elimination of what might appear to imply indifferentism or laicism, and the importance of education for the exercise of freedom and responsibility. The section on religious freedom in the light of Scripture would be revised. The limits of religious freedom would be made more precise. The duty of searching for truth as well as the rights of the Church would be more strongly affirmed.

At the conclusion of De Smedt's summation, the Secretary-General announced that, by decision of the Moderators, an immediate vote would be taken on the religious freedom schema. The Fathers were asked the following question: "Does it please the Fathers that the already amended text on religious freedom should be taken as the basis for a definitive declaration after further amendments in the light of Catholic doctrine on the true religion and proposed amendments which will be subsequently approved according to the norms of Council procedure?" The only choice in the vote was between approval and disapproval; there was no provision for approval with reservation. When the votes were counted, the result was a landslide victory for the progressives: 1,997 votes were cast in favor of the motion, 224 against, and one vote was invalid. Announcement of the result was greeted by long applause.

The lopsided margin of the vote obscures the drama of the situation before the event. Due to the impression of strength created by the conservative opposition, there had been considerable uncertainty whether or when a vote would take place. Indeed, at a meeting of the Coordinating Commission and Moderators on the previous evening, Monday, September 20, a proposal for an immediate vote on the religious freedom schema failed to carry.

The vote on Tuesday was secured by the intervention of the Pope himself. Summoning Cardinal Tisserant, chairman of the Council presidency, Cardinal Agagianian, presiding Moderator of the day, and Archbishop Felici, the secretary-general, to his apartment Tuesday morning, the Pope indicated his wish for a preliminary vote on the religious freedom schema. The Pope approved the formula for the vote drawn up by the Secretariat, adding the clause which guaranteed subsequent approval of amendments "according to the norms of Council procedure."[66] Thus the Secretariat was assured of full jurisdiction, and no change could affect the substance of the Declaration if the Council voted preliminary approval by the required two-thirds majority.

In virtue of the rule permitting interventions after the close of debate by those who represented at least seventy Fathers, four speeches the next day, Wednesday, September 22, provided something of an anticlimax to the debate on religious freedom.[67] Archbishop Wojtyla, in the name of the bishops of Poland, argued that since the position of the Church on religious freedom is founded on revelation and at the same time in harmony with reason, it was not necessary to separate the arguments from both.[68] Moreover, since the Council is concerned with the right of the human person in religious matters, it ought to declare man's responsibility in the use of this right. As a consequence, limits to religious freedom should be founded on the principles of the moral law.

Bishop Michel Doumith of Sarba (Lebanon) thought that the concept of the confessional state, which the text sought to justify, was altogether equivocal.[69] The equivocation was said to consist in this, that the same words could apply to both Christian and non-Christian confessional states, although the two classes of states differ in an important respect. The Christian confessional state implies only a priority of honor and favor, while a non-Christian confessional state necessarily implies discrimination in essential rights. The whole reference, therefore, should be dropped.

Bishop Giocondo Grotti, O.S.M., of Acre e Purús (Brazil) made a very brief comment on the schema.[70] He expressed the desire that the vote of the day before would not be exaggerated out of context, and that the gracious assurances of De Smedt would be carried out.

The last speaker of the day and of the debate, Bishop Ancel, ranks with Cardinals Urbani and Alfrink as a most influential contributor to the subsequent revision of the schema.[71] In the name of more than one hundred bishops of France, Ancel proposed to found religious freedom on man's obligation to seek truth and to show the connection between that obligation and religious truth itself. Ancel argued that every man is held to seek truth, to adhere to it, and to conform his whole life to its demands; this principle is very often affirmed in Scripture in various ways.

But for man to be able to satisfy this obligation it is necessary that he enjoy not only psychological freedom but also immunity from all coercion. This is why not only is there no opposition between religious freedom and the obligation to seek truth, but religious freedom is founded on this obligation, and the obligation demands religious freedom. Thus the argument from man's obligation to seek truth will reinforce the principle of religious freedom and reassure those who fear religious indifferentism and subjectivism.

The public debate on religious freedom was now over, and the overwhelmingly favorable vote made the future of the schema entirely secure. But the welter of suggestions from the Fathers would not make the task of revision easy. And there was now very little time to do this before the end of the fourth and last session of the Second Vatican Council. The outcome, however, was inevitable, and the suspense over.

Notes

1. Xavier Rynne, *The Fourth Session* (New York: Farrar, Straus and Giroux, 1966), p. 50.
2. "Relatio, pars alters," Schema declarationis de libertate religiosa [*textus re-emendatus*] (Rome: Vatican Polyglot Press, 1965), pp. 40–52. Spellman's speech was submitted as written intervention DL, 1. (Mimeographed by the Secretariat, the Murray files.) All but thirteen speeches of the debate can be found summarized (eleven are reported integrally) in *La Documentation Catholique*, October 17, 1965, cols. 1763–1802.
3. DL, 2.
4. DL, 3.
5. On the U.N. Declaration of Human Rights, see *supra*, p. 92, n. 10.
6. DL, 4.
7. DL, 5.
8. DL, 6.
9. DL, 7.
10. DL, 8.
11. DL, 9.
12. DL, 10.

13. DL, 11.
14. DL, 12.
15. DL, 13.
16. DL, 14.
17. DL, 37.
18. DL, 15.
19. DL, 16.
20. DL, 17.
21. DL, 18.
22. DL, 19.
23. DL, 20.
24. DL, 21.
25. DL, 22.
26. DL, 23.
27. DL, 24.
28. DL, 25.
29. DL, 26.
30. DL, 27.
31. DL, 28.
32. DL, 29.
33. DL, 30.
34. DL, 31.
35. DL, 32.
36. DL, 33.
37. DL, 34.
38. DL, 35.
39. DL, 36.
40. DL, 38.
41. In December, 1961, the Third Assembly of the World Council of Churches at New Delhi, India, adopted a statement on religious freedom. That statement endorsed a broad freedom to bear public witness to one's religion and to preach to others, subject only to the requirements of public order. A note distinguished Christian witness from unworthy means of proselytizing. See *Vatican II: La liberté religieuse*, eds. Hamer and Congar, Annexe III, pp. 261–63.
42. DL, 76.
43. DL, 40.
44. DL, 39.
45. DL, 42.
46. DL, 41.
47. DL, 63.
48. DL, 64.
49. DL, 65.
50. DL, 66.
51. DL, 67.
52. DL, 68.
53. DL, 69.

54. DL, 70.
55. DL, 71.
56. DL, 72.
57. DL, 73.
58. DL, 74.
59. DL, 75.
60. DL, 99.
61. DL, 100.
62. DL, 98.
63. DL, 97.
64. For an account of the day's events and their background, see Rynne, *op. cit.*, pp. 47–50 and *La Documentation Catholique*, cols. 1797–98. Agagianian was mistaken on the number of speakers; including De Smedt, there were only sixty-one before the call for a standing vote.
65. Copy of De Smedt's summation, the Murray files; summarized in *La Documentation Catholique, loc. cit.*
66. On the Pope's addition to the voting formula, see Rynne, p. 49.
67. On the rule permitting speeches after the close of debate, No. 4 of the additions of July 2, 1964 to the Council rules, see *La Documentation Catholique*, August 2, 1964, col. 982.
68. DL, 89.
69. DL, 88.
70. DL, 91.
71. DL, 90.

IX

Final Revisions and Adoption

BESIDES THE OPINIONS EXPRESSED in the debate, the Secretariat received sixty-eight written interventions by September 27, the day on which it took up the task of revising the *textus reemendatus*.[1] Even after that date, the Secretariat continued to receive interventions, and the total, including those of the debate, eventually reached 201.[2] The special subcommission set up to revise the text studied the corrections proposed by the Fathers, and after full discussions at three plenary sessions, the Secretariat adopted many of the changes proposed by the subcommission.[3] Thus was the fifth conciliar text on religious freedom, the *textus recognitus*, constituted.

The first change in the new text was the subtitle: the "freedom" to which the schema asserted the right of persons and communities was now expressly qualified as "social and civil."[4] At the request of the Fathers, these words were added to make clear that the freedom in question in the schema did not concern the relation of men to truth or to God, or the relations between the faithful and authorities in the Church, but the relations among persons in human and civil society.[5]

After noting that the contemporary demand for freedom in human society chiefly regards the quest for values proper to the human spirit, especially religious values, the introductory first section of the schema added a frank profession of Catholic faith.[6] The text expressed the Council's belief that God has made known

155

to mankind the way in which men are to serve Him, and that this one true religion subsists in the Church. Thus, since all men are held to seek truth, especially in what concerns the worship of God, and to embrace the truth they come to know, and to hold fast to it, they are also bound by a sacred duty to embrace and profess the Catholic faith, as far as they are able to recognize it.

Where the *textus re-emendatus* disavowed religious subjectivism and indifferentism, the *textus recognitus* expressed the Council's belief that the duties cited in the preceding paragraph affect and bind the human conscience, and that "truth cannot impose itself except by virtue of its own truth, as it makes its entrance into the mind at once quietly and with power."[7] On the other hand, religious freedom, which men demand as necessary to fulfill their duty of worshiping God, concerns immunity from coercion in civil society. Therefore it evidently leaves untouched the Catholic doctrine on the one true religion, the one Church of Christ, and the moral duty of men toward the Church. By acknowledging this freedom as a right proper to the human person, the text intended to develop papal doctrine on his inviolable rights and the constitutional order of society.

By the vote of September 21 the Secretariat was bound to perfect the *textus re-emendatus* "in the light of the Catholic doctrine on the true religion." These words, the Secretariat felt, required the Declaration to show in a more explicit way that religious freedom did not absolve man and society from their moral duties toward the Catholic religion. Therefore in the introduction, the *textus recognitus* expressed the faith of the Council in the uniqueness of the Church. Whether this specific statement was ecumenically desirable, or even required by the Council vote of September 21, is questionable. But, at any rate, it certainly absolved the Declaration from the charge of favoring subjectivism or indifferentism, at least in any obvious sense.

The first chapter of the *textus recognitus* took up the general principle of religious freedom.[8] Like its predecessor, the text defined the object of religious freedom as immunity from coercion.[9] No one may be compelled to act against his conscience, nor may he be impeded from acting according to conscience. This right of the human person to religious freedom should be recognized in the constitutional law governing society and should thus become a civil right. Moreover, the right to religious freedom has its foundation in the very dignity of the human person.[10]

Here the new text offered its main argument to show how religious freedom has its foundation in the dignity of the human person.[11] As persons endowed with reason and free will and bearing the consequent privilege of personal responsibility, all men are impelled by their nature and morally obliged to seek truth, especially religious truth. They are held to adhere to the known truth and to order their whole lives according to the demands of truth. But men cannot satisfy this obligation in a manner appropriate to their nature unless they enjoy immunity from external coercion as well as psychological freedom. Religious freedom thus has its foundation in the very nature of the human person, not in his subjective disposition. Therefore the right to immunity continues to exist even in those who do not live up to the obligation of seeking truth and adhering to it, provided that the just requirements of public order are observed.

The text anticipated the difficulty of establishing a right to religious freedom for the complacent man from the right and duty to seek truth. To meet it, the text attempted to root the right to immunity in the nature of man rather than his subjective disposition. Search for truth indeed proceeds from a deep drive of man, not a subjective whim; accordingly, man may claim a natural right to search for truth. But does this establish the right of a complacent man to communicate his views? The text concluded abruptly and without explanation that it does: "*In consequence* . . . the right to . . . immunity continues to exist even in those who do not live up to their obligation of seeking truth and adhering to it."[12] (Italics added.)

This argument for religious freedom from the right and duty to seek truth, of course, is the argument advanced on several occasions by Colombo and Ancel, both members of the subcommission of the Secretariat charged with the task of revising the *textus re-emendatus*. As previously indicated, the argument will not establish the right of all men to religious freedom if it is too simply stated. How does the right to search for truth give a right to communicate what is false, or even what may be known to be false? How does the right to search for truth give a man complacent in the possession of what he thinks is true a right to communicate his views, whether true or false? To be convincing, the argument must be fixed in a social and political context. As social dialogue and exchange, search for truth requires the political condition of freedom; in this context *every* man may claim, within the limits of public order, a right to immunity from coercion in all expression that concerns the order of truth, and religious truth in particular.

The general theme of this argument was expanded in succeeding paragraphs.[13] Since the highest norm of human life is the divine law, and since man participates in this law, every man has the duty, and therefore the right, to seek truth in religious matters, in order that he may prudently form for himself, by the use of suitable means, right judgments of conscience. Here the social nature of the search for truth was affirmed: inquiry is to be free, carried on by teaching, communication, and dialogue; thus men assist one another in the quest for truth.

Relating truth to action, the text explained that man perceives the imperatives of the divine law through the medium of conscience and is bound to follow his conscience faithfully in all his activity in order that he may come to God, for whom he was created. It follows that he is not to be forced to act against his conscience, nor is he to be restrained from acting in accordance with his conscience, especially in religious matters. No merely human power can either command or prohibit the internal, free acts by which man sets the course of his life directly toward God. Moreover, since the social nature of man requires that he give external expression to his internal acts of religion, that he participate with others in religious matters, and that he profess his religion in community, the human person may not be denied the free exercise of religion in society, provided that the requirements of public order are observed.

In the last place, the text offered a shortened version of the constitutional argument.[14] Religious acts, whereby men direct their lives to God in public and in private from a sense of conviction, of their nature transcend the order of terrestrial and temporal affairs. Therefore governments must be said to transgress their limits if they impede or direct such acts.

Thus the *textus recognitus* integrated the argument from man's right and duty to follow conscience and the argument from the

social nature of man and religion under the primacy of the argument from man's right and duty to seek truth; the constitutional
argument was simply appended as a further consideration.[15] The
progressive evolution of the argumentation for the principle of
religious freedom in the last three texts was significant. In the
textus emendatus five different arguments were enumerated, although the dignity of man and the correlative constitutional principle held the primacy. In the *textus re-emendatus* the arguments
were organized around two clearly distinguished aspects of religious freedom: the right not to be forced to act against conscience and the right not to be impeded from acting according
to conscience. Again, the dignity of man and the correlative constitutional principle enjoyed a primacy in establishing the critical
second aspect of religious freedom. But in the *textus recognitus*
the arguments were more broadly fused, the distinction between
the two aspects of religious freedom blurred, and the constitutional
principle reduced to the status of an ancillary argument.

In fact, the role of rational argumentation was progressively
de-emphasized and less space accorded to it in the successive texts.
Thus the *textus recognitus* unequivocally affirmed the right of all
men to religious freedom, demanded its recognition in the constitutional law of human society, and founded the right on the
dignity of the person. Only then did the text undertake a further,
more specific analysis of how and why human dignity requires
religious freedom. This procedure, in accord with the purpose of
a conciliar declaration on religious freedom, left to professional
theologians, philosophers, and political scientists the task of critically evaluating specific arguments. It was the affirmation of the
principle of religious freedom which the Council proclaimed un-
reservedly to the faithful and the world.

In applying the principle of religious freedom to religious communities, the *textus recognitus* added two specifications: religious
communities should not be impeded in the nomination and trans-
fer of ministers or in the construction of buildings for religious
uses.[16] On the rights of parents to determine the content of religious instruction given to their children, the text added the
specification that governments violate the rights of parents if
children are compelled to attend lessons not in accord with the
religious persuasions of their parents.[17]

The *textus recognitus* commended the care of religious freedom not only to citizens generally, as had the *textus re-emendatus,* but also to social groups, to the Church, and to other religious communities.[18] It also stated more directly as to form, if no less vaguely as to content, that governments should help to create conditions favorable to the fostering of religious life.

But the most significant change in this section was on the confessional state. Where the *textus re-emendatus* had admitted the legitimacy of the legal establishment of a particular religion categorically, the *textus recognitus* admitted the legitimacy of such an institution only hypothetically: *if,* in view of peculiar historical circumstances, special legal recognition is granted to a particular religion, religious freedom must be preserved.[19] Thus the text avoided either affirming or denying that formal legal establishment is consistent with religious freedom. Many Council Fathers considered any form of establishment fundamentally at odds with the principle of religious freedom, but many others considered the institution fully compatible. Since there was no conciliar consensus on the question, the *textus recognitus* was satisfied to insist on the universal validity of the principle of religious freedom and admit only hypothetically the legitimacy of the confessional state. The text also made sufficiently clear that the institution of legal establishment is a product of historical circumstance, not a matter of theological doctrine.

There was little change in the section on the limits to religious freedom, but greater care was taken to avoid any false interpretation or unjust use of the text by governments disposed to violate the religious freedom of their citizens.[20] To avoid the implication of opposition between the requirements of personal responsibility and those of the public order, the text did not divide the limits on religious freedom into two classes, one moral and the other juridical. Rather, the text explained progressively what concerns individuals, groups, and governments in the matter. Individuals and groups are held by the moral law to take account of the rights of others, of their duties to others, and of the common welfare of all. For their part, governments have the right to act according to the juridical norms which necessities of public order, founded on objective morality, demand. Public order requires the effective protection and peaceful integration of the rights of all citizens, adequate care of that honorable public peace which comes about when men live together in good order and in true justice, and the proper custody of public morality. Thus the public order which may require restrictions on religious freedom is not any kind of public peace which exists or could exist, but rather the public peace which comes from living together in good order and in true justice.

At the end of the first chapter of the schema, the *textus recognitus* repeated the warning of the preceding text on respect for lawful authority and the responsible exercise of freedom.[21] It added the conclusion that religious freedom should have as a purpose and aim that men may act with greater responsibility in fulfilling their duties in society.[22] Thus the text here stressed the social responsibility that religious freedom entails. Although the religious purpose of religious freedom is obvious enough, its social function deserved special attention.

The second chapter of the schema considered the principle of religious freedom in the light of revelation.[23] At the outset, the *textus recognitus* attempted to make clear the nature of the relationship between the two.[24] Although revelation indeed does not affirm expressly the right to immunity from external coercion in religious matters, it does nonetheless disclose the dignity of the human person in its fullness. It gives evidence of the respect which Christ showed toward the freedom of man in fulfilling his duty of belief in the word of God. It gives us lessons, too, in the spirit which disciples of such a Master ought to recognize and follow in every situation.

In the new arrangement of the schema, the section on the act of faith, incorporated almost verbatim from the *textus re-emendatus*, was inserted before the section on the example of Christ and the Apostles.[25] This was done to show more clearly the connection between religious freedom and the freedom proper to the act of faith. Thus the example of Christ and the Apostles is offered as an illustration of the general principles on which the doctrine of religious freedom is based.

In tracing the ministry of Christ, the new text developed more fully the theme that He did not coerce His hearers.[26] Christ certainly denounced the incredulity of those who heard Him, but He left vengeance to God on the day of judgment. When He sent His

Apostles into the world, He affirmed that those who did not believe would be condemned. But, noting that cockle had been sown amid the wheat, He gave orders that both be allowed to grow until the harvest at the end of the world. He refused to be a political messiah, ruling by force; He preferred to be called the Son of Man, who came to serve and to give His life as a ransom for many. He recognized the power of government and its rights when He commanded that tribute be given to Caesar. Lastly, in completing the work of redemption on the Cross, by which He achieved salvation and true freedom for men, He brought His redemption of mankind to perfection. He bore witness to the truth, but He refused to impose it by force on those who denied it. Thus the *textus recognitus* cited two of the most celebrated scriptural passages in the history of church-state literature: the parable of the tares and the tribute to Caesar.

In tracing the ministry of the Apostles, the new text showed more fully how they followed the example of Christ.[27] They strongly proclaimed the salvific plan of God for all men, but they also respected weaker souls, even when in error. Thus they made clear the personal responsibility of each one before God and his obligation to obey conscience. As the Master, so the Apostles recognized legitimate civil authority. At the same time, however, they did not fear to speak out against governing powers opposing the will of God.

The new text was more modest in its description of how the Church followed the footsteps of Christ and the Apostles.[28] It confessed openly and in a spirit of penance that, in the life of the People of God, as it made its pilgrim way through the vicissitudes of human history, there were at times ways of acting which were less in accord with the spirit of the gospel and even opposed to it. The confession was brief and unspecific, but its intention was clear. Not only did the text admit that Christian rulers and churchmen had erred in appealing to coercion in defense of the faith, it also admitted that the Church herself, the People of God, had erred in this matter. Thus, although particular institutions of repression may be understood in the context of history, they are by no means to be justified.

Succeeding sections on the freedom of the Church and the duty of the Church and the conclusion incorporated without significant change the corresponding sections of the *textus re-emendatus*.[29] In the article on the freedom of the Church, two proposed changes, which would have subtly undermined the schema, were narrowly averted.[30] One would have described the Church's freedom as a condition rather than a principle of relations between Church and state, thus implying that the Church required more of the state in principle than her freedom. The second would have acknowledged only that in a regime of religious freedom the Church obtains a *de facto* stable condition for the independence necessary in filling its mission; thus it would have implied that a regime of religious freedom does not provide the Church with a *de jure* stable condition.

On Friday, October 15, as the Council prepared to recess for a week, the Secretary-General announced that balloting on the amended schema on religious freedom would begin the week of October 25.[31] On Saturday, October 16, the Secretary-General announced that the new text on religious freedom would be distributed during the recess.[32] As scheduled, Bishop De Smedt introduced the revised text to the Council on Monday, October 25, and the voting took place on the succeeding two days.[33]

There were six votes October 26 on the first eight articles of the Declaration.[34] On the introductory first article the vote was 2,031 for, 193 against, eight invalid; on Articles 2 and 3 (the general principle of religious freedom) the vote was 2,000 for, 228 against, six invalid; on Articles 4 and 5 (freedom of religious communities and parental rights in religious education) the vote was 2,026 for, 206 against, four invalid; on Articles 6, 7, and 8 (care of religious freedom, its limits, and its responsible use) the vote was 2,034 for, 186 against, three invalid. The favorable outcome was overwhelming, but the two subsequent summary votes, which admitted the expression of reservation, made clear that a large number of Fathers were less than enthusiastic with the text. On Articles 1 to 5 taken together the vote was 1,539 for, 65 against, 543 for with reservation, and fourteen invalid; on Articles 6 to 8 the vote was 1,715 for, 68 against, 373 for with reservation, and five invalid.

There were five votes the next day on the last seven articles of the Declaration.[35] On Articles 9 and 10 (the roots of religious freedom in revelation and the freedom of the act of faith) the vote was 2,087 for, 146 against, and five invalid; on Articles 11 and 12 (the example of Christ and the Apostles and the practice of the Church) the vote was 1,979 for, 254 against, and five invalid; on Articles 13 to 15 (freedom of the Church, her duty, and conclusion) the vote was 2,107 for, 127 against, and five invalid. Again, the two subsequent summary votes, which admitted the expression of reservation, revealed that the overwhelmingly favorable votes on individual articles were deceptive. On Articles 9 to 12 taken together the vote was 1,751 for, 60 against, 417 for with reservation, and eight invalid; on Articles 13 to 15 the vote was 1,843 for, 47 against, 307 for with reservation, and five invalid.

Thus the Council approved the text of the Declaration, in whole and in each part, by more than the required two-thirds vote. Only specific amendments to the approved text were now permissible, and the large number of reservations expressed when the votes allowed indicated that they would not be lacking. Indeed, four thousand petitions proposed nearly six hundred revisions before the Secretariat completed the final text at the plenary sessions of November 8 and 9.[36]

Despite the number of amendments proposed, only fifty-nine changes were made in the final text, and of these only a few were of any significance.[37] In the introductory first article, after the opening recognition of the contemporary consciousness of human dignity, a new sentence was inserted: correlative to contemporary man's demand for freedom, he also demands that constitutional limits be set to the powers of government in order that there may be no encroachment on the rightful freedom of the person and of associations.[38] The final text thus asserted at the outset the constitutional context of religious freedom. By reinstating this sentence of the *textus emendatus,* the final text partially rescued the consitutional principle from the limbo to which it had been consigned in the *textus recognitus.*

Many Fathers were afraid that the first article's profession of the Church's role in the salvation of men and the corresponding duties of men toward the Church would make the Declaration less intelligible or less acceptable to non-Catholics. Indeed, the confession of faith did not seem either theoretically necessary to the subject of religious freedom or practically effective as a palliative to the conservative opposition in the Council. But the

Secretariat argued that, in a matter of such moment for the pastoral office of the Church, the Council ought to show clearly and sincerely how the moral duties toward the true religion remain to be fulfilled by the faithful when religious freedom is acknowledged. The Secretariat also felt bound by the vote of October 26 specifically accepting the whole of the first article.[39] At any rate, however inopportune, the confession of the Church's faith did not weaken the Declaration's affirmation of the principle of religious freedom or add to what non-Catholics already knew was integral to Catholic belief.

Many Fathers were concerned that the text appeared to approve a laicist attitude by governments toward religion, as if they ought not to care for that part of the common good which concerns the exercise of religion by citizens. To accommodate these Fathers, the Secretariat accepted two amendments.[40] First, while continuing to deny the competence of the state to direct or impede religious acts, the final text affirmed in Article 3 that governments ought indeed to take account of the religious life of the people and show it favor, since the function of government is to make provision for the common welfare.[41] This affirmation, of course, is deliberately vague; it does not make clear whether the government should merely aid religiously oriented activities performing secular functions and accommodate religious activities in specific circumstances when justified by equitable considerations indicating no intention to prefer religious belief over disbelief (*e.g.*, military chaplains), or whether governments should formally prefer belief over disbelief as a matter of general public policy. As from the beginning, the establishment question continued to brood over the Declaration on Religious Freedom, here in a more subtle form than the classic model of the confessional state.

Second, at the beginning of the section on the care of religious freedom (Article 6), the final text added an introduction: "The common welfare of society consists in the entirety of those conditions of social life under which men enjoy the possibility of achieving their own perfection in a certain fullness of measure and also with some relative ease" and "chiefly in the protection of the rights, and in the performance of the duties, of the human person."[42] This affirmation is a two-edged sword. The first edge, on the amplitude of the common good, serves to introduce the statement of the succeeding paragraph that governments ought to provide conditions favorable to the fostering of religious life. Again, this relation of government to religion is left deliberately ambiguous. The second edge, however, on the protection of human rights, makes abundantly clear that the right to religious freedom is an integral, indeed principal, part of the common good. Hence, whatever the government's role in fostering religious life, it must safeguard the right to religious freedom. By means of this two-edged affirmation, the text implicitly both disavowed the nineteenth-century concept of the "policeman state" and justified the narrow concept of public order as the only limit to the free exercise of religion.

To the section in Article 4 condemning "proselytism," or unworthy forms of religious propagation, the final text added a summary judgment: such a manner of acting would have to be considered an abuse of one's own right and a violation of the rights of others.[43] The final text accented the condemnation of "proselytism" in the hopes of calming the fears of bishops from lands of traditionally Catholic culture whose masses were uneducated. The text did not, however, clarify the ambiguous description of what was condemned as a dishonorable or unbecoming means of persuasion.

No significant change and only fourteen insignificant changes were introduced into the second chapter of the Declaration, on religious freedom in the light of revelation.[44] One hundred and seventy-seven Fathers had requested that the whole scriptural doctrine developed in Article 11 be either corrected or omitted because it was partisanly, sometimes infantilely, explained.[45] But the Secretariat judged that because the text of the article had been specifically accepted by the required two-thirds majority, it was not to be omitted.[46] Moreover, although Scripture does not directly speak of the doctrine on religious freedom, Christian revelation offers a remote foundation and leaven for the principle. The explanation, the Secretariat argued, is also of great value for dialogue with separated brothers, with whom Catholics share Scripture as a source of faith.[47]

On Wednesday, November 17, the final text on religious freedom was distributed to the Fathers, and the voting on the Secretariat's disposition of the amendments was scheduled for Friday,

November 19.[48] As scheduled, there were five votes Friday, four on individual parts and one on the whole of the final text.[49] On Articles 1 to 5 the vote was 1,989 for, 246 against, and seven invalid; on Articles 6 to 8 the vote was 1,957 for, 237 against, and six invalid; on Articles 9 to 12 the vote was 1,989 for, 217 against, and four invalid; on Articles 13 to 15 the vote was 2,033 for, 190 against, and five invalid; and on the whole text the vote was 1,954 for, 249 against, and thirteen invalid. The approval of the Declaration was again overwhelming; only the formal vote and promulgation remained before it was constituted an act of the Second Vatican Council.

The concluding formalities took place on Tuesday, December 7, 1965.[50] At a public session in Saint Peter's basilica, the Declaration on Religious Freedom achieved final passage (the vote was 2,308 for, 70 against, and eight invalid) and proclamation by Pope Paul VI. Thus after six conciliar texts, five years of conciliar gestation, four conciliar votes, and three conciliar debates, the Second Vatican Council formally adopted the Declaration on Religious Freedom. The Declaration was hardly an earth-shaking intellectual, political, or theological event; it only recognized the consensus of modern thought, national constitutions, and professional theologians on principles of religious freedom. Indeed, nineteen hundred and sixty-five, two-thirds of the way to the twenty-first century, seemed rather late to lay a nineteenth-century problem to rest. It is also true that the final text was neither perfect nor the best of the series of conciliar texts, especially in the construction of the argument for the principle of religious freedom. But the Declaration did strongly endorse religious freedom without ambiguity or quibble. There could be no doubt now in the mind of anyone where the Church stood on the question of religious freedom.

At the solemn closing ceremony of the Second Vatican Council on December 8, the Pope addressed messages to different groups.[51] The second, directed to rulers and read by Cardinal Liénart, referred specifically to the Declaration:

> In your earthly and temporal city, God constructs mysteriously His spiritual and eternal city, His Church. And what is it that this Church asks of you, after nearly two thousand years of all sorts of vicissitudes in her relations with you, the powers of the earth? What

does the Church ask of you today? In one of the major texts of the Council, she has told you: she asks of you nothing but freedom—the freedom to believe and to preach her faith, the freedom to love God and to serve Him, the freedom to live and to bring to men her message of life.[52]

The Church had always asked earthly powers for freedom to preach the gospel. Now the Church made clear that that was all she asked. This was an altogether fitting summary of the Declaration on Religious Freedom.

Notes

1. "Relatio, pars prima," *Schema de libertate religiosa* [*textus recognitus*] (Rome: Vatican Polyglot Press, 1965), p. 31.
2. Mimeographed by the Secretariat, the Murray files.
3. "Relatio," pp. 31–32.
4. *Textus recognitus*, p. 3.
5. "Relatio," p. 25.
6. *Textus*, p. 3.
7. *Ibid.*, p. 4.
8. *Ibid.*, pp. 4–11.
9. *Ibid.*, p. 4.
10. *Ibid.*, p. 5.
11. *Ibid.*
12. *Ibid.*
13. *Ibid.*, pp. 5–6.
14. *Ibid.*, p. 7.
15. On October 5 Murray suffered a lung collapse, which forced him to the sidelines of subsequent Secretariat deliberations on drafting the *textus recognitus*. Murray discounts as highly improbable that he would have had much influence on the *textus recognitus* even if he had been present at all the Secretariat deliberations. In any event, Murray did return to action in time to consider the petitions for final revision of the Declaration.
16. *Textus*, pp. 7–8.
17. *Ibid.*, p. 8.
18. *Ibid.*, p. 9.
19. *Ibid.*
20. *Ibid.*, p. 10.
21. *Ibid.*, p. 11.

22. *Ibid.*

23. *Ibid.*, pp. 11–17.

24. *Ibid.*, pp. 11–12.

25. *Ibid.*, p. 12.

26. *Ibid.*, pp. 12–13.

27. *Ibid.*, pp. 13–14.

28. *Ibid.*, pp. 14–15.

29. *Ibid.*, pp. 15–17.

30. "Relatio, pars altera," p. 66. Cf. the October 5 draft of the *textus recognitus*, pp. 14–15. (Mimeographed by the Secretariat, the Murray files.)

31. Xavier Rynne, *The Fourth Session*, pp. 172.

32. *Ibid.*, p. 174. The text was distributed on October 22. See Pavan, "The Declaration on Religious Freedom," *Information Documentation on the Conciliar Church*, Doss. LXVI–XXVIII (November 30, 1966), p. 1.

33. Rynne, pp. 175–76.

34. "Expensio modorum, pars prima," *Schema declarationis de libertate religiosa: modi et textus* [*denuo recognitus*] (Rome: Vatican Polyglot Press, 1965), p. 25. There is a typographical error on the fifth vote (534 for 543); cf. Rynne, p. 175.

35. "Expensio modorum, pars altera" [*textus denuo recognitus*], p. 64.

36. For the dates of the Secretariat plenary sessions, see "Expensio modorum, pars prima," p. 26. Copies of the proposed amendments, duplicated by the Secretariat, are in the Murray files.

37. "Elenchus modorum acceptorum," [*textus denuo recognitus*], pp. 81–85.

38. *Textus denuo recognitus*, p. 5; Appendix I, p. 186. Cf. *textus emendatus*, p. 3.

39. "Relatio" [*textus denuo recognitus*], p. 22.

40. *Ibid.*

41. *Textus*, p. 7; Appendix I, p. 190.

42. *Ibid.*, p. 8; Appendix I, p. 192.

43. *Ibid.*, Appendix I, p. 191.

44. *Ibid.*, pp. 10–13; Appendix I, pp. 194–199.

45. Amendment ML-11, 3. (Duplicated by the Secretariat, the Murray files.)

46. "Expensio modorum, pars altera," p. 68.

47. "Relatio," p. 21.

48. Rynne, p. 245.

49. *Ibid.*, p. 247.

50. *Ibid.*, p. 250.

51. *The Documents of Vatican II*, pp. 728–37.

52. *Ibid.*, p. 730.

X

Religious Freedom: Retrospect and Prospect

THE DECLARATION ON RELIGIOUS FREEDOM had to travel a long, rough, and winding road before December 7, 1965. On the one hand, the conservative opposition was formidable; it made up for lack of numbers by well-placed position and cohesion. On the other, the liberal majority was deeply split on how to articulate a rationale for the principle of religious freedom; four different schools of thought vied for primacy in the argument. The task of drafting a statement on religious freedom was further complicated by different conceptions of the purpose of a statement on religious freedom. Although all the proposed conciliar texts defined religious freedom as immunity from coercion, many bishops and theologians wanted to do more than lay the nineteenth-century constitutional problem to rest. Indeed, especially at and between the Third and Fourth Sessions of the Council, the division of the majority delayed approval of the Declaration far more than the arguments or maneuvers of the conservative opposition.

The conservative argument was quite simple. On the level of theory, the conservatives argued that society no less than the individual must worship and serve God as He wishes to be worshiped and served. Since the Catholic Church is the unique instrument of God's plan for salvation, a "Catholic" state must, under ideal conditions, protect its citizens from religious error by the use of its coercive power. Therefore the "Catholic" state cannot accept as a matter of principle the right of all individuals and groups to the freedom of religious exercise; it can only tolerate public non-Catholic religious exercises as a matter of practice. On the level of authority, the conservatives cited the many statements of the nineteenth-century papacy adverse to the principle of religious freedom, distinguished the relevant statements of Pius XII, and argued against the liberal interpretation of John XXIII's dictum in *Pacem in terris*.

The conservatives' paternal concept of political society failed to distinguish the secular from the sacred and the state from society. Moreover their appeal to papal authority was both too literal minded with respect to the nineteenth-century papacy and too strained with respect to Pius XII and John XXIII. The conservatives did not lack intelligence; they lacked historical consciousness. Because they themselves were more historically conditioned than they realized, they did not recognize the evolution of human institutions and human consciousness in the Church as well as political society. Happily, the conservative thesis never commended itself to even a sizable minority.

As for the liberal majority, there were four basic lines of argument. The first sought to establish the principle of religious freedom from the right and duty to follow conscience. Conservatives and many liberals contended that this argument constituted an illicit transition from the subjective world of individual conscience to the objective world of social interaction. An argument for religious freedom must prove not only the right of the individual not to be compelled to act against his conscience, but also his right not to be impeded from acting according to conscience. The argument for religious freedom from the right and duty to follow conscience clearly raises the question of whether an individual's action is in fact good or bad for society, and without appeal to the objective realities of man's personal dignity as a free agent and the corresponding constitutional limitation of the state in matters of religion is vulnerable to the conservative thesis that religious error harms the common good. Moreover, the argument does not give any ground for the insincere conscience to claim a right to religious freedom, invites the state to judge which consciences are sincere, and thus risks making religious freedom a concession from the state rather than a right. The argument from the right and duty to follow conscience was central to the first two conciliar texts.

Indeed, the second text seemed to call the dictate of a sincere conscience a divine call. To this argument the two texts coupled another argument from the freedom required by the act of faith, but the latter was admittedly inadequate to establish the right to freedom of religious exercise.

The third text introduced a sharply different line of argument, based on the dignity of the human person and the corresponding constitutional principle of the state's incompetence in matters of religion. Since the subjective state of conscience is irrelevant to the dignity of the person, the principal argument of the third text is applicable to all men. Conscious of the social and political context of human freedoms, the third text was particularly concerned to establish the general right to act in society according to conscience as well as the right not to be coerced to act against conscience, which even the conservative opposition conceded. The fourth text, although restructured, adopted the same perspective.

While the specific objections to the argument from the right and duty to follow conscience could not be brought against the main argument of the third and fourth texts, the latter was subjected to attacks both from the conservative opposition and from many liberals. In addition to their other, fundamental objections to any affirmation of the principle of religious freedom, conservative opponents condemned the implication of the third text's denial of competence to the state in religious matters for the question of legal establishment. Many liberals also feared that the constitutional argument of the third and fourth texts limited too severely the state's interest in promoting religious values in society. Moreover, many liberals thought the argument too political and legal; they complained specifically that the argument was not theological, that the appeal to Scripture did not enjoy its rightful primacy. The so-called French view proposed as an alternative that the Declaration begin with the scriptural and patristic doctrine on the freedom of man and then offer arguments for religious freedom from reason. In this view, the Declaration ought to speak out of the treasury of Catholic teaching by proclaiming the truth on the freedom of man from the riches of Holy Scripture rather than by arguing elaborately and principally from reason.

There were many difficulties with the method and argument proposed by the French critics. Although religious freedom is connected with the general freedom of man and the freedom of the sons of God, it is not identical with these and requires its own argument. The scriptural doctrine on the dignity of man and his freedom by God's grace is for the believer deeper than that which is open to reason, but there is evidently a great difference between the scriptural doctrine and the contemporary concept of religious freedom. Civil freedom of religious exercise may be demanded by the freedom proclaimed in the word of God, but it cannot be deduced in any formal way from the latter as a juridical consequence. Moreover, since the Council wanted to speak to all men, not only the Christian faithful, when it spoke on religious freedom, it could not ignore the fact that contemporary man understands the question best as one formally juridical, political, and ethical, a question to be solved by rational arguments confirmed by experience. For these reasons, the French critics' line of argument was never adopted by a majority of the Secretariat or the Council.

A fourth line of argument, from man's right and duty to seek truth, was proposed by Colombo and Ancel, introduced into the third and fourth texts in a subordinate position, and given primacy in the fifth and final texts. But this argument will not establish the right of all men to religious freedom if it is not fixed in a social and political context, since it must conclude to the right to communicate what is in fact false, or even known to be false, and to the right of a complacent man to communicate his religious views, whether true or false. To be convincing, the argument must rely on the fact that search for truth, as social dialogue and exchange, requires the political condition of freedom. Only in this context may *every* man claim, within the limits of public order, a right to immunity in all expression that concerns the order of truth, and religious truth in particular. The argument for religious freedom from the right and duty to search for truth thus must have recourse to the constitutional principle of the limited competence of government in relation to the quest for values proper to the human spirit. Fortunately, despite the primacy of the fourth line of argument in the Declaration, the constitutional principle was never deleted and was at least partially restored in the final text.

There was, of course, the tantalizing alternative of affirming the principle of religious freedom without elaboration and without argument. At first sight this appeared to have the merit of uniting all factions of the liberal majority behind the principle, leaving the articulation of arguments to theologians. But it became less attractive as the tenacity and subtlety of the conservative opposition became manifest. The Council could ill afford the appearance of compromise or equivocation if it wished to convince men of good will of the Church's commitment to human freedom. Hence elaboration and argument was judged necessary.

The final Declaration was the product of compromise. The first line of argument, from the right and duty to follow conscience, was represented, although in a subsidiary rather than a central role; the second line of argument, based on the constitutional principle, was also represented, although not as centrally as in the third and fourth texts; the third line of argument, from Scripture, constituted the entire lengthy second chapter, although it did not enjoy the primacy; the fourth line of argument, from the right and duty to seek truth, of course, held undisputed first place, in both position and the number of lines devoted to it, although the other lines of argument were also included. Whatever the compromises in the composition of the Declaration's argument, however, its affirmation of the principle of religious freedom is absolutely unequivocal. Now there can only be question of the Church's growth in understanding the meaning of religious freedom and its concrete application to complex situations.

Despite the clarity of the Declaration's affirmation of the principle of religious freedom, there are a number of ambiguities in its application of the principle. First, the Declaration's condemnation of "proselytism," that is, the use of unworthy means in spreading a religious faith, is couched in unspecific and nonobjective language. To condemn "any manner of action which might seem to carry a hint of coercion or of a kind of persuasion that would be dishonorable or unworthy" is to offer a pretext for the abuse of religious freedom to public authorities so disposed.[1] The Declaration would have done better if it specifically condemned slander, libel, deceit, bribes, threats, etc. Such a condemnation would not be open to the abuse to which the actual text is vulnerable.

Second, the Declaration does not touch the question of the right of governments to act as *parens patriae* in the religious interests of the illiterate masses who are a regrettable reality in certain areas of traditionally Catholic culture.[2] The Declaration is concerned with freedom of religious exercise in a society in which citizens have attained a minimum level of intellectual consciousness, not with the "hard case" of primitive masses in certain countries. Still, if the state has no competence in religious matters, and if religious groups employ no slander, libel, deceit, bribes, threats, etc., to spread their faiths, it is difficult to see how the state has any legitimate interest as *parens patriae* to justify action in behalf of the religious faith of the illiterate.

Third, the Declaration's limitation of religious exercise by the requirements of "public order" requires analogous application to different societies. Although the text's limiting concept of public order is relatively clear, objective, and specific, it obviously has different import for paternal than for democratic societies. What might disturb public peace in Franco's Spain would not necessarily do so in the United States. In addition, as questions of public policy on birth control in this country amply demonstrate, matters of public morality can involve religious as well as purely rational perspectives.

Fourth, the Declaration carefully avoids any commitment on the question of legal establishment. It insists only that if special legal recognition is given to one religion, it must be given without any legal intolerance of other religions.[3] One may argue that legal establishment is inconsistent with the equal dignity of persons and the incompetence of the state in religious matters, but the Declaration does not make the argument. The text does, however, at least make clear that the institution of establishment is the product of historical circumstance, not a matter of theological doctrine.

Related to the question of legal establishment is that of financial and other assistance to religious activities. On this question, the Declaration is deliberately vague: governments ought "to take account of the religious life of the people and show it favor," and "to help create conditions favorable to the fostering of religious life."[4] These comments imply that governments are to do more than safeguard the religious freedom of all their citizens. But what? The possibilities range from financial aid to religiously oriented institutions performing secular functions and accommodation of expressly religious activities in specific circumstances where there is implied no preference of one religion over another or of belief over disbelief to legally institutionalized preference of religion and general, proportionately equal, subsidies to the religious activities of all faiths. For obvious reasons, the conciliar Declaration chose to avoid this political thicket of church-state relations.

From the beginning, it was evident that the Declaration's affirmation of the principle of religious freedom posed a difficult problem in the development of doctrine, since no one could deny the *prima-facie* adverse position of the nineteenth-century papacy on the issue. Of course, from the purely juridical point of view, the Church had never definitively accepted the nineteenth-century papal position and could, therefore, reverse that position without abandoning any article of faith. Such an observation is accurate enough but radically inadequate; it ignores the dynamic historical process in which and through which the Church progressively articulates her consciousness of the word of God.

Indeed, the contrast between the teaching of John XXIII and the teaching of Leo XIII on religious freedom is no more startling than the contrast between the teaching of Leo and that of Boniface VIII on the relation of the temporal and spiritual powers. In the famous bull *Unam sanctam*, Boniface argued that temporal power was in the hands of kings "at the nod and sufferance of the priest," that temporal authority is subject to the spiritual power, and that the spiritual power has the right to institute and judge terrestrial power.[5] Indeed, Boniface told the envoys of Albert of Hapsburg in April of the year following *Unam sanctam* that "no earthly power has anything except what it receives from the ecclesiastical power," and that "all powers . . . are from Us, as the Vicar of Jesus Christ."[6] Leo XIII explicitly rejected this medieval conception of relations between Church and state. Leo clearly distinguished between the spiritual and temporal societies and insisted on the "excellence and nobleness" of each:

The Almighty, therefore, has given charge of the human race to two powers, the ecclesiastical and the civil, the one being set over divine, and the other human things. Each in its kind is supreme, each has fixed limits within which it is contained, limits which are defined by the nature and special object of the province of each, so that there is, we may say, an orbit traced out within which the action of each is brought into play by its own native right.[7]

Like Boniface, Leo used historically conditioned theological language to implement the teaching of doctrinal truth. Boniface was contesting the caesaropapism of Philip the Fair, and Leo the absolute autonomy of the individual conscience and the juridical omnipotence of the state proposed by the nineteenth-century Latin liberals. But the theologies employed by both were defective, although historically intelligible. In the context of the political ideology of the *respublica Christiana* and the accepted authenticity of the spurious Donation of Constantine, Boniface failed to distinguish the autonomy of the secular order; in the context of paternalism, Leo failed to distinguish the state from society and to draw the necessary conclusion for Church-and-state relations from the admitted autonomy of the secular order. With the historical evolution of human consciousness, the inadequacy and inaccuracy of the theologies of both Leo and Boniface became evident. Leo recognized the defects of Boniface's theology. (Pius XII openly labeled Boniface's theology a "medieval conception . . . conditioned by the times."[8]) The Declaration on Religious Freedom goes a step further and recognizes the inadequacy and inaccuracy of Leo's theology.

Like all things human, the Church is subject to the law of growth; like all human consciousness, the Church grows in and through the historical process. This means that the present has both continuity and discontinuity with the past. Against the argument of the conservative opposition to the Declaration from the papal statements of the last century, the liberal majority understandably stressed the elements of continuity. Now, with the need for polemic past, it is possible to recognize fully the radical discontinuities, even contradictions, in the life of the pilgrim Church on the issue of religious freedom. In view of the depth of these discontinuities, it is fair to describe this growth in the Church's consciousness as a genuine evolution, *i.e.*, not merely a linear increase of understanding but a passage from one discrete stage of thought to another without apparent logical connections. The Declaration on Religious Freedom acknowledged this historical growth of human consciousness in its opening paragraph: "A sense of the dignity of the human person has been impressing itself more and more deeply on the consciousness of contemporary man" and "the demand is increasingly made that men should act on their own judgment, enjoying . . . a responsible freedom."[9] The Council not only took note of contemporary man's desire for freedom; it also specifically approved that desire in the matter of religious exercise.

To rest content with a retrospective history and critique of the Declaration on Religious Freedom would be a mistake. Of course, such a history and critique is necessary, and it is the focus of this work. But to fail to look forward to the Declaration's import for the present and the future would abdicate the creative role of intelligence, return theology to its preconciliar state of merely annotating magisterial statements, and frustrate the spirit of *aggiornamento*, which was the chief aim of the Council. The Declaration laid to rest a nineteenth-century polemic; it accepted belatedly, well beyond the middle of the twentieth century, civilized man's long-standing contemporary consciousness of the value of religious freedom. The task now before the Church is to confront new moments of history, not to replay a recording of her own voice. Indeed, the Declaration itself is a symbol of the change to which the Church must be always open.

The most obvious case of contemporary concern is with the acceptance and the implementation of the Declaration by the governments of those nations of traditionally Catholic culture which have up to the present denied the right of non-Catholics to the full freedom of religious exercise. The Spanish government has drafted a new law which purports to guarantee the right of all religious groups to religious freedom, public and private, subject only to the necessities of public order.[10] Although this action is long overdue, and although the proposed law would maintain or impose many unnecessary and odious restraints on the freedom of non-Catholic religious groups in the name of "public order," it will, when consummated and enforced, go far to liquidate the most offensive instance of restrictions on the religious freedom of non-Catholics by "Catholic" states. The world, Catholic and non-Catholic, looks forward to adoption and enforcement of the proposed law's liberal features, but must regret that the compliance of the Spanish government with the conciliar Declaration on Religious Freedom will be inadequate even when the new law is in force.

With the attitude of Catholics toward the basic issue of freedom of religious exercise no longer in doubt, conflict among religious groups is likely to center on public morals. This conflict will involve not only "Catholic" nations but also other nations whose code of public morality still reflects the consensus of the last century. A century ago, except for attitudes in the United States toward gambling and drinking, Catholics and non-Catholics were scarcely distinguishable in their code of public morals; today, of course, they differ on many socially important moral questions, e.g., divorce, abortion. As non-Catholics press for the liberalization of existing legislation in matters of public morals, there is likelihood of sharp conflict between non-Catholics and Catholics. If Catholics resist proposed reforms, they may be charged with seeking to impose their religious views of morality on non-Catholics.

Such a charge would be an oversimplification of a complex issue. Catholics have as much right to resist proposals for liberalization which they deem harmful to the moral ethos of the community as non-Catholics have to press for those that they deem necessary or timely. But the argument must be rational. Catholics must hear and weigh the reasons advanced for revising the community's moral judgment and especially for reforming coercive legislation which deals with matters of public morality. Human law, as a determination of practical reason, must take full measure of the evolution of human society and human consciousness, the inherent ambiguity of many moral questions, the possibility of enforcing coercive legislation, the weakness of human nature, and the consensus of a people.

On the other side of the equation, citizens must weigh the magnitude of the dangers which prompt coercive action. The state should be especially zealous to prohibit acts which deprive other citizens of what is rightfully theirs. Thus the state should protect the rights of each citizen to his life, liberty, and property. Just how much beyond this the state should go will depend. Some restrictions, of course, will be required of actions (e.g. divorce, polygamy, consumption of alcohol, solicitation) which prove seriously harmful or a serious nuisance to the commonwealth, even when the actions do not necessarily deprive others of their rights. But what restrictions of which activities should depend on how widespread the activity is and how bad the results are. No magic formula will offer a substitute for the painstaking effort of human prudence.

The difficulties inherent in political dialogue on a code of public morality illustrate the more general political problem left unfinished by an affirmation of the principle of religious freedom. Since religious freedom is essentially negative in concept, the positive task of forging political unity among citizens of different religious persuasions remains. Here the quickening spirit of religious charity and the exacting exercise of political reason is required. There is a deeper harmony of godly and brotherly love which Catholics and non-Catholics must achieve. They must overcome through charity and reason their religious and ideological separation from one another; they must move out of isolation into communication, out of estrangement into understanding, and out of hostility into cooperation. This harmony is the unfinished and never finished work to which all men of good will, as citizens of a common city, must aspire.

As a result of current movements of social protest in the United States and the prominent participation of clerics and religious, the American political community is confronting a new dimension of the age-old problem of asserted rights to disobey laws in the name of conscience. Citizens in Western society have long reserved the right to disobey laws deemed unjust and, ultimately, to revolt against a government deemed tyrannical when the degree of injustice to self or fellow citizens outweighs the consequences of resistance to other individuals or to society. What is new in the contemporary American scene is the asserted right to disobey an admittedly just law in order to protest another law or system of laws deemed unjust. The calculus of casuistry necessary in these cases of civil disobedience is similar to that of the more traditional cases of disobeying allegedly unjust laws and revolting against tyranny: the degree of alleged injustice in a law or system of laws must be weighed against the cost of particular acts of disobedience to individual citizens and to the community, including the disvalue of encouraging disobedience to all law. Such a calculus is outside the focus of this work and requires a special study of its own.

The Declaration does explicitly mark and encourage the religious responsibility of citizens for the society in which they live: "Religious freedom . . . ought to have this further purpose and aim, namely, that men may come to act with greater responsibility in fulfilling their duties in community life."[11] Of course, the Declaration does not consider specifically the phenomenon of civil disobedience; it would have been inappropriate for the Council of the universal Church in its statement on the general subject of religious freedom to comment on the peculiar problem of the United States. But this problem is clearly pertinent to the Declaration's affirmation of the right to act according to conscience in religious matters and its invitation to the religious consciences of men to exercise social concern.

The Declaration's qualification that conscience act responsibly can be applied to cases of civil disobedience: prudence is necessary on the part of individuals participating in acts of civil disobedience and on the part of society judging these acts. Individuals cannot appeal to the rights of conscience as a formula of absolution from their obligation as citizens to justify rationally disobedience of society's laws. On the other hand, society cannot simply appeal to citizens' general obligations to obey legal prescriptions without weighing the actuality and degree of the injustice alleged by the civil disobedients. In any case, clerics and religious can claim no special charism exempting them from the obligation of justifying rationally their disobedience. Still less can they plead "benefit of clergy" if society disallows particular acts of civil disobedience.

The Declaration on Religious Freedom blesses the modern transition of the last two centuries from sacral to secular society. Before the American and French revolutions, the sacral concept of society dominated the Christian era in various forms: the Roman and successor empires, medieval Christendom, the post-Reformation confessional states, and the absolute monarchies. But by the end of the nineteenth century the demise of sacral society in the Western world was sealed. The new secularity distinguished sharply between the terrestrial order of human endeavor and the transcendent order of divine initiative.

The Church was slow to recognize the validity of this transition because of the guise which the idea of secularity assumed in the course of its historical realization in Latin Europe. Indeed, nineteenth-century Latin liberals sought to substitute an antisacral, not merely a secular, society for the sacral society of the *ancien régime*. Yet, for all their limitations, the liberals of the last century were working to realize a genuine advance for human society. Even Leo XIII acknowledged this development though he was undoubtedly unconscious of its full meaning, by distinguishing clearly the origin, jurisdiction, and responsibilities of the temporal and spiritual societies. Happily, the Declaration on Religious Freedom ratifies the evolution of human society and human consciousness toward secularity and all its consequences.

The Declaration denies the central principle of sacral society, *viz.*, that a government is in any sense defender of a people's faith. On the contrary, it affirms the right of all persons and groups to freedom of religious exercise and even insists that governments must protect and promote this freedom. Religious freedom is thus declared not only a sacred but also a secular value, and that is why governments are called on to guarantee and defend it. Unlike the nineteenth-century Latin liberals, who tended to consider religious exercise in society hostile to secular values, the Declaration affirms that religious exercise in society complements and strengthens secular values. More important, it affirms that religious freedom, as a freedom of the human person, is a proper secular value and a paramount concern of the secular order.

The Declaration also repudiates the sacral concept of society in several other respects. As indicated above, it admits legal establishment of a particular religion only in the context of religious freedom for all and as a matter of historical circumstance. It further disavows the sacral concept of society by asserting that the "freedom of the Church is the fundamental principle in what concerns the relations between the Church and governments and the whole civil order,"[12] not merely a necessary condition, as the conservative thesis maintained. Speaking to those charged with the authority and responsibility of governing the nations of the world, Pope Paul VI emphasized the centrality of this dictum in the Declaration: the Church asks of the powers of the earth only freedom![13] Where the medieval *respublica Christiana* made government a sacral function, the Church today asks of government only the freedom to carry out her mission within secular society.

In one aspect of the distinction between the secular and sacral orders, however, the Declaration is silent. It states clearly the incompetence of the state in matters of religion, but it does not explicitly disavow the competence of the Church in matters of the secular order. Of course, the sacral order has the right and obligation to judge the morality of governmental policies and practices and to press for social justice. But it can claim no privileged insight into the solution of practical problems of the secular order. This is the sole responsibility of citizens in rational dialogue. The Constitution on the Church expressly makes this point, which the Declaration on Religious Freedom only implies: "It must be recognized that the temporal sphere is governed by its own principles."[14]

With the basic work of differentiating the sacral and secular orders effected in history and blessed by the Church, a new, more formidable task of synthesis confronts Christians, who are members of both orders. The secular must be distinguished from the sacred, but they must also be integrated in the thought and action of citizens whose destiny transcends the earthly city. In the sacral society this process of integration was so total that it confused the identity of the two orders; in the secular society a new synthesis is necessary which will respect the proper independence and autonomy of each. The integrity of the believer as a rational human being requires the effort. To decline it would invite intellectual and practical schizophrenia. Indeed, the Constitution on the Church strongly commends this search for harmony: "Because the very plan of salvation requires it, the faithful should learn how to distinguish carefully between those rights and duties which are theirs as members of the Church and those which are theirs as members of human society. Let them strive to harmonize the two, remembering that in every temporal affair they must be guided by a Christian conscience."[15]

Not only is the Declaration on Religious Freedom significant for the secular order, it also has meaning for the internal life of the Church. Although the Declaration nowhere treats explicitly freedom in the Church, and one introductory report disclaimed any intention to treat the subject,[16] it stands as symbol of change, a recognition of the historical evolution of human institutions and human consciousness. In this context the Church's affirmation of the value of freedom in the polity is bound to influence the evolution of freedom in the Church herself. The relation of freedom to authority clearly depends on the nature of the community involved. Since the Church and the polity are communities with different, if complementary, goals, the relation of freedom to authority in the one cannot be applied without distinction to the other. But since freedom is a value inherent in the dignity of the human person, it must exist in every community as far as possible.

The Constitution on the Church affirms "the dignity and freedom of the sons of God, in whose hearts the Holy Spirit dwells as in His temple."[17] As the People of God, "they have the same filial grace and the same vocation to perfection," and the layman "by reason of the knowledge, competence, or outstanding ability which he may enjoy, is permitted and sometimes even obliged to express his opinion on things which concern the good of the Church."[18] The Decree on the Laity expands on the latter, somewhat condescending, invitation to lay freedom of thought and action in the life of the Church:

> . . . the Holy Spirit, who sanctifies the People of God through the ministry and the sacraments, gives to the faithful special gifts as well. . . . From the reception of these charisms, or gifts, including those which are less dramatic, there arise for each believer the right and the duty to use them in the Church and in the world for the good of mankind and for the upbuilding of the Church. In so doing, believers need to enjoy the freedom of the Holy Spirit, "who breathes where he wills" (Jn. 3:8).[19]

But "they must act in communion with their brothers in Christ, especially with their pastors."[20]

There's the rub. What are the functions of authority in the postconciliar Church? The Council indeed reasserted the horizontal, interpersonal lines of community and recognized that the vertical, juridical lines of superior-subject are inadequate to express the reality of the Church as the People of God. Yet authority still has essential functions in the Church because the People of God is a community: bishops must preach the word of God, preside over the worship and sacramental life of the Christian people, and guide the community in the way of salvation. In carrying out these functions, authority must stimulate reflection on the faith of the Christian community and direct through dialogue the Christian work of witness and service. But if stimulating Christian reflection and directing Christian work belong to the role of authority in the Church, restraint will also be found necessary in the progress of the pilgrim Church toward the heavenly Jerusalem according to the universally valid principle of as much freedom as possible and only as much restraint as necessary. Indeed, necessary or unnecessary, restraint is a regrettable consequence of human limitations and sinfulness, conditions not restricted to either laity or clergy. The possibilities of unnecessary restraint, however, could be narrowed by institutionalizing quasi-judicial agencies to arbitrate certain areas of conflict between freedom and authority within the Church.

The Declaration on Religious Freedom has an exemplary import for freedom in the Church as well as an ideological rapport with it. Liberal Catholic voices, especially in France, were heard even in the nineteenth century: Montalambert, Dupanloup, and Acton argued their case within the Church for the principle of religious freedom, and to all appearances lost. But the dissent from the "official" thesis of the nineteenth-century papacy not only swelled to a crescendo by the middle of the twentieth century, it also enjoyed the intellectual leadership of philosophers like Maritain and theologians like Murray. Indeed, a non-Catholic observer noted before the Council that "it would be an understatement to say that, for one book or article in favor of the traditional doctrine, ten have been published defending . . . religious freedom."[21] This long-suffering chorus of dissent within the Church was vindicated in the Declaration. As a result, dissenters in other matters of theological opinion are more likely to find an open forum of expression.

If the Second Vatican Council closed one chapter of the Church's history with the Declaration on Religious Freedom, it opened another. To the problems of freedom now facing Church and state, Christian citizens must bring the spirit of religious charity and a commitment to rational dialogue.

Notes

1. Declaration on Religious Freedom, Article 4; Appendix I, p. 191.
2. See John C. Murray, S.J., "La Declaration sur la Liberté religieuse," *Nouvelle Revue Théologique*, January 1966, p. 67.
3. Declaration, Article 6; Appendix I, p. 192.
4. Declaration, Articles 3 and 6; Appendix I, pp. 190 and 192.
5. *Enchiridion Symbolorum, Definitionum et Declarationum de rebus fidei et morum*, eds. Henry Denzinger *et al.* (33rd ed.; Freiburg im Breisgau: Herder, 1965), p. 280.
6. *Monumenta Germaniae historica*, Leges, sect. IV, tom. IV, part 1, p. 139.
7. Leo XIII, *Immortale Dei*, ASS, LV (1885), p. 166; the translation is from *The Church Speaks to the Modern World: The Social Teachings of Leo XIII*, ed. Etienne Gilson, p. 167.
8. Pius XII, Address to the 10th International Congress of Historical Studies, AAS, XLVII (1955), p. 678.
9. Declaration, Article 1; Appendix I, p. 187.
10. See *The New York Times*, November 23, 1966, p. 1. For indications of restrictive features in the proposed Spanish law on religious freedom, see *America*, January 7, 1967, and *The National Catholic Reporter*, February 15, 1967, p. 5.
11. Declaration, Article 8; Appendix I, p. 194.
12. Declaration, Article 13; Appendix I, p. 197.
13. Paul VI, Closing Message to Rulers, *The Documents of Vatican II*, p. 730.
14. Dogmatic Constitution on the Church, Article 36; *Documents*, p. 63.
15. *Ibid.*
16. See "Relatio, pars altera," [*textus recognitus*], p. 74. According to Murray, this disavowal expressed the will of the Pope, which was communicated to the Secretariat by Colombo.
17. Dogmatic Constitution, Article 9; *Documents*, p. 25.
18. Dogmatic Constitution, Articles 32 and 37; *Documents*, pp. 58 and 64.
19. Decree on the Apostolate of the Laity, Article 3; *Documents*, pp. 492–93.
20. *Ibid.*
21. A. F. Carillo de Albornoz, *Roman Catholicism and Religious Liberty* (Geneva: World Council of Churches, 1959), p. 8.

Appendix I

DECLARATION ON RELIGIOUS FREEDOM*

On the Right of the Person and of Communities to Social and Civil Freedom in Matters Religious

1. A sense of the dignity of the human person has been impressing itself more and more deeply on the consciousness of contemporary man.[1] And the demand is increasingly made that men should act on their own judgment, enjoying and making use of a responsible freedom, not driven by coercion but motivated by a sense of duty. The demand is also made that constitutional limits should be set to the powers of government, in order that there may be no encroachment on the rightful freedom of the person and of associations. This demand for freedom in human society chiefly regards the quest for the values proper to the human spirit. It regards, in the first place, the free exercise of religion in society. This Vatican Synod takes careful note of these desires in the minds of men. It proposes to declare them to be greatly in accord with truth and justice. To this end, it searches into the sacred tradition and doctrine of the Church—the treasury out of which the Church continually brings forth new things that are in harmony with the things that are old.

First, this sacred Synod professes its belief that God Himself has made known to mankind the way in which men are to serve Him, and thus be saved in Christ and come to blessedness. We believe that this one true religion subsists in the catholic and

---

* The translation is that of Fr. John Courtney Murray, S.J., from *The Documents of Vatican II*, eds. Walter M. Abbot, S.J., and Joseph Gallagher (New York: America, 1966), pp. 675–96.

apostolic Church, to which the Lord Jesus committed the duty of spreading it abroad among all men. Thus He spoke to the Apostles: "Go, therefore, and make disciples of all nations, baptizing them in the name of the Father, and of the Son, and of the Holy Spirit, teaching them to observe all that I have commanded you" (Matt. 28: 19–20). On their part, all men are bound to seek the truth, especially in what concerns God and His Church, and to embrace the truth they come to know, and to hold fast to it.

This sacred Synod likewise professes its belief that it is upon the human conscience that these obligations fall and exert their binding force. The truth cannot impose itself except by virtue of its own truth, as it makes its entrance into the mind at once quietly and with power. Religious freedom, in turn, which men demand as necessary to fulfill their duty to worship God, has to do with immunity from coercion in civil society. Therefore it leaves untouched traditional Catholic doctrine on the moral duty of men and societies toward the true religion and toward the one Church of Christ. Over and above all this, in taking up the matter of religious freedom, this sacred Synod intends to develop the doctrine of recent popes on the inviolable rights of the human person and on the constitutional order of society.

Chapter I

GENERAL PRINCIPLE OF RELIGIOUS FREEDOM

2. This Vatican Synod declares that the human person has a right to religious freedom. This freedom means that all men are to be immune from coercion on the part of individuals or of social groups and of any human power, in such wise that in matters religious no one is to be forced to act in a manner contrary to his own beliefs. Nor is anyone to be restrained from acting in accordance with his own beliefs, whether privately or publicly, whether alone or in association with others, within due limits. The Synod further declares that the right to religious freedom has its foundation in the very dignity of the human person, as this dignity is known through the revealed word of God and by

reason itself.[2] This right of the human person to religious freedom is to be recognized in the constitutional law whereby society is governed. Thus it is to become a civil right.

It is in accordance with their dignity as persons—that is, beings endowed with reason and free will and therefore privileged to bear personal responsibility—that all men should be at once impelled by nature and also bound by a moral obligation to seek the truth, especially religious truth. They are also bound to adhere to the truth, once it is known, and to order their whole lives in accord with the demands of truth. However, men cannot discharge these obligations in a manner in keeping with their own nature unless they enjoy immunity from external coercion as well as psychological freedom. Therefore the right to religious freedom has its foundation not in the subjective disposition of the person, but in his very nature. In consequence the right to this immunity continues to exist even in those who do not live up to their obligation of seeking the truth and adhering to it. Nor is the exercise of this right to be impeded, provided that the just requirements of public order are observed.

3. Further light is shed on the subject if one considers that the highest norm of human life is the divine law—eternal, objective, and universal—whereby God orders, directs, and governs the entire universe and all the ways of the human community, by a plan conceived in wisdom and love. Man has been made by God to participate in this law, with the result that, under the gentle disposition of divine Providence, he can come to perceive ever increasingly the unchanging truth. Hence every man has the duty, and therefore the right, to seek the truth in matters religious, in order that he may with prudence form for himself right and true judgments of conscience, with the use of all suitable means.

Truth, however, is to be sought after in a manner proper to the dignity of the human person and his social nature. The inquiry is to be free, carried on with the aid of teaching or instruction, communication, and dialogue. In the course of these, men explain to one another the truth they have discovered, or think they have discovered, in order thus to assist one another in the quest for truth. Moreover, as the truth is discovered, it is by a personal assent that men are to adhere to it.

On his part, man perceives and acknowledges the imperatives of the divine law through the mediation of conscience. In all his activity a man is bound to follow his conscience faithfully, in order that he may come to God, for whom he was created. It follows that he is not to be forced to act in a manner contrary to his conscience. Nor, on the other hand, is he to be restrained from acting in accordance with his conscience, especially in matters religious. For, of its very nature, the exercise of religion consists before all else in those internal, voluntary, and free acts whereby man sets the course of his life directly toward God. No merely human power can either command or prohibit acts of this kind.[3] However, the social nature of man itself requires that he should give external expression to his internal acts of religion; that he should participate with others in matters religious; that he should profess his religion in community.

Injury, therefore, is done to the human person and to the very order established by God for human life if the free exercise of religion is denied in society when the just requirements of public order do not so require.

There is a further consideration. The religious acts whereby men, in private and in public, and out of a sense of personal conviction, direct their lives to God transcend by their very nature the order of terrestrial and temporal affairs. Government, therefore, ought to take account of the religious life of the people and show it favor, since the function of government is to make provision for the common welfare. However, it would clearly transgress the limits set to its power were it to presume to direct or inhibit acts that are religious.

4. The freedom or immunity from coercion in matters religious which is the endowment of persons as individuals is also to be recognized as their right when they act in community. Religious bodies are a requirement of the social nature both of man and of religion itself.

Provided the just requirements of public order are observed, religious bodies claim freedom in order that they may govern themselves according to their own norms, honor the Supreme Being in public worship, assist their members in the practice of the religious life, strengthen them by instruction, and promote institutions in which they may join together for the purpose of ordering their own lives in accordance with their religious principles.

Religious bodies also have the right not to be hindered, either by legal measures or by administrative action on the part of government, in the selection, training, appointment, and transferral of their own ministers, in communicating with religious authorities and communities abroad, in erecting buildings for religious purposes, and in the acquisition and use of suitable funds or properties.

Religious bodies also have the right not to be hindered in their public teaching and witness to their faith, whether by the spoken or by the written word. However, in spreading religious faith and in introducing religious practices, everyone ought at all times to refrain from any manner of action which might seem to carry a hint of coercion or of a kind of persuasion that would be dishonorable or unworthy, especially when dealing with poor or uneducated people. Such a manner of action would have to be considered an abuse of one's own right and a violation of the right of others.

In addition, it comes within the meaning of religious freedom that religious bodies should not be prohibited from freely undertaking to show the special value of their doctrine in what concerns the organization of society and the inspiration of the whole of human activity. Finally, the social nature of man and the very nature of religion afford the foundation of the right of men freely to hold meetings and to establish educational, cultural, charitable, and social organizations, under the impulse of their own religious sense.

5. Since the family is a society in its own original right, it has the right freely to live its own domestic religious life under the guidance of parents. Parents, moreover, have the right to determine, in accordance with their own religious beliefs, the kind of religious education that their children are to receive. Government, in consequence, must acknowledge the right of parents to make a genuinely free choice of schools and of other means of education. The use of this freedom of choice is not to be made a reason for imposing unjust burdens on parents, whether directly or indirectly. Besides, the rights of parents are violated if their children are forced to attend lessons or instruction which are not

in agreement with their religious beliefs. The same is true if a single system of education, from which all religious formation is excluded, is imposed upon all.

6. The common welfare of society consists in the entirety of those conditions of social life under which men enjoy the possibility of achieving their own perfection in a certain fullness of measure and also with some relative ease. Hence this welfare consists chiefly in the protection of the rights, and in the performance of the duties, of the human person.[4] Therefore the care of the right to religious freedom devolves upon the people as a whole, upon social groups, upon government, and upon the Church and other religious communities, in virtue of the duty of all toward the common welfare, and in the manner proper to each.

The protection and promotion of the inviolable rights of man rank among the essential duties of government.[5] Therefore, government is to assume the safeguard of the religious freedom of all its citizens, in an effective manner, by just laws and by other appropriate means. Government is also to help create conditions favorable to the fostering of religious life, in order that the people may be truly enabled to exercise their religious rights and to fulfill their religious duties, and also in order that society itself may profit by the moral qualities of justice and peace which have their origin in men's faithfulness to God and to His holy will.[6]

If, in view of peculiar circumstances obtaining among certain peoples, special legal recognition is given in the constitutional order of society to one religious body, it is at the same time imperative that the right of all citizens and religious bodies to religious freedom should be recognized and made effective in practice.

Finally, government is to see to it that the equality of citizens before the law, which is itself an element of the common welfare, is never violated for religious reasons, whether openly or covertly. Nor is there to be discrimination among citizens.

It follows that a wrong is done when government imposes upon its people, by force or fear or other means, the profession or repudiation of any religion, or when it hinders men from joining or leaving a religious body. All the more is it a violation of the will of God and of the sacred rights of the person and the family of nations when force is brought to bear in any way in order to destroy or repress religion, either in the whole of mankind or in a particular country or in a specific community.

7. The right to religious freedom is exercised in human society; hence its exercise is subject to certain regulatory norms.

In the use of all freedoms, the moral principle of personal and social responsibility is to be observed. In the exercise of their rights, individual men and social groups are bound by the moral law to have respect both for the rights of others and for their own duties toward others and for the common welfare of all. Men are to deal with their fellows in justice and civility.

Furthermore, society has the right to defend itself against possible abuses committed on pretext of freedom of religion. It is the special duty of government to provide this protection. However, government is not to act in arbitrary fashion or in an unfair spirit of partisanship. Its action is to be controlled by juridical norms which are in conformity with the objective moral order. These norms arise out of the need for effective safeguard of the rights of all citizens and for peaceful settlement of conflicts of rights. They flow from the need for an adequate care of genuine public peace, which comes about when men live together in good order and in true justice. They come, finally, out of the need for a proper guardianship of public morality. These matters constitute the basic component of the common welfare: they are what is meant by public order. For the rest, the usages of society are to be the usages of freedom in their full range. These require that the freedom of man be respected as far as possible, and curtailed only when and insofar as necessary.

8. Many pressures are brought to bear upon men of our day, to the point where the danger arises lest they lose the possibility of acting on their own judgment. On the other hand, not a few can be found who seem inclined to use the name of freedom as the pretext for refusing to submit to authority and for making light of the duty of obedience. Therefore this Vatican Synod urges everyone, especially those who are charged with the task of educating others, to do their utmost to form men who will respect the moral order and be obedient to lawful authority. Let them form men, too, who will be lovers of true freedom—men, in other words, who will come to decisions on their own judgment and

in the light of truth, govern their activities with a sense of responsibility, and strive after what is true and right, willing always to join with others in cooperative effort.

Religious freedom, therefore, ought to have this further purpose and aim, namely, that men may come to act with greater responsibility in fulfilling their duties in community life.

Chapter II

RELIGIOUS FREEDOM IN THE LIGHT OF REVELATION

9. The declaration of this Vatican Synod on the right of man to religious freedom has its foundation in the dignity of the person. The requirements of this dignity have come to be more adequately known to human reason through centuries of experience. What is more, this doctrine of freedom has roots in divine revelation, and for this reason Christians are bound to respect it all the more conscientiously. Revelation does not indeed affirm in so many words the right of man to immunity from external coercion in matters religious. It does, however, disclose the dignity of the human person in its full dimensions. It gives evidence of the respect which Christ showed toward the freedom with which man is to fulfill his duty of belief in the word of God. It gives us lessons, too, in the spirit which disciples of such a Master ought to make their own and to follow in every situation. Thus further light is cast on the general principles upon which the doctrine of this Declaration on Religious Freedom is based. In particular, religious freedom in society is entirely consonant with the freedom of the act of Christian faith.

10. It is one of the major tenets of Catholic doctrine that man's response to God in faith must be free. Therefore no one is to be forced to embrace the Christian faith against his own will.[7] This doctrine is contained in the word of God, and it was constantly proclaimed by the Fathers of the Church.[8] The act of faith is of its very nature a free act. Man, redeemed by Christ the Savior and through Christ Jesus called to be God's adopted son,[9] cannot give his adherence to God revealing Himself unless the Father draw him to offer to God the reasonable and free sub-

mission of faith.[10] It is therefore completely in accord with the nature of faith that in matters religious every manner of coercion on the part of men should be excluded. In consequence, the principle of religious freedom makes no small contribution to the creation of an environment in which men can without hindrance be invited to Christian faith, and embrace it of their own free will, and profess it effectively in their whole manner of life.

11. God calls men to serve Him in spirit and in truth. Hence they are bound in conscience, but they stand under no compulsion. God has regard for the dignity of the human person whom He Himself created; man is to be guided by his own judgment and he is to enjoy freedom. This truth appears at its height in Christ Jesus, in whom God perfectly manifested Himself and His ways with men. Christ is our Master and our Lord.[11] He is also meek and humble of heart.[12] And in attracting and inviting His disciples, He acted patiently.[13] He wrought miracles to shed light on His teaching and to establish its truth. But His intention was to rouse faith in His hearers and to confirm them in faith, not to exert coercion upon them.[14] He did indeed denounce the unbelief of some who listen to Him; but He left vengeance to God in expectation of the day of judgment.[15] When He sent His Apostles into the world, He said to them: "He who believes and is baptized shall be saved, but he who does not believe shall be condemned" (Mark 16:16); but He Himself, noting that cockle had been sown amid the wheat, gave orders that both should be allowed to grow until the harvest time, which will come at the end of the world.[16] He refused to be a political messiah, ruling by force;[17] He preferred to call Himself the Son of Man, who came "to serve and to give his life as a ransom for many" (Mark 10:45). He showed Himself the perfect Servant of God;[18] "a bruised reed he will not break, and a smoking wick he will not quench" (Matt. 12:20). He acknowledged the power of government and its rights when He commanded that tribute be given to Caesar. But He gave clear warning that the higher rights of God are to be kept inviolate: "Render, therefore, to Caesar the things that are Caesar's, and to God the things that are God's" (Matt. 22:21). In the end, when He completed on the Cross the work of redemption whereby He achieved salvation and true freedom for men, He also brought His revelation to completion.

He bore witness to the truth, but He refused to impose the truth by force on those who spoke against it.[19] Not by force of blows does His rule assert its claims.[20] Rather, it is established by witnessing to the truth and by hearing the truth, and it extends its dominion by the love whereby Christ, lifted up on the Cross, draws all men to Himself.[21]

Taught by the word and example of Christ, the Apostles followed the same way. From the very origins of the Church, the disciples of Christ strove to convert men to faith in Christ as the Lord—not, however, by the use of coercion or by devices unworthy of the gospel, but by the power, above all, of the word of God.[22] Steadfastly they proclaimed to all the plan of God our Savior, "who wishes all men to be saved and to come to the knowledge of the truth" (I Tim. 2:4). At the same time, however, they showed respect for weaker souls even though these persons were in error. Thus they made it plain that "every one of us will render an account of himself to God" (Rom. 14:12), and for this reason is bound to obey his conscience.[23] Like Christ Himself, the Apostles were unceasingly bent upon bearing witness to the truth of God. They showed special courage in speaking "the word of God with boldness" (Acts 4:31) before the people and their rulers.[24] With a firm faith they held that the gospel is indeed the power of God unto salvation for all who believe.[25] Therefore they rejected all "carnal weapons."[26] They followed the example of the gentleness and respectfulness of Christ. And they preached the word of God in the full confidence that there was resident in this word itself a divine power able to destroy all the forces arrayed against God[27] and to bring men to faith in Christ and to His service.[28] As the Master, so too the Apostles recognized legitimate civil authority. "For there exists no authority except from God," the Apostle teaches, and therefore commands: "Let everyone be subject to the higher authorities . . . : he who resists the authority resists the ordinance of God" (Rom. 13:1–2).[29] At the same time, however, they did not hesitate to speak out against governing powers which set themselves in opposition to the holy will of God: "We must obey God rather than men" (Acts 5:29).[30] This is the way along which countless martyrs and other believers have walked through all ages and over all the earth.

12. The Church therefore is being faithful to the truth of the gospel, and is following the way of Christ and the Apostles when she recognizes, and gives support to, the principle of religious freedom as befitting the dignity of man and as being in accord with divine revelation. Throughout the ages, the Church has kept safe and handed on the doctrine received from the Master and from the Apostles. In the life of the People of God as it has made its pilgrim way through the vicissitudes of human history, there have at times appeared ways of acting which were less in accord with the spirit of the gospel and even opposed to it. Nevertheless, the doctrine of the Church that no one is to be coerced into faith has always stood firm.

Thus the leaven of the gospel has long been about its quiet work in the minds of men. To it is due in great measure the fact that in the course of time men have come more widely to recognize their dignity as persons, and the conviction has grown stronger that in religious matters the person in society is to be kept free from all manner of human coercion.

13. Among the things which concern the good of the Church and indeed the welfare of society here on earth—things, therefore, which are always and everywhere to be kept secure and defended against all injury—this certainly is pre-eminent, namely, that the Church should enjoy that full measure of freedom which her care for the salvation of men requires.[31] This freedom is sacred, because the only-begotten Son endowed with it the Church, which He purchased with His blood. It is so much the property of the Church that to act against it is to act against the will of God. The freedom of the Church is the fundamental principle in what concerns the relations between the Church and governments and the whole civil order.

In human society and in the face of government, the Church claims freedom for herself in her character as a spiritual authority, established by Christ the Lord. Upon this authority there rests, by divine mandate, the duty of going out into the whole world and preaching the gospel to every creature.[32] The Church also claims freedom for herself in her character as a society of men who have the right to live in society in accordance with the precepts of Christian faith.[33]

In turn, where the principle of religious freedom is not only proclaimed in words or simply incorporated in law but also given sincere and practical application, there the Church succeeds in achieving a stable situation of right as well as of fact and the independence which is necessary for the fulfillment of her divine mission. This independence is precisely what the authorities of the Church claim in society.[34] At the same time, the Christian faithful, in common with all other men, possess the civil right not to be hindered in leading their lives in accordance with their conscience. Therefore a harmony exists between the freedom of the Church and the religious freedom which is to be recognized as the right of all men and communities and sanctioned by constitutional law.

14. In order to be faithful to the divine command "Make disciples of all nations" (Matt. 28:19), the Catholic Church must work with all urgency and concern "that the word of God may run and be glorified" (II Thess. 3:1).

Hence the Church earnestly begs of her children that, first of all, "supplications, prayers, intercessions, and thanksgivings to be made for all men. . . . For this is good and agreeable in the sight of God our Savior, who wishes all men to be saved and to come to the knowledge of the truth" (I Tim. 2:1–4).

In the formation of their consciences, the Christian faithful ought carefully to attend to the sacred and certain doctrine of the Church.[35] The Church is, by the will of Christ, the teacher of the truth. It is her duty to give utterance to, and authoritatively to teach, that Truth which is Christ Himself, and also to declare and confirm by her authority those principles of the moral order which have their origin in human nature itself. Furthermore, let Christians walk in wisdom in the face of those outside, "in the Holy Spirit, in unaffected love, in the word of truth" (II Cor. 6:6–7). Let them be about their task of spreading the light of life with all confidence and apostolic courage, even to the shedding of their blood.[36]

The disciple is bound by a grave obligation toward Christ his Master ever more adequately to understand the truth received from Him, faithfully to proclaim it, and vigorously to defend it, never—be it understood—having recourse to means that are incompatible with the spirit of the gospel. At the same time, the charity of Christ urges him to act lovingly, prudently, and patiently in his dealings with those who are in error or in ignorance with regard to the faith.[37] All is to be taken into account—the Christian duty to Christ, the life-giving word which must be proclaimed, the rights of the human person, and the measure of grace granted by God through Christ to men, who are invited freely to accept and profess the faith.

15. The fact is that men of the present day want to be able freely to profess their religion in private and in public. Religious freedom has already been declared to be a civil right in most constitutions, and it is solemnly recognized in international documents.[38]

The further fact is that forms of government still exist under which, even though freedom of religious worship receives constitutional recognition, the powers of government are engaged in the effort to deter citizens from the profession of religion and to make life difficult and dangerous for religious communities.

This sacred Synod greets with joy the first of these two facts, as among the signs of the times. With sorrow, however, it denounces the other fact, as only to be deplored. The Synod exhorts Catholics, and it directs a plea to all men, most carefully to consider how greatly necessary religious freedom is, especially in the present condition of the human family.

All nations are coming into even closer unity. Men of different cultures and religions are being brought together in closer relationships. There is a growing consciousness of the personal responsibility that weighs upon every man. All this is evident. Consequently, in order that relationships of peace and harmony may be established and maintained within the whole of mankind, it is necessary that religious freedom be everywhere provided with an effective constitutional guarantee, and that respect be shown for the high duty and right of man freely to lead his religious life in society.

May the God and Father of all grant that the human family, through careful observance of the principle of religious freedom in society, be brought by the grace of Christ and the power of the Holy Spirit to the sublime and unending "freedom of the glory of the sons of God" (Rom. 8:21).

Notes

1. Cf. John XXIII, encyclical *Pacem in terris*, April 11, 1963. AAS, LV (1963), p. 279; *ibid.*, p. 265; Pius XII, radio message, December 24, 1944, AAS, XXXVII (1945), p. 14.
2. Cf. *Pacem in terris*, *loc. cit.*, pp. 260–61; Pius XII, radio message, December 24, 1942, AAS, XXXV (1943), p. 19; Pius XI, encyclical *Mit brennender Sorge*, March 14, 1937, AAS, XXIX (1937), p. 160; Leo XIII, encyclical *Libertas praestantissimum*, June 20, 1888, *Acts of Leo XIII*, Vol. VIII (1888), pp. 237–38.
3. Cf. John XXIII, *Pacem in terris*, *loc. cit.*, p. 270; Paul VI, radio message, December 22, 1964, AAS, LVII (1965), pp. 181–82.
4. Cf. John XXIII, encyclical *Mater et magistra*, May 15, 1961, AAS, LIII (1961), p. 417; *Pacem in terris*, *loc. cit.*, p. 273.
5. cf. *Pacem in terris*, pp. 273–74; Pius XII, radio message, June 1, 1941, AAS, XXXIII (1941), p. 200.
6. Cf. Leo XIII, encyclical *Immortale Dei*, November 1, 1885, ASS, XVIII (1885), p. 161.
7. Cf. *Corpus iuris canonici*, c. 1351; Pius XII, allocution to prelate auditors and other officials and administrators of the tribune of the Holy Roman Rota, October 6, 1946, AAS, XXXVIII (1946), p. 394; *idem*, encyclical *Mystici corporis*, June 29, 1943, AAS, XXXV (1943), p. 243.
8. Cf. Lactantius, *Divinarum Institution*, Bk. V, Ch. 19: *Corpus Scriptorum Ecclesiasticorum Latinorum*, Vol. XIX, pp. 463–64, 465: PL VI, pp. 614 and 616 (Ch. 20); Saint Ambrose, *Epistola ad Valentianum Imp.*, *Epistola* 21: PL, XVI, p. 1005; Saint Augustine, *Contra Litteras Petiliani*, Bk. II, Ch. 83; CSEL, LII, p. 112; PL, XLIII, p. 315; C. 23, q. 5, c. 33 (ed. Friedberg, Vol. I, col. 939); *idem, Epistola* 23: PL, XXXIII, p. 98; *idem, Epistola* 34; PL, XXXIII, p. 132; *idem, Epistola* 35; PL, XXXIII, p. 135; Saint Gregory the Great, *Epistola ad Virgilium et Theodorum Episcopos Massiliae Galliarum*, Register of Letters I, 45: MGH, Ep. I, p. 72: PL, LXXVII, pp. 510–11 (Bk. I, Letter 47); *idem, Epistola ad Johannem Episcopum Constantinopolitanum*, Register of Letters III, 52: MGH, Ep. I, p. 210: PL, LXXVII, p. 649 (Bk. III, Letter 53); D. 45, c. 5 (ed. Friedberg, Vol. I, col. 160); Council of Toledo IV, c. 57: Mansi, X, p. 633; D. 45, c. 5 (ed. Friedberg, Vol. I, cols. 161–62); Clement III: X., V, 6, 9 (ed. Friedberg, Vol. II, col. 774; Innocent III, *Epistola ad Arelatensem Archiepiscopum*: X., III, 42, 3 (ed. Friedberg, Vol. II, col. 646).
9. Cf. Eph. 1:5.
10. Cf. John 6:44.
11. Cf. John 13:13.

12. Cf. Matt. 11:29.
13. Cf. Matt. 11:28–30; John 6:67–68.
14. Cr. Matt. 9:28–29; Mark 9:23–24; and 6, 5–6; Paul VI, encyclical *Ecclesiam Suam*, August 6, 1964, *AAS*, LVI (1964), pp. 642–43.
15. Cf. Matt. 11:20–24; Rom. 12:19–20; II Thess. 1:8.
16. Cf. Matt. 13:30 and 40–42.
17. Cf. Matt. 4:8–10; John 6:15.
18. Cf. Isa. 42:1–4.
19. Cf. John 18:37.
20. Cf. Matt. 26:51–53; John 18:36.
21. Cf. John 12:32.
22. Cf. I Cor. 2:3–5; I Thess. 2:3–5.
23. Cf. Rom. 14:1–23; I Cor. 8:9–13; 10:23–33.
24. Cf. Eph. 6:19–20.
25. Cf. Rom. 1:16.
26. Cf. II Cor. 10:4; I Thess. 5:8–9.
27. Cf. Eph. 6:11–17.
28. Cf. II Cor. 10:3–5.
29. Cf. I Pet. 2:13–17.
30. Cf. Acts 4:19–20.
31. Cf. Leo XIII, letter *Officio Sanctissimo*, December 22, 1887, *ASS*, XX (1887), p. 269; *idem*, letter *Ex Litteris*, April 7, 1887, *ASS*, XIX (1886–87), p. 465.
32. Cf. Mark 16:15; Matt. 28:18–20; Pius XII, encyclical *Summi pontificatus*, October 20, 1939, *AAS*, XXXI (1939), pp. 445–46.
33. Cf. Pius XI, letter *Firmissimam constantiam*, March 28, 1937, *AAS*, XXIX (1937), p. 196.
34. Cf. Pius XII, allocution *Ci Riesce*, December 6, 1953, *AAS*, XLV (1953), p. 802.
35. Cf. Pius XII, radio message, March 23, 1952, *AAS*, XLIV (1952), pp. 270–78.
36. Cf. Acts 4:29.
37. Cf. John XXIII, *Pacem in terris*, pp. 299–300.
38. *Ibid.*, pp. 295–96.

Appendix II

CHRONOLOGY OF THE DECLARATION ON RELIGIOUS FREEDOM

December 27, 1960: A subcommission of the Secretariat for Christian Unity meets at Fribourg, Switzerland, and adopts De Smedt's draft on religious freedom as the basis for future discussion.

February 2, 1962: Pope John convokes the Second Vatican Council.

June 18, 1962: Cardinal Bea submits the revised Fribourg draft to the Central Commission, and the Theological Commission submits its own schema on the subject to the same body.

July 1962: Pope John creates an *ad hoc* commission to reconcile the two drafts.

July 15, 1962: The Secretariat submits a compromise draft to the *ad hoc* commission.

August 2, 1962: Negotiations between the Secretariat and the Theological Commission collapse.

February 16–18, 1963: The Secretariat adopts a new draft on religious freedom.

May 30, 1963: The Secretariat approves a revision of the February draft.

July 4, 1963: The Secretariat incorporates the draft on religious freedom into the schema on ecumenism as Chapter V.

November 12, 1963: The Theological Commission votes to release Chapter V for conciliar consideration.

November 19, 1963: Chapter V is distributed to the Council Fathers; De Smedt gives the introductory report.

November 21, 1963: Conciliar consideration of Chapter V is postponed.

December 4, 1963: The Second Session closes without consideration of Chapter V.

February 27–March 7, 1964: The Secretariat weighs the interventions of Council Fathers at Ariccia, Italy, and adopts a
new draft on religious freedom.

September 23, 1964: The Secretariat presents the new text as a
declaration appended to the schema on ecumenism.

September 23–25, 1964: The Council debates the Declaration on
Religious Freedom.

October 9, 1964: Secretary-General Felici writes Bea to announce
the appointment of a mixed commission to examine and revise the Declaration.

October 13, 1964: Pope Paul assures Cardinal Frings that the
Declaration will remain under the Secretariat's jurisdiction
and provides for its examination by a joint committee composed of representatives of the Secretariat and the Theological Commission.

November 17, 1964: The *textus emendatus* of the Declaration is
distributed to the Council Fathers.

November 19, 1964: Cardinal Tisserant announces postponement
of a vote on the Declaration until the Fourth Session; the
Pope upholds Tisserant's action.

February 18–28, 1965: Experts of the Secretariat prepare revisions
of the Declaration at Monte Mario, Italy.

February 28–March 6, 1965: A plenary session of the Secretariat at
Ariccia constitutes the *textus re-emendatus*.

September 15–21, 1965: The Council debates religious freedom
again.

September 21, 1965: The Council votes approval of the *textus
re-emendatus* as the basis for a definitive declaration.

October 25, 1965: The *textus recognitus* is introduced to the
Council.

October 26 and 27, 1965: The Council votes approval of the
textus recognitus.

November 8 and 9, 1965: The Secretariat completes the final text.

November 19, 1965: The Council approves the final text.

December 7, 1965: The Council formally votes and promulgates
the Declaration on Religious Freedom.

Index